Material Girls
Women, men and work

Lindsey German

Material girls

Women, men and work
Lindsey German

bookmarks publications

Material Girls: Women, men and work – Lindsey German
First published October 2007
Bookmarks Publications Ltd
c/o 1 Bloomsbury Street, London WC1B 3QE
Copyright © Bookmarks Publications

ISBN 1905192177
ISBN 9781905192175

Printed by Cambridge Printing
Cover illustration by Matt Kenyon
Cover design by John-Henry Barac
Typesetting by Bookmarks Publications

Contents

In memory of my sister, Mary Cox

Acknowledgements

I would like to thank all those from whom I gained so many insights that helped in writing this book. I am grateful to Jane Shallice, Elaheh Rostami Povey, Chris Bambery, Chris Harman, Marnie Holborow, Hannah Dee and Carmel Brown for comments on the original draft. I would also like to thank Patrick Ward for helping with research, and Mary Philips, Peter Robinson, John-Henry Barac and Farah Reza for production and design of the book. Mark Thomas did a very thorough and persistent, as well as sympathetic job of editing. A very special thank you must go to Judith Orr, who has always encouraged me to finish the book and has helped me in many practical as well as political ways. I am very grateful to her.

This book took rather longer to write than I expected, because the war on terror intervened. Two people who certainly did not help its progress were George Bush and Tony Blair, who ensured that my past six years have been very busy organising the Stop the War Coalition. The experiences I gained doing so, however, have also helped with the book, especially the chapter on war, and I would like to thank my colleagues in Stop the War for their help and understanding while I have been writing.

Finally, I would like to thank my partner, John Rees, who also read and commented on the manuscript. That, however, does not do justice to the love and support he has given me, as well as the criticism, which has helped sustain me in my writing and political work over the years.

Introduction:
a revolution stalled

TWENTY first century women are represented to us in a number of different images. There are the career women, as sharply tailored as any man, who have proved that they are as good as men, if not better, and who have overcome sexist barriers to get to the top. There are the supermodels, frail and precious, presenting an impossible picture of female beauty and launching thousands of anxious diets among teenage girls. There are the ladettes, the binge drinkers and Essex girls, out for a good time on the same terms as men. There are the single women who reject marriage, monogamy and motherhood, at least until they hear their biological clock ticking.

These women are all making it in a man's world. Nothing in these images suggests any problems: nothing's going to stop them now, not poverty, or dirt or misery, or failure in education, or unemployment, or rape or anorexia. Occasionally these parts of the real world impinge on the images, but never for very long.

The assumption behind them is one that is sometimes described as post-feminist, that women faced inequality in the past but that this has now been overcome. Women can do any job, can do better than boys in education, can express their own sexuality, and can choose to have children or not. They don't have to be held back by insecurity, lack of confidence, staid convention or Betty Friedan's "problem that has no name".[1]

If millions of women don't match the image, then they have to catch up. Make yourself look ten years younger, exhorts one television show; dress to keep your man and impress your work colleagues, says another; sell yourself as a manager who can be as tough as any man, demands a third.

The philosophy is self-help – change or suffer the consequences. It's taken for granted that any successes or failings are those of the individual, not of society. They don't tell you that however much you change, a lot of people are going to fail – by the exacting standards of these role models anyway. That's because by definition most of us can't be winners and because we're operating much of the time with one hand tied behind us. In particular, women's oppression and inequality are not a thing of the past – they are still very much with us. Yet these images are not by any means a fabrication. They are distorted pictures of a stalled revolution, the reflection of real changes in women's lives that opened up the promise of liberation but have never delivered on that promise.

While a small number of women have hit the jackpot from the 1980s onwards, most have struggled to stand still or have even gone under. "Top jobs" are still a male preserve in government and parliament, in the City of London, among the top judiciary and in business. According to the Equal Opportunities Commission, at the current rate of progress it will take 60 years to reach an equal number of female directors in FTSE 100 boardrooms and another 40 *general elections* before women hold an equal number of parliamentary seats.[2]

However, while the lack of women in these positions speaks eloquently of the discrimination throughout society, it is hardly in the same league as the structural inequality that leaves millions of women at the bottom of the pile. Even full time women workers will earn £4 for every £5 earned by a man. Part timers have wages which on average are only two thirds those of men.[3] The structure of women's employment means that "women's work" and low paid work are often synonymous, with many of those occupations also having the largest number of women in the bottom ten for wages. The pressure on married women, and mothers in particular, to work increased rapidly during the 1990s. At the same time, the level of satisfaction among working women with children about their hours fell sharply from just over half who were highly satisfied in 1992 to only 29 percent in 2001.[4]

Sexual discrimination at work, supposedly outlawed more than 30 years ago by the Sex Discrimination Act, is only one part of women's continued inequality. The often degrading images of women, the sale of sex in its various manifestations on a scale undreamt of a generation ago, the widespread use of porn and sexual images on the internet and other media, all create an atmosphere where women's sexuality is seen as something to be bought and sold and where women are regarded as sexual objects. The figures for rape convictions, now at an all time and unacceptable low, suggest a society where the tolerance of women's much more open sexuality only applies until women demand the right not to be sexually assaulted because of how they dress or behave.

These inequalities and many more are the reality behind the images. Women's lives are hard: that's true on a global scale. Women routinely and in their hundreds of thousands leave their own children and families to travel round the world to look after other people's children.[5] Those who stay in countries like the Philippines find themselves employed in factories under sweatshop conditions, subject to long hours, poor wages and conditions, and high levels of sexual harassment. Work on the land and in the home falls disproportionately on women, who do the majority of unpaid work in the world.

The hard life stretches far beyond: women's work outside the home is harder in Britain as well. Women work long and unsocial hours, do shift work on unprecedented scales outside wartime, travel longer to go to work, and are subject to the tyranny of the clock and electronic supervision in white collar and professional work as well as in factories. A report in 2007 by the Equalities Review found that the people who face most discrimination at work are mothers with young children. Lone mothers with a child under 11 are 45 percent less likely to be employed than a man with a partner, while mothers who have a partner are 40 percent less likely to be in work than men in relationships.[6]

The big question about 21st century women is, why, when things have changed so much in the past half century or so, do women remain at the bottom of the pile? Many of those sympathetic to women's plight would answer with one word: oppression. Women suffer specifically because they are women. But that conclusion opens up many new questions – why are women oppressed and why can't the changes in their lives overcome that oppression? Is it just a man's world because it has always been a man's world?

That's a very popular view of the world, expressing as it does the "common sense" of millions of people. However, it is unsatisfactory because it is a static way of looking at male/female relationships, and does not take into account the many ways in which individual men and women, as well as society as a whole, have changed in quite fundamental ways, even though these changes still leave men on top. Biology is no longer women's destiny as it was for thousands of years. Today women have the ability to choose marriage and motherhood. They also have the ability to have their children cared for by others while they work as doctors, lorry drivers, or even go off and climb mountains. Women have entered new roles, and in the process men and women have changed, sometimes willingly, sometimes not.

We do ourselves no favours by pretending this is not so, or by trying to reduce differences to biology or genetics. Do men like barbecuing because there is some deep-rooted memory within them which takes them back to the Stone Age, or is there something rather more to do with the modern sexual division of labour that accounts for it? Are women in "caring" jobs in large numbers because they love children and old people, or are these the jobs which fit round their role in the family, and which remain "women's jobs" because of their low pay and low status? The simplistic answers to where women's oppression comes from sound amusing enough – "men are from Mars, women are from Venus" – or "just like a bloke" – but they mirror the traditional sex stereotyping which women and some men have repeatedly fought against in order to achieve independence. It may be progress of a sort to say "just like a bloke" instead of the saying common half a century ago of "just like a girl" that reinforced sexual stereotypes of girls and summed up an attitude to women as docile, decorative, and undemanding.[7] However, it doesn't really lead to a strategy that can change "blokes" from their traditional behaviour or point the way forward for women.

Instead we should try to understand why particular societies produce particular sorts of behaviour and why our particular society has opened up to some extent for women but has failed to deliver liberation. Inequality is the hallmark of class society, an inequality based not on natural shortages of resources but on the wealth of the society being produced, owned and controlled in an unequal way. In the 19th century Frederick Engels wrote his book *Origin of the Family, Private Property and the State* which linked the production of a surplus of wealth in society (in other words more wealth than simply covered the consumption needs of its inhabitants) to the creation of private property in the hands of a minority. These people established institutions to maintain their rule, including the family. Engels regarded the development of class society as "the world historic defeat of the female sex".[8]

Today the family is still a central institution of capitalist society, argued over by politicians, blamed for much that goes wrong with children and young people. However, it would be wrong to see the family as unchanging or women's position within it as static and passive. In fact the family has undergone great changes even in the past few decades. Even more tellingly, the lives of women are profoundly different from even 50 years ago and they are changing all the time.

The aim of this book is to demonstrate just how profound these changes have been. Attitudes to sex and sexuality have been revolutionised, to such an extent that young people today would find it hard to recognise their grandparents' time. In the repressive dictatorships of Spain and Portugal which existed until the mid-1970s, sexual images were prohibited. Bikinis were banned from beaches in Franco's Spain. Before the 1960s abortion was illegal in Britain, as was gay sex between consenting adults, and divorce was expensive and restrictive. The theatre was subject to censorship, as were books such as *Lady Chatterley's Lover* or *Last Exit to Brooklyn*. It was only during the 1960s that even sometimes quite small steps towards liberalisation began. Work has also been transformed for women, who work longer hours, get themselves educated and qualified for work, enter new trades and professions, and have social lives outside the home and family.

The family as it was could simply not survive the above changes without also undergoing profound change. Despite record low marriages, many women deciding not to have children, and very high rates of divorce, the family has emerged bruised and battered to remake itself around the fulltime working mother rather than the full time housewife. Much of that change has been for the worse. The conditions under which women have gone out to work, and under which the family and personal relationships have changed, have impacted on children's lives. A wide ranging report by UNICEF, the children's organisation, on children's wellbeing in 21 industrialised countries, found that the United Kingdom came bottom in an assessment of child wellbeing. Relative child poverty stood at over 15 percent in the south European countries of Spain, Portugal and Italy, but also in Ireland, the US and Britain.[9] For one of the richest countries in the world to receive such an appalling assessment of the condition of its children is an indictment of government policies over the past decades, and of the neoliberal policies which are creating greater inequality across the world.

Relations between men and women and children have also changed in far reaching ways, which some people believe will lead to a greater equality between the sexes as women "catch up" with men, while others think this will disadvantage men.

Yet these very profound changes have not resulted in real equality in women's personal lives and their place in society. This book also attempts to find answers to the question, why not? The promise of equality has certainly been there. The development of capitalism during the 20th century saw enormous transformations in women's lives. The two world wars profoundly altered women's work patterns and the perceptions of work which women had. The creation of a welfare state was a recognition that government and state had to intervene in the lives of women and their families in order to ensure the health, education and wellbeing of children. Improvements in housing and schools, the development of a health service, the provision of publicly owned utilities, high standards of public health, were all campaigned for and implemented throughout the 20th century but reached their high point during the post-war 1945 Labour government, which put this welfare capitalism at the centre of its aspirations.

The more far-sighted sections of Britain's rulers understood that this was money well spent: to maintain a productive and relatively contented workforce necessitated expenditure on keeping that workforce housed, healthy and educated to at least basic levels of literacy and numeracy. The state therefore provided resources to improve the lives of families, and especially of their children. The 1945 Labour government is most famous for its introduction of the National Health Service, but other provisions included free milk and orange juice for children, the expansion of secondary education and an extensive programme of house building. These were added to already existing provisions introduced from 1909 onwards, which included council house building, national insurance, old age pensions and family allowances to help compensate for the high costs of having children.

Women benefited from the extension of the welfare state in a number of ways. They formed an ever growing part of the workforce in much of the public sector, especially in areas such as health and education. Along with immigrant workers, usually from the Caribbean or from south Asia (many of whom were, of course, women), women became part of a new layer of workers, often initially on a part time basis. They also saw a general improvement in their lives: the birth rate fell throughout the 20th century, improvements in medical care meant fewer deaths in childbirth or child mortalities, and access to contraception gradually improved, culminating in the reforms of the 1960s and 1970s, which allowed legal abortion for medical and social grounds, and much greater access to free contraception.

Education has also been a great source of emancipation for women. Whereas still at the beginning of the 20th century a woman in higher education was a rare species, who had often had to battle social and family prejudice and pressure, even when she had overcome the economic constraint that denied virtually all but the wealthy access to universities and colleges. That began to change by the 1950s, when women began to take advantage of free education in order to equip themselves with qualifications so that they could work as teachers, nurses, lecturers and civil servants, and these occupations grew rapidly from the 1960s onwards.

Major social forces all helped to propel women towards change: war, the great boom following the Second World War which opened up jobs and education for women, and the mass migration that accompanied it which broke up traditional families and sent individual family members across the world. In turn, women's ideas changed as result of these changing circumstances and they began to think of themselves and the world around them in different ways.

This led to moves for greater rights for women: laws to defend their workforce participation, to prevent financial and legal discrimination against them, to allow them rights as mothers while they were workers. Many sections of the media and society began to accept what would once have seemed daring or extreme views: that women could become bosses, that they didn't have to get married, or that having open attitudes to sexuality didn't harm educational or job prospects.

Some of the demands of women's liberation could therefore be achieved, but only so far. Time and again those proposing such demands came up against the limits of class society. At their root was the clash between demands for equality, whether they were for free nurseries or equal pay, and the refusal of employers and governments to accede seriously to these demands, for fear that the costs would eat into their profits and make them uncompetitive with their rivals. It seemed to many who campaigned in the 1960s and 70s that such demands could become extensions of the welfare state – that it was as logical to pay for nurseries as for family allowances. However, employers and governments did not just fear competition. They also recognised that women's unpaid labour in the home allowed them to be treated as they were at work. Because so many women cared for children without being paid, it was easier to get away without providing paid childcare. The tacit assumption was that since women had a breadwinner to provide for them, wages for women could be set lower. An end to sexual exploitation remains a dream, while the "sex industry" is big business and sex, including the requisite stick thin models, sells all the goods that lead to profits in the first place.

So women's emancipation goes so far, but no farther. A small number of women can make it on men's terms. A much larger number of women can live better than their grandmothers. But the right to work has become the right to be exploited on the same basis as men, only for less money. The right to sexual freedom has become the right for women's bodies to be sold in every lap dancing bar and on every magazine cover. We can't redress this just by changing the individual behaviour of men – indeed it could be argued that the behaviour of some men is worsened by the signals they get from the media and other social institutions. We have to change the society which spends billions on weapons and war, which allows growing gaps between rich and poor, but which expects childcare on the cheap or absolutely free, and which expects women to work for less than men.

Women's liberation had the aspiration to change the world when it began in the late 1960s but ultimately it has not succeeded. Whatever theoretical contribution it made in its early years, it was incapable of practically engaging the mass of working class women who suffer most in our society. That increasingly led supporters of women's liberation away from activity and towards the idea of gaining positions in politics or academia in order to advance feminist ideas. This means that they failed to confront the structures of class society which lead to the oppression of women. I see this failure as the inability of the women's movement to link up with wider forces, centrally the working class movement, which had the organisation, potential and need to fight the inequality created by class society.

Hence the widening of the gap between women who can at least aspire to having it all, and the mass of women who see the small gains that they had made in the long boom submerged by cuts, privatisation and precarious employment.

We are seeing the limits of liberation in a society where the profit motive is king and where the lives of men, women and children are subjugated to the needs of profit. How to change that is a question with which people have been grappling for hundreds of years. The aim of this book is to try to explain our victories and defeats, and to point to some steps which we can take in order to go from where we are now to where we want to be.

Sex: the peculiarities of the English

IT's hard to avoid seeing or talking about images of sex in Britain today. In an age of digital technology we can, if we want to, conjure up images on every computer screen which would once have been confined to the seediest back streets. For a handful of gangsters and dealers in underground pornography, there was always plenty of money to be made from selling sex. Now the big money is made by corporations, and sex has been repackaged as fun for nearly all the family. "Ironic" burlesque dancers appear on chat shows, strippers perform at female film stars' birthday parties and lap dancing clubs spring up in the business areas of big cities – an expensive fun night out for men and women. Cherie Blair, the former prime minister's wife, declares she and Tony regularly enjoy sex five times a night. Anyone not joining in the sexual revolution as decreed by media and advertisers is seen as hopelessly old fashioned or prudish.

It wasn't always like this. The transformation in attitudes to sex and sexuality over the space of just two generations has been remarkable, so that even middle aged people in Britain today can remember a time when a very different set of morals and family values prevailed. Few then would have predicted then that by the beginning of the 21st century Britain would have become a country so strongly identified with relaxed attitudes to marriage, morality and sexuality. Yet this is exactly what has happened.

Most obviously, far fewer people today are living in conventional two parent families than even 30 years ago. By the spring of 2005 nearly a quarter of children (24 percent) lived in a family headed by a lone parent, compared with just 7 percent as recently as 1972.[1] And while up to the mid-1980s many single mothers had once been married but were now divorced, today an increasing number have never been married.[2] Equally, there has been a huge increase in the numbers of unmarried women who are living with a partner (cohabiting), with the proportion of women aged under 60 doing so nearly doubling between 1986 and 2005 from 13 percent to 24 percent.[3] Perhaps not surprisingly then, by 2005 more than four out of every ten live births in Britain occurred outside marriage, more than *four times* the proportion in 1974.[4] This represents a radical departure from the dominant norm for most of the 20th century where, with the exception of the two world wars and their immediate aftermath, nearly all births took place inside marriage. Britain is now renowned for some of the most extreme figures relating to sexual behaviour. Divorce rates in Britain are at twice the rate of any other EU country,[5] while teenage pregnancies are the highest in Europe – twice as high as Germany, three times as high as France and six times as high as those of the Netherlands.[6]

How do we explain these enormous changes? Why does Britain have such a peculiarly high number of women who divorce, or cohabit with their partners rather than marry, or bring up children alone as single parents? As we shall see, the secret lies in the wider social changes that have taken place over the last half century and more.

Chaste Britannia

When the pioneering gynaecologist Helena Wright asked her working class patients in the 1930s what they got out of making love, most of them blinked uncomprehendingly. Sex was much more likely to be something which men wanted, and women suffered. The combination, especially for working class women, of ignorance and a fear of pregnancy was enough to deny many women any pleasure from sex at all. The difference from modern women was total. As Helena Wright says, today "the contrast is extraordinary. The girl's face shines brilliantly and she says, 'Oh, Doctor, it's glorious'".[7] As late as the early 1950s the results of an investigation of English attitudes could prompt their author to write, "I very much doubt whether the study of any other urban population would produce comparable figures of chastity and fidelity." He regarded these figures as remarkable.[8] They are even more so with the hindsight of sexual developments over the past 50 years.

It is hard now to imagine a world where so much that we now take for granted did not exist or was not acknowledged to exist. It is hard to imagine a vocabulary that for most people did not include terms like "orgasm" or descriptions of various sexual acts. It is hard to imagine a time when the only pills associated with conception were evil looking dangerous ones taken as crude abortion-inducing drugs. It is hard to imagine a working class morality where an "illegitimate" child born outside marriage carried a terrible burden of shame not just on the mother but her whole family too, and was regarded as one of the worst disasters that could befall them. Yet that was the world in which the majority of the working class lived for a large part of the 20th century.

Steve Humphries in his brilliant study *A Secret World of Sex* argues that there was effectively a taboo on premarital sex which lasted from the Victorian age right through to the 1950s in Britain. All the institutions which shaped society, from the state and the church to the family itself, were strongly opposed to "promiscuity". The only people who really escaped these strictures were the very rich – who could and did do as they pleased – and the very poor, who were beyond the reach of bourgeois respectability.[9] While this proscription on sex outside marriage was never wholly successful, and became much less so as the 20th century wore on, it firmly placed a stamp of approval on certain sorts of behaviour while strictly outlawing others. This was a world of intense sexual self-restraint and guilt, with its rituals of long periods of engagement or courting, a strong social disapproval of premarital sex and a high marriage age. In the Edwardian period the average marriage age was the highest recorded at that point, at 27 for men and 26 for women. This was a society where older adults exercised very strong control over youth.[10] This was also the era that saw the spreading of the cult of the white wedding and the virgin bride, from its origin as an upper class habit in the late 19th century into wider sections of society.[11]

But as Humphries suggests, this period of extraordinary sexual conservatism, far from being the product of a timeless and "traditional" moral and sexual code, only lasted a comparatively short time and was relatively recently imposed. The narrowness, sexual prudishness and strict norms which characterised working class and much of middle class Britain can be dated from the heyday of empire, around the 1880s, through to the aftermath of the Second World War. Indeed, it could well be argued that the sexual habits and customs of today have more in common with those of the 17th, 18th and early 19th centuries than with those of the late 19th and first half of the 20th century. There is evidence that for much of early modern history, in the period prior to industrialisation in Britain, attitudes to marriage and childbirth within marriage were often much more laissez faire and libertarian than in the century preceding the 1950s. So in the 18th and early 19th centuries marriages were conducted "over the broomstick" in some parts of the country, meaning that informal agreement to marriage without the sanction of religious blessing was regarded as enough; common law marriage agreed by a handclasp was frequent.[12] Divorce, like marriage, was also a much more impromptu matter. Jumping back over the broomstick within a year by the man or woman dissolved the marriage.[13] In Scotland you could be married in front of any witness, hence the popularity of weddings conducted by the blacksmith in the border town of Gretna Green. Attempts were made to wipe out these arrangements and to regularise the sexual and marital relations of the poor. Lord Hardwicke's Act in 1753 required most people to now marry in the Anglican Church: "After 1754 no vow other than that made in the Church of England, Quaker meetings or a Jewish synagogue had any legal standing as marriage".[14]

But the real turning point was the industrial revolution. Sexual pleasure was now to be subordinated to the work ethic. Legal and social changes were increasingly successful at ensuring sexuality was regulated through marriage and other laws. Around the middle of the 19th century illegitimacy ratios declined "and would not reach early-nineteenth-century levels until the 1960s".[15] There was "a pronounced tendency for couples to return to legal matrimony" so that "by the turn of the [20th] century the clergy could congratulate themselves on the return of the people to their altars".[16]

The new industrial system, based on exploitation in the factories, was increasingly underpinned by a narrow, conventional and monogamous sexuality where the family became one of the bulwarks of society, a centre of social control rather than sexual experimentation. The factory imposed a regular working day and a new discipline of timekeeping, in contrast to the older agricultural patterns of work. It also required the increased policing of the workforce's sexual habits. The dominant religions, the newly developing state education system, and the regulation of the poor through the workhouse system, all took as their fundamental tenets that sexual "licence" was wrong and that work should be the dominant ethic. The capitalist state, whose growing powers were extending into areas once considered private, now took on a new role of officially sanctioning marriage and childbirth. All of this suited the new industrial capitalism. The Italian Marxist Antonio Gramsci described the attitude of the American car magnate Henry Ford in the 1930s in terms that apply could just as well to Victorian Britain:

It is worth drawing attention to the way in which industrialists (Ford in particular) have been concerned with the sexual affairs of their employees and with their family arrangements in general. One should not be misled, any more than in the case of [alcohol] prohibition, by the "puritanical" appearance assumed by this concern. The truth is that the new type of man demanded by the rationalisation of production and work cannot be developed until the sexual instinct has been suitably regulated and until it too has been rationalised.[17]

As we shall explore in more detail in the next chapter, this new narrow sexual code rested on the emergence of a new family structure. It came to involve both the separation of work from home and the creation of a sexual division of labour where men worked and earned a wage able to provide for a family, at least in theory, while women and at least younger children were removed from the labour market.

Sexual activity was, of course, not solely confined to marriage and the family. Prostitution was rife in Victorian Britain – without it the respectable and narrow bourgeois marriage could not have existed.[18] Child abuse existed at horrific levels, with incest widespread in overcrowded slums and child prostitution not uncommon. Poor women in particular suffered sexual abuse at the hands of their employers. Above all, millions of ordinary people continued to have "illicit" sex:

sex outside marriage, in addition to marriage, and with people of the same sex. But they faced a world of double standards, where public flouting of such behaviour often meant becoming a social outcast and losing family, home and employment. It was sex constrained by the morality of the time and is part of the female experience which is "hidden from history".

We can assume from our own time and from what we know about women then that many women did enjoy sex and were not just the passive victims of male passion as is sometimes portrayed. But they found it very hard to express their sexuality or indeed to talk about or read about anything connected with sex. Society as a whole did not publicise or generalise that experience – indeed it did its very best to hide and repress it, to make those who participated in sexual activity outside certain narrow norms of sex within marriage feel ashamed or outcast. Newspapers such as the *News of the World* could make their name and achieve a wide circulation by reporting prurient stories of brothels, scandalous divorces and celebrity affairs, which were not reported widely in other media.

It was, of course, women who bore the brunt of the double standards over sex. Women who were "seduced" by evil men were the recipients of patronising charity from groups like the Salvation Army. Even worse was the treatment of those who were considered to have enjoyed sex, or had taken up with more than one man. They were regarded as promiscuous or even known as amateurs – meaning amateur prostitutes. If young, such women could be placed in care – often effectively little different from a prison or the workhouse. The horror stories that have emerged in recent years, where women who became pregnant in the 1920s and 1930s could be consigned to mental hospitals and kept there for decades, are luckily fairly rare. But they are still common enough to demonstrate what draconian measures awaited women who transgressed the norms of society and who did not have friends or family to support them.

Saturday night and Sunday morning
But there were significant changes in British society that were beginning to undermine the stranglehold of this narrow code of monogamy and sexual self-restraint. New ways of living created new attitudes to the family, children and sexuality. However, these coexisted for many people with the old attitudes and constraints which

still continued to exercise a powerful hold. The tensions that resulted were played out in the lives of millions of people.

One sign was that many more young men and women were beginning to engage in sex before marriage. The evidence provided by Eustace Chesser of women's sexual habits, for example, shows an increase in sexual activity short of full intercourse, or "petting" (non-coital sex). A survey comparing the engagement in premarital non-coital sex of women born before 1904 and the decade following (1904-1914) reveals a sharp rise among the younger women, up from 7 percent to 22 percent and then a further rise to 29 percent for the women born in the decade after that (1914-1924). Figures for participation in premarital sexual intercourse itself also tell a similar story, with the corresponding figures for the same age groups being 9 percent (born before 1904) rising to 36 percent (1914-24) and then rising again to 39 percent (1914-24).[19]

Similarly dramatic changes took place in the US at the same time, as one survey of middle class college girls demonstrated. It showed that of those surveyed nearly 90 percent of women born before 1890 were virgins at marriage compared with 74 percent of those born in the following decade. But of those born between 1900 and 1910, only 51 percent were virgins at marriage and of those born after 1910 just 32 percent were.[20]

These figures suggest a fairly rapid weakening in the hold of the conventional morality on sexual practice in the period around the First World War, and of a much more dramatic rise in premarital sex during the 1920s. The explanation lies in the fact that the sexual constraints among British workers were less to do with religious beliefs but instead were much more based on the strong secular habits of a society noted for its stability and lack of wider political or social upheaval.

Before the First World War the ties of home and employer on working class women were often very strong. Courtship was controlled from the home and the parents expected a say in their children's choice of partner. Opportunities for sex were often few and far between in overcrowded working class households and in closely-knit communities where there was little geographical separation between work, home and social life. The main possibility of working women leaving home then was to go into domestic service, and this was probably the main opportunity to engage in sex as well. Indeed in 1911 nearly half of all illegitimate children born in Britain were born to women in domestic service.[21] Some of these were the result of often unwilling relationships between servants and the men of the household, but many resulted from relationships with other servants.

But during the 1920s and 30s increasing numbers of single women were employed in new industries across the expanding light industrial sector, geared to the production of consumer goods, as well as the growing numbers of white collar jobs.[22] This acted to weaken the ideological bonds which had been so important in policing relationships, particularly of the young, as they acquired a greater degree of independence than ever before.

Other changes in working class living conditions also played a part. Already by the early 20th century popular newspapers brought wider images of women and men and of life in general to a mass readership. More importantly, so did the developing cinema, which both in its films and in the lives of its stars opened up new vistas for millions of working people around the world. There were changing expectations about the role of women, too: the fight for women's suffrage took off in the years preceding the First World War, and limited suffrage for women was granted in 1918.

The general raising of living standards and conditions also raised expectations about personal lives. Physical improvements such as decent water and sanitation in houses made it easier for people to live in clean conditions. The spread of electricity to most homes, which took place in the period between the two wars, also made a difference to cleanliness, the use of labour saving domestic devices, and higher levels of comfort. The development of fast public transport also led to more men and women working further away from home, with many going to live in suburban or overspill areas where their houses were more likely to be modern, more spacious and easier to clean.

Some of the prevailing ideas about women's role in society also began to be undermined in other ways. Even the entry of a very small number of mostly upper class women into the handful of universities had an impact. In a society that had defined women's role almost exclusively either as one of working class drudgery or upper class decorative idleness this acted to widen the horizons not just of the few women who benefited from higher education, but also of a layer beneath them who had aspirations to a career and who now saw a very different role for themselves.

All this began to have an effect on many people's relationships. By the inter-war years there was much more expectation that marriage itself should be a partnership and that its sexual element should be a source of pleasure rather than just a duty. Already in the US there were greater expectations over the role sex should play in marriage and a rise in the publication of sex manuals that tried to advise their readers on a more active and fulfilling sex life.[23] By the 1930s in Britain there was also a new literature emphasising sexual pleasure and sexuality in marriage.[24]

Attitudes to children changed too. In the 50 or 60 years after 1870, when the Education Act marked compulsory if very limited working class education, there were very dramatic changes to the family and children within it. Before the period of full time education for children, and when child labour still existed in many areas, children were a source of income for the family from relatively early in life. The growing length of time spent at school meant children became much more of a financial burden on the family. In addition, improvements in health and childcare standards contributed to a reduction in infant mortality. As this happened, so families tended to have fewer children: those who were born were more likely to survive to adulthood and were sufficiently costly to make having large numbers impossible. The beginning of availability of contraceptive advice and more state provision in caring for pregnant mothers and their babies also contributed to the changes.[25] As Diana Gittins says:

> Economic, political, demographic and ideological changes resulted in a very different position, status and meaning attached to the family and children in the early 20th century. Children were now much more of an economic burden than an asset to working class families. A prolonged period of dependence and compulsory schooling meant that the time during which a child could actually contribute to the family income was less than before. Through government legislation, the media and the education system, however, the importance of women bearing and rearing healthy children as their one essential role in society was emphasised in one way or another continuously. Successful womanhood was becoming virtually synonymous with successful motherhood.[26]

The greater interest in sexuality within marriage and the fairly sharp reduction in fertility and childbirth rates which took place in the early 20th century all meant a change in sexual attitudes. The idea that sexuality should be strictly controlled and subject to detailed custom and practice in its regulation; that marriage should be the pinnacle of social achievement; and that the old should control the young, was being eroded by events. But these new attitudes were still conditioned by the past and many of the old ideas still held a great deal of sway. Increasingly, these changes created a clash between the dominant ideology and the new realities of people's lives, especially among the working class and particularly among the young.

So many women still felt that sex was something dirty or dangerous. Working class expressions speak volumes: women would describe themselves as "falling" pregnant, implying some kind of fault or sin.[27] Husbands would "want their way" in relationships where sex was seen as something to be endured.[28] Nevertheless, while sexual intercourse outside marriage was still as widely frowned upon, it was frequently practised. However, this often occurred not in conditions of the participants' own choosing, but determined by the situation in which young working class people found themselves: living at home – unable to afford cars which were still the preserve of the well off, they had few opportunities to have sex. The most common form of sexual intercourse pre-war was therefore the "knee trembler" – sexual intercourse standing up, often outdoors, which was "fast, furtive and rarely fulfilling for young women".[29] A Mass Observation survey published in 1945 gives some sense of how widespread this was in "Worktown", the northern industrial town it studied:

In Worktown we must walk along the backstreets at night... There, at scattered intervals along the walls, will be closely-linked couples, standing, one or two in each back. Sexual intercourse enjoyed in this way (as common in winter as summer) is generally known as 'having a knee trembler'.[30]

Any chance of moving to more relaxed or intimate surroundings would probably have been welcomed. In the inter-war years more young people began to be mobile and if in work many had sufficient money to at least occasionally go away for a seaside holiday. Better transport, including working class ownership of motorbikes, meant that couples could escape the scrutiny of neighbours and relatives, at least for a few days. Increasingly the trend became for courting couples to spend holidays together in resorts such as Blackpool. This obviously allowed greater opportunities for sex, despite the draconian nature of some boarding house regimes.[31] Another study by Mass Observation in "Seatown" in 1937 shows why the big seaside resorts had a reputation for "easy" sex. The beaches were crowded with courting couples late at night. Between 11.30 and midnight 120 couples were sitting on the promenade and embracing, another 42 were standing and embracing and a further 46 were lying on the sand and embracing.[32] It is impossible to know how far the Mass Observation reporters took their research but this seems a fairly large number of couples by the standards of today. Steve Humphries argues that the survey actually underplayed the amount of sexual activity taking place, and that the casual workers who took jobs in towns like Blackpool were more likely to be involved in such activity.[33] Certainly some evidence – for example, a Lancashire mill girl's diary from the 1930s shows a high level of "pick-ups" while on holiday in Blackpool – would suggest that such trips were made with this activity very much in mind.[34]

However, these changes were greatly at odds with what was still considered socially acceptable. Family and social pressure still remained to avoid sex outside marriage, to avoid pregnancy outside marriage at all costs, and to stick to the norms of courting, engagement and marriage. The ideology inside the working class, carried by mothers and older women in particular, reinforced this. The notion that no man would respect you if you slept with them, and that a woman who had been "used" sexually would stay on the shelf, were widespread. Connected with them was the idea that if you "got into trouble" it was your own fault – "you've made your bed and now you must lie on it," was a common refrain. "Shotgun weddings" – arranged and carried out within the early months of pregnancy – were quite common in the first half of the 20th century.[35]

It is hard now to reconcile the harshness of many working class (and middle class) responses to unmarried pregnancy within the family. Many young girls were thrown out of their families and lived in near destitution. There were threats of the workhouse.[36] A young Lancashire woman who became pregnant in 1940 and was abandoned by her boyfriend was put in the workhouse by her mother. "My mother put me in the workhouse because she thought it was wrong what I had done. When you were put in there, while the time come to have your baby, you had to work. But I couldn't work because I was ill".[37] Young pregnant women could be detained under the Mental Deficiency Act of 1913 and subject to the most terrible conditions. Part of the reason for such sharp responses was that government and social institutions frowned on premarital sex and devised punitive responses supposedly to counter it. But partly it also reflected the attitudes of working class families. There was sometimes a terrible sense of shame and betrayal inside the family, especially within the "respectable" working class. One Lancashire woman remembers the attitude in her family towards her brothers:

> He'd [her father] have killed them…he would have seen there'd have been no shenanigans. There wouldn't have been no flying their kites and then changing their minds. They'd have had to marry the girl, if she'd been good enough to do that with, she'd have been good enough to marry and that would have been Dad's lot.[38]

Another man said that if you couldn't marry a woman you had made pregnant, the least you could do was emigrate. A woman interviewed said her sister had drowned herself when she discovered she was pregnant.[39] These reactions may not have been typical but they were not unique within the working class. They expressed a fear of pregnancy and the shame associated with it which has to be seen in the context of insecurity and poverty within the working class. People just about kept their heads above water, and dreaded themselves or any of their family being pulled down into destitution. Sometimes the family was simply already too poor to support a daughter who could not work and another mouth to feed. Either way, these attitudes and this behaviour created a dread inside the working class that the punishment for "illicit" sex could be dire indeed.

So how did people enjoy sex but avoid pregnancy? For much of the first half of the 20th century they relied on non-manual methods of contraception: abstention, the rhythm method (avoiding intercourse during ovulation), abortion, and withdrawal (coitus interruptus). Obviously these methods were often more difficult for unmarried women – but access to sheaths, pessaries or diaphragms was even more restricted. A survey at the Manchester and Salford Mothers' Clinic in 1928-33 of married women also revealed a level of class differences in the approach to contraception. While 35 percent of routine non-manual (white-collar) women workers used no contraception, the figure rose to 50 percent for the unskilled working class. Use of the sheath was highest among skilled manual workers and lowest among routine non-manual workers (18 percent and 9 percent).[40] The most favoured method – coitus interruptus – was used by 33 percent of skilled manual workers, 24 percent of routine non-manual and 15 percent of unskilled manual. So the most common method of contraception was at the same time one of the least satisfying and the most risky. The sense of sexual disappointment it caused can be summed up by one Lancashire woman, married in 1950, who described the experience of coitus interruptus thus: "It was like getting off at the roundabout instead of going to Morecambe".[41]

However, another very common traditional method of contraception was even more unsatisfying and considerably more dangerous – that of abortion. Figures for abortion – although impossible to be highly accurate – were by all accounts huge. In 1914 it was estimated that 100,000 working class women took abortifacients every year, and by just before the Second World War a government investigation estimated the number of illegal abortions performed each year at between 44,000 and 60,000.[42] If self-induced miscarriages are added to that figure, the total could have been between 110,000 and 150,000 a year – comparable with figures today but in a much smaller population.[43]

The number of miscarriages among unskilled manual working class women was double that among skilled workers in Manchester and Salford in the late 1920s and early 1930s. Diana Gittins estimates that a very high proportion of these were in fact abortions, given that the government's own survey, of the Interdepartmental Committee on Abortions, estimated that at least 40 percent of all miscarriages in the 1930s were in fact a result of induced abortion.[44] This committee was set up in the 1920s and reported just before the Second World War. It confirmed various other contemporary studies which showed that between 16 and 20 percent of all pregnancies ended in abortion. It was concluded that this was most likely to happen because of economic problems. Most of these abortions were performed on married women, suggesting that they were used as a means of limiting the family size, rather than escaping scandal – obviously a consideration for single pregnant women. Indeed it seemed that "abortion is relatively more common in the case of mothers in the higher age groups than in the case of younger mothers".[45]

Overall contraception remained very difficult for many people to gain access to, and knowledge of contraception, as well as sex and sexuality, was often abysmal. Many thought that contraceptive sheaths were faulty, that manufacturers were obliged by law to make a fixed proportion defective; or that Catholic pharmacists made holes in them. Women were encouraged by pioneering clinics to equip themselves with contraceptive devices but in the inter-war years most working class women did not take up the offer.[46]

Even doctors were ignorant of contraceptive techniques and of little help in dealing with ignorance or embarrassment, apart from a small number of specialists, and government approached the question half heartedly, unwilling to offend religious or other vested interests. So the increased interest in sexuality was not met with any informed response and most people struggled to find answers to the most basic questions. Little wonder that in 1938-39 nearly a third (30 percent) of all women conceived their first child before marriage, a figure that rose to 42 percent of under 20s who were pregnant at marriage.[47]

For all the new developments and changing attitudes towards sex and the role of women in the first half of the 20th century, and especially in the inter-war period, this was still a society quite unprepared for what was to take place in the next few years.

Two events would play a crucial role in the final overthrow of the sexual codes established in the Victorian period; the Second World War and the sexual and social revolution of the 1960s. In between the 1950s seemed to offer a restoration of sexual conservatism, but in retrospect it was nothing more than a temporary triumph for the old order. As we have seen, the strength of marriage and engagement and the disapproval of extramarital sexual activity up to the 1950s, speak not of centuries of tradition but of the success with which the British ruling and middle class had imposed their views of morality on the industrial working class by using the instrument of the family. The strange feature of the post-war period was, however, how quickly it suddenly changed.

From war time to boom time: the prelude to the 60s

The Second World War was paradoxically one of the high points of many women's lives. It meant a radical upheaval as in both Britain and the US women were drawn into the workforce in unprecedented numbers. State legislation ensured that by 1943 one in two of all British women were working or in the military. Women between the ages of 18 and 50 had to register at employment offices and women workers were directed to essential jobs. Wages for women rose dramatically as they took on traditional "men's jobs" in the war industries.[48] Women found they had a freedom never available to most of them before. Working long hours, living away from home in increasing numbers, finding their husbands conscripted and fighting abroad, they had enough money to be able to go out and be independent in a limited way. All this had an impact on breaking down the old morals and sexual attitudes. But perhaps the greatest impetus to rapid change in this direction was the terrible effect of war, the immediate threat of being bombed or of losing loved ones through fighting, the sense that there was no point in waiting to have sex or to marry because there might not be another chance.

The war saw some remarkable changes. The rate of unmarried births rose in the final few years of the war. Whereas unmarried births represented around 4 to 5 percent of all live births before the war, by the end of it the rate had doubled.[49] Divorces rose, reaching their peak in the few years immediately following the end of the war. There was a major scare about the rising incidence of venereal disease (VD). One of the major factors in producing more relaxed attitudes to relationships and to sex was the influx of allied troops into Britain, most notably GIs from the US. The GIs earned £750 a year compared with less than £100 for a British soldier, and they had access to consumer goods not easily available in Britain such as stockings, sweets and cigarettes. It was estimated that Americans in Britain had fathered 70,000 babies by 1945, and 20,000 women in Britain applied to be US soldiers' wives.[50] The Americans tended to be more advanced sexually. According to Sheila Rowbotham, the GIs:

> were extremely puzzled by the British custom of making love standing up, fully clothed, in dark side streets or parks...problems came about because of the Americans' upfront persistent courting methods and refusal to take "no" for an answer, which led to

complaints of sexual molestation. Margaret Mead was sent over to apply her knowledge as an anthropologist to the clash in sexual attitudes. She concluded that British girls had little experience of the dating and flirting to which Americans were accustomed from their school days.[51]

However, many British women took to these new customs enthusiastically. The openness of many women's relationships was frowned on sometimes by neighbours and families and by those in authority. Advertisements against VD tended to blame "loose women" rather than men for the disease and the response of one Mass Observation interviewee about one of his neighbours gives some flavour of the disapproval mixed with fear which greeted the activity of some women:

There's a woman in the house where I'm staying bringing men home every night. And he knows – he *knows* what's going on – in the army he is. Who's going to come back to that? There'll be some messes there will – little kids and all. And what about them that's earning £4 or £5 a week – women – are they going to settle to nothing a week when their old man comes back?[52]

Divorce figures shot up to 60,000 in the year 1946-47, reflecting the broken relationships resulting from the war. Although this was a freak figure resulting from wartime experience, it frightened government and authorities, who were already in something of a state of moral panic over issues such as teenage pregnancy and VD. The National Marriage Guidance Council was therefore given state assistance, in preference to the Family Planning Association, which was what the Home Office wanted.[53]

In the post-war world most people did settle down into families again, encouraged by the state and the media who placed much stress placed on getting things "back to normal" after the war. A stable home life was supposed to deal with all social ills. Anyone who deviated from this norm was likely to be seen as a social problem. Women's unorthodox role during wartime was hidden, and although there was much more discussion about sex and related issues, the dominant assumption was that it would be strictly heterosexual and that it would be within marriage.

The practical fashions of the 1940s gave way to the "new look" inspired by Christian Dior – a return to long full skirts, tight nipped waists and formal "feminine" fashions. The ideology of the media and advertisers stressed that a woman's most important role was as mother and wife, and for some years many people bought into this idea. After all, the years of unemployment and war seemed far behind, living standards were rising, and there was more housing being built every year which could be turned into the "perfect home".

For a time it all seemed to work. The divorce figures went down and white weddings were all the rage. The typical family was made up of a mum and dad with usually two or three children. Engagements were long;[54] births outside wedlock were regarded as scandals. Far from marriage dying out or being seen as irrelevant, it was growing in popularity. More people married than ever before, and tended to do so younger. There was very strong pressure to conform, especially when there were children involved. In a survey in 1947 asking about unmarried couples living together, 86 percent disapproved or gave only conditional acceptance. As one study put it in the 1950s, "Marriage meant family; and family meant marriage. The rates of illegitimacy and cohabitation were at the lowest points in over a century".[55]

But it was impossible for everything to go back into the box again. For one thing, the post-war economic boom led people to have much higher expectations of living standards. They wanted a job, a home, a family, and even some of the new consumer durables like washing machines which became more widely available in the 1950s. Throwing out the old living conditions meant throwing out some of the old attitudes. This all further reinforced the idea that marriage should be a partnership and that sex – at least within marriage – should be pleasurable for both partners and should not necessarily be tied to procreation. While there was pressure from the top of society for women to continue to have families, and the official ideology was very much against single children ("only" children as they were called), most people resisted the propaganda for larger families. Secondly, married women were increasingly going out to work in the late 1940s and early 1950s, at least part time, and this meant a growing disjuncture between the dominant values which prevailed in the 1950s and the growing reality of women's lives. This was an explosive mix.

Most obviously, the position of women was changing. At least a minority of women had some life outside the home, tended to have smaller families and were becoming better educated. The sexual conservatism which pervaded British society was weakening dramatically but was still there. Sex was still not much discussed in public and the stigma against unmarried mothers continued. But many people began to feel that these kinds of attitudes were antiquated, and the growing acceptance of the need for pleasurable sex within marriage led to some questioning why the same could not also apply outside marriage.

Perhaps most importantly, the 1950s saw the emergence of a new phenomenon: the teenager. As for most young people, sex was a central concern, not least because in this fairly sexually repressive society it was always frowned upon and its importance denied. So teenagers developed their own counter-cultures, centred on rock music, in which sexuality played a very central part. Despite being frowned on by the institutions of the establishment, a booming capitalist society also saw a major marketing opportunity. They could use advertising to encourage certain limited sexual rebellion and could package as commodities the desires and wishes of teenagers. Records, clothes, films, motorbikes and scooters were products which expressed some of the rebellious attitudes and aspirations of young people. In turn the mass consumption of these commodities created a "youth culture". They thus helped to encourage and spread that rebellion, and to create the idea that everyone was behaving in this way. Conservative family values were one of the main objects of rebellion. The growth of this youth culture created a major paradox inside Western capitalist society. It meant that the conservative consumer society built on the fruits of the post-war boom also contained the seeds of its own downfall.

The great leap forward

It is no coincidence that the movements and attitudes of the 1960s – with the sexual revolution at their heart – marked a rebellion of young against old. It could hardly have been otherwise in a society where the old had dominated the young for the previous six decades. Now all the old values were subverted – the work ethic, patriotism, deference and, of course, sexual conservatism. The young were in a position where they did not have to just submit to the wishes of the old. So in the 1960s:

There were a million more unmarried people in the age range 15 to 24 than ten years previously – a 20 percent increase. And they wielded a new economic power. Average real wages increased by 25 percent between 1938 and 1958, but those of adolescents by twice this. And though they disposed of only some 5 percent of total consumer spending, they were the biggest purchasers of certain commodities – 42 percent of record players, 29 percent of cosmetics and toiletries, 28 percent of cinema admissions.[56]

At the same time, they tended to be dependent on their parents longer, through the raising of the school leaving age and the broadening of higher education. This led to greater tensions between parents and their children. So too did the more open attitude to sex, denounced as "permissiveness" by much of society and the subject of continued controversy and debate. For most young people, there were still many restrictions on sex. Indeed, what dominated theory and practice was very often ignorance. Sex education in schools was much more widespread than it had been before the war, but was still inadequate in many instances. Films like *Tom Jones*, *Alfie*, *The Knack*, *Saturday Night and Sunday Morning* all showed a more open and casual attitude to sex than 1950s cinema had done, but they hardly amounted to sex education. Indeed, the abortion scene in *Alfie* shows the dangers of illicit sex rather than any cost-free consequence.

Sexual intercourse was continuing to take place at an ever younger age. So whereas for women born between 1931 and 35 the median age of first intercourse was 21, for those born between 1941 and 45 the median had fallen to 19 years.[57] But the sexual experience for many does not appear to have changed too much. As a survey carried out in the mid-60s showed, for most people their early sexual experience was often conducted by trial and error. Sex "just happened": when penetrative sex occurred for the first time it was unpremeditated for four fifths of girls and boys. By 15, only one in 50 girls and one in 20 boys had had intercourse. First intercourse was not pleasurable for half of boys and two thirds of girls.[58] But the fact was that many taboos in behaviour had been lifted by the 1960s.

Marriage too tended to be at a younger age and by 1972 one in three of those marrying who had not previously been married were teenagers. This trend seems to be associated with access to sex and reveals the persistence of certain taboos on sex, or at least childbirth, outside marriage; at the same time it acted as a challenge to those same taboos. Figures from 1969-70 showed that one third of teenage brides were pregnant and 43 percent of all births conceived before marriage were to teenagers. Perhaps even more remarkably, only just over half (54 percent) of such births were subsequently legitimised by marriage in the period 1964-70. Illegitimate births were at 5.8 percent in 1961 (slightly up on 5 percent in 1951) – but by 1976 the figure was 9 percent.[59] This does not necessarily suggest a greater awareness of sexuality or greater control by women over their bodies, but it does suggest a much greater willingness to reject "old fashioned morals".

There were four major changes in women's lives which began to have an influence on their attitudes. Firstly, the numbers of women gaining access to higher education grew sharply in the 1960s and by 1970/1 there were 173,000 female undergraduates.[60] There they encountered on the one hand liberal attitudes on a whole range of issues which encouraged them to think differently about their role as women. Did they have to see their future as marriage and mother-hood or were there alternatives at least for educated and independent women? On the other hand, they were subject to petty restrictions on their life styles and sex lives which created great frustration and anger. Women undergraduates who were caught with a man in their room could be expelled from the college. In France the restriction on men visiting women's rooms was one of the issues which led directly to the great student explosion of May 1968.[61] The contradiction between the widening of horizons through education and the continued treatment of young adult students as children in their personal lives highlighted the ludicrous situation this new generation faced. In addition, the pos-sibility of sexual experimentation, of having more than one partner, and of connecting questions of sexuality with wider questions of social change, all led to a generation of women and men challenging the dominant ideas of women's subordination and sexual conformity.

The second influence on women's attitudes was the existence of an unprecedented level of control women now had over their own bodies – above all through much more widely available contracep-tion. For the first time in history it was possible to separate out procreation from sexual enjoyment. It is hard today, when younger women have had this much greater control over their bodies for the past few decades, to fully grasp what a huge difference this made at the time. It allowed women to liberate their choices about sexuality from the strictures of society and for many women who were young in the 1960s it was absolutely decisive in shaping their lives. The decline in the birth rate and the trend towards smaller families were notable throughout the 20th century, but the 1960s marked a turning point as new forms of contraception became available to the mass of women. These contraceptives did not depend in any way on a male partner, they were hidden and they did not involve embarrassing interruptions in sexual foreplay. Some medical problems with the oral contraceptive pill and much more with the various coil contraceptives became more apparent over the years. But nevertheless these developments represented a tremendous step forward in allowing women to be able to experiment sexually.

Thirdly, there was the impact of the liberalisation of laws relating to abortion, divorce and homosexuality. While the limitations of these laws were apparent from the beginning, they marked a breakthrough both for individuals directly affected but also for the general attitudes of society.[62] As Jeffrey Weeks has written:

> What was taking place in the 1960s was not a simple reform of outdated laws, but a major legislative restructuring, marking an historic shift in the mode of regulation of civil society. And at the heart of these changes were the great series of reforms of the laws relating to sexual behaviour, amounting to the most significant package of legislative changes on morality of over half a century.[63]

The increasing visibility and self-confidence of many gays and lesbians, with growing numbers refusing to stay in the closet, had a significant impact on sexual attitudes across society. It was probably the most threatening development to the dominant ideology about sexuality. The idea that all sex was happy and heterosexual was dealt a major blow and was replaced, at least in radical circles, with the acceptance of a wide and divergent range of sexuality.[64]

Finally, and perhaps most significantly was the change in the position of women at work. The post-war boom from the late 1940s to the mid-1970s drew in a huge new reserve of female labour. While in the 1950s in countries such as Britain much emphasis was on part time married women workers who could partially fill the gaps in a booming economy, the new generation of women were encouraged more and more to train and educate themselves for full time work.

Marriage and motherhood became an interruption in work outside the home rather than the end of it. Women had access to their own work and their own income, however limited this might be. Women's role at work meant again a thoroughgoing change in ideas – the view that women were meant to be simply decorative or always in the home could not be sustained. The 1960s also produced the great social movements for change that marked the first major challenge to the post-war consensus in the West. Out of these movements came those for women's liberation – and gay liberation – and these helped to ensure that the questioning of the old order brought with it a new sexual radicalism and experimentation.

The women's movement also created an awareness of sexuality that went far beyond what had been previous discussed openly in society for most people. By the start of the 1970s books like *The Myth of the Vaginal Orgasm* and *The Female Eunuch* were enthusiastically polemicising for a different and more adventurous female sexuality. The movement promoted new ways of looking at sexuality, and also led to a new approach to marriage, divorce, childbirth, abortion and other questions related to women's sexual control. Shere Hite's *The Hite Report* investigated and reported on female sexuality from an independent and feminist point of view. Other feminists highlighted the hidden horrors of domestic violence or of rape. The obvious message was that women had a right – and often a necessity – to escape from the supposed haven of the nuclear family to which they were meant to aspire.[65] The slogans of the period summed up the changes: "A woman's right to choose"; "YBA wife?"; "How dare you assume that I'm heterosexual?"; while a tea towel produced by the feminist magazine *Spare Rib* bore the slogan, "It begins when you sink in his arms, and ends with your arms in his sink".

But the more open moral climate of the 1970s soon met with a backlash. The second half of the 1970s saw successive attempts to restrict abortion. These attempts were unsuccessful because they went against the trends of the time, although without people mobilising they could have made more headway. James Callaghan's Labour government stressed the need for a strong family and for a return to more conventional education. The 1980s were much worse. The Aids epidemic, which began in the early part of that decade, was used as a means of attacking promiscuous sex and especially gay sex. Aids was referred to by all sorts of bigots from

Margaret Thatcher to the religious right as a gay plague – the punishment of the permissive society was death and disease. This religious fundamentalism was coupled with a total refusal to confront the real issues that could have prevented the spread of Aids – most obviously by explaining to people in sexually explicit language how to avoid passing on the disease. The fear and confusion created by the virus led to some changed sexual behaviour by both gays and straights, but did not alter the trend towards more openness about sexuality. It was, however, part of a move towards a more conservative establishment political discourse.

In any society there are sometimes contradictory developments taking place at any one time: the development of industry and work, and how that affects people's circumstances, their jobs and lives, leads to many material changes in people's situations. At the same time, these developments often involve conflicts with the ideas and institutions which have been created in the past. Many of the changes in society are hotly contested and argued over. In the 1980s it seemed that these two sometimes moved in opposite directions: right wing ideas often appeared to dominate in areas such as the legal control of sexuality, but at the same time people were not deterred from living the more "permissive" lives that had sprung up in the previous two decades. So by the 1990s bigoted measures such as Clause 28 of the Local Government Act, which banned the "promoting of homosexuality" in schools, could continue to coexist alongside the creation of much larger and more open gay communities, at least in big cities such as London and Manchester. Government ministers could spout the virtues of the family while numbers of marriages fell to record lows and more people than ever lived outside the traditional family.

Behind these developments were a number of very important features. Sex and sexuality had been separated from procreation, so people naturally asked why they couldn't gain sexual enjoyment in the way that they wanted – and what did it have to do with anyone apart from the individuals concerned? Whereas for previous generations there were all sorts of material constraints on sexual experimentation, by the 1980s and 90s there were far fewer. Young people tended to go to work later in life than their ancestors. Student numbers were expanding all the time, the majority of those in higher education living away from their parents. They might have limited finances, but they had time and opportunity to discover their sexuality. Young people in general had more time, money and independence than their grandparents or parents. Particularly important in this were young women. Often in essentially similar positions in college or at work to young men, and able to avoid unwanted pregnancy, women have expressed an interest in sex which has shocked many people. What is novel about all this is not that young women have an interest in sex, but that they now have the ability to do something about it. Women's assertiveness in this situation is a demand for the right to be treated equally with men, sexually as well as legally or financially.

Has it all gone too far?

By the beginning of the 21st century there were clear enough signs of certain permanent trends in love, marriage and sexuality. It was no longer the norm for people to abstain from sex before marriage – those who "saved themselves" for marriage became a smaller and smaller minority.[66] Marriage itself had changed dramatically. Whereas, as we have seen, for some of the 19th century and much of the 20th, premarital sex was taboo, now the norm was a form of "trial marriage" with few social sanctions on either side if they broke the relationship – especially if children were not yet involved. Whereas in the 1950s only 1 percent of women in Britain marrying for the first time had lived with the man first for an extended period, by the early 1980s this rose to 21 percent.[67] Of those born between 1933 and 1942 in the US, 84.5 percent of men and 93.8 percent of women married without living with their partner beforehand; but of those born between 1963 and 1974 – only 30 years later – these figures had slumped to 33 percent of men and 35.3 percent of women.[68] As John Gillis has pointed out, "The new cohabitation has many of the features of the old betrothal. It was an extended rite of transition…which was brought to a ritual conclusion when the couple decided it was time to incorporate themselves into the adult world of mothers and fathers".[69]

Talk about sex and sexuality also tends to be more open and sexual practice more widespread and varied. Here there are marked differences between the generations. Only 3 percent of women who started having sex in the 1950s had ten or more partners during their lifetime, while 10 percent of women starting intercourse in the 1970s claimed this figure.[70] While half a sample of 45 to 59 year olds in the early 1990s cited "being in love" as a reason for first intercourse, this reason declined through the age groups, to only 37.5 percent of women aged 16 to 24.[71] Attitudes to oral sex point to the changes which have taken place. A survey in the early 1990s revealed that even among 18 to 24 year olds, the proportion who have ever had oral sex exceeds that of those over 45. So while 76.7 percent of 18 to 24s had ever experienced it, this rose to 87.8 percent of 25 to 34s but fell to 61.8 percent of 45 to 59 year olds. Indeed, oral sex looked to be on a par with vaginal intercourse. In the age group 16 to 24, of those who had ever experienced vaginal intercourse, 85 percent had also experienced oral sex. In the US oral sex appears to be increasing among virgins with 25 percent of virgin boys and 15 percent of virgin girls having given or received oral-genital stimulation.[72] Despite the prevalence of men demanding "blow jobs" from women in Hollywood films, it seems the vast majority of oral sexual acts are reciprocal.[73]

But despite all this, the manifestations of sexuality that are so prevalent today cannot be said to add up to sexual liberation. We are sold particular images of sex and sexuality which conform to certain stereotypes about men and women but which reinforce unequal attitudes or oppressive relationships: images of violence, dominance and submission, and rape. The dominant view of sex is far from one of equality and openness. Sex in all of its manifestations is seen as a commodity to be bought and sold on the market. Pornographic films, DVDs, magazines, lap dancing clubs, phone sex, lad magazines with semi-pornographic contents, male strippers, entertainment for stag and hen nights, internet sex, sex contact listings in magazines, expensive women's underwear, sex toys and upmarket ice cream as a sex aid are only some of these new commodities. Most of them are advertised openly and are easily available to those with the necessary money. They have made millions for big business in the past 20 years. Most of them trade on the greater openness and awareness about sex and sexuality, and many of them hint at a more erotic, once forbidden world of sexual pleasure which can create liberation and release from the old stereotypes.

They rarely live up to this promise. Despite the substantial sums of money spent on these goods and services, they remain apart from their consumers – on film, at the end of a phone line, strutting a dingy stage or staring from a computer screen. Any intimacy or love or closeness in sexual relations is missing. Old sexist activities are dressed up as fun in other areas as well. Sleazy old stripping is reborn as lap dancing in expensive clubs patronised by businessmen and those on outings from City banks. The presence of women in the audience is supposed to make this cultural development acceptable. The 200 clubs which now exist in Britain mark "the invention of a branch of the sex industry considered not the slightest bit exploitative, nor remotely damaging to women".[74] The lap dancing clubs, however, do not break the mould of the old exploitative strip joints or brothels – rather they repackage it for credit card customers. The main objection to this commercialisation of sexuality cannot simply be the profits which have been made out of the greater sexual openness, objectionable though they may be. It is that a human relationship, something which should bring pleasure to the vast majority of men and women, has a price like a piece of meat or a second hand car and has been turned into another commodity. This process degrades the women and men directly involved in its production and display, but it also degrades the rest of us, since sexuality is turned into a series of objects and commercial relationships rather than being a natural expression of human relations.

For many women who campaigned for sexual freedom as central to women's liberation and who demanded the right to read and watch whatever we wanted, the developments over sexuality promote mixed feelings. You can't help feeling that someone else is getting the benefit of women's sexual freedom. The young feminist writer Ariel Levy in her book *Female Chauvinist Pigs* points out that our role models – or at least the role models thrust upon us – are increasingly the porn artists, strippers and lap dancers who seem to be defining sexuality and what it is to be sexual in our era:

> Both men and women alike seem to have developed a taste for kitschy, slutty stereotypes of female sexuality resurrected from an era not quite gone by. We don't even think about it any more, we just expect to see women flashing and stripping and groaning everywhere we look.[75]

Again, if this was about women expressing themselves sexually and nothing more it would be fine. Instead women are expected to be sexual and enjoy sex – but in ways that commercial interests imagine that men want them to do (which may not be what men want at all):

Women are currently encouraged to be "active" in male ways, rather than their own – for example, performing actions that demonstrate intercourse is making them more and more excited…"initiating" sexual activities long defined to be "sexual" by men, "acting hot" wearing "sexy" shocking outfits etc.[76]

While any of these may be the pinnacle of sexual fulfilment for some men and women, they also not coincidentally represent the way sex is supposed to be according to those who package it. As Levy says:

We have to ask ourselves why we are so focused on silent girly-girls in G-strings *faking* lust. This is not a sign of progress; it's a testament to what's still missing from our understanding of human sexuality with all of its complexity and power.[77]

Young women wearing "babe" or "bitch" T-shirts may be displaying a knowing post-modern irony but it doesn't always seem like that. Isn't it great, we are told, that women can get off with men in the way that men have traditionally got off with women: pick ups in bars, one night stands, and then not waiting around for them to call? Yes, it is better than it was, but it remains far short of what it *could* be. And sometimes it isn't even that great: that's when sexual freedom is turned against women and used to attack women's rights on a wider scale. The example of attitudes to rape over the past three decades serves to make the point.

Rape

Until the women's movement and the generally heightened atmosphere around women's rights in the early 1970s, rape was not regarded as a political issue. It became one after a series of prominent cases where it was widely felt that judges and other representatives of the legal system were treating women who were victims of sexual assault as though they had brought this upon themselves. A young Northern Ireland woman, Noreen Winchester, imprisoned for killing her father who had repeatedly raped her and her sister, became a symbol of the women's movement. The case of a guardsman released after raping a 17 year old because the judge felt that he "allowed his enthusiasm for sex" to get the better of him caused further outrage. The Yorkshire Ripper case in the late 1970s, where police failed to find the killer of prostitutes in Leeds and surrounding towns, politicised a horrific series of murders.[78]

These cases and others like them led to changes in police procedure and the law on rape. The first Rape Crisis Centre opened in 1976. Susan Brownmiller's book *Against our Will* became a key work of the women's movement. While there are many criticisms which can be made of Brownmiller's theoretical framework, especially her statement that rape is "a conscious process of intimidation by which all men keep all women in a state of fear", her book is a serious study which tries to locate rape in a social context of war and racist dominance.[79] In recent years there has been a backlash against ideas such as hers, reflecting the demise of the radical feminism which gave them impetus, but also reflecting a growing criticism of women's sexual behaviour. Katie Roiphe's *The Morning After* attacked the whole concept of "date rape": "If I was really standing in the middle of an epidemic, a crisis, if 25 percent of my female friends were really being raped, wouldn't I know it?"[80] Well, maybe she wouldn't be the first sympathetic shoulder to cry on, especially since her view is that "there is a gray area in which someone's rape may be another person's bad night".[81] High profile cases where men were acquitted of rape were used to suggest that the women had asked for it, with a marked willingness on the part of the authorities and media to blame the sexual behaviour of the women.

So the wheel has turned full circle. While women 30 years ago would have been denounced for wearing "provocative" clothing and so contributing to their own rape, they are now victims of the general easing of sexual attitudes. Because many women wear "provocative" clothes and are prepared to meet men in bars or hotels, they seem to have little or no protection against rapists who assume that women having the right to consent to sleep with anyone they choose means they consent to sleep with everyone.

The effects of this change in ideology can be detected in the record low levels of conviction for rape. Amid-much talk of women who cry rape unfairly and ruin the lives of men, there is far less sensational reporting in the media that many women who are raped do not report it. Some feel it is too shameful to report, others that they will not be believed and others suspect that the police and/or courts will not be sympathetic. It is hard to disagree when considering the figures. More rapes than ever are reported, so between 2001 and 2005 the number of reported rapes rose by just under 4,000 (9,734 to 13,712), while the proportion of suspects convicted fell from 6.57 percent to 5.31 percent.[82] Two thirds of reported rapes do not even go beyond investigation, and of those cases that finally get to court between one third and a half end in acquittal. These figures are so low that they mean that any rapist has a very good chance of getting away with it.

The double bind

Sexual freedom was never meant to be about women just becoming equal with men – after all, that would always have required women to have adopted many of men's sexual and social characteristics. It was about how men and women changed so that their sexuality became really equal with no assumptions of prejudice or inferiority. The limits of sexual liberation in the 20th century were precisely that this did not happen and that women's main form of sexual assertion is to imitate or to replace men. Why are we so far away from sexual liberation even after 40 years of liberalisation and more sexual openness?

One reason is that capitalist society continues to generate sexual repression and this in turn gives rise to double standards. While sex is one of the strongest human feelings and is the central act of human reproduction, it is constantly denied the arena of open and honest discussion within capitalism. Even in Britain today, where sex and sexuality are supposedly so open, we talk about it constantly but only in a stereotypical, commercialised "non-language". We know that many people feel too repressed to talk about their sexuality. We know that openness is not possible for many gays and lesbians, who for social, family, work or religious reasons feel that they have to stay in the closet. There is still a great deal of ignorance about sex and sexuality, and about sexual disease. Many people feel uncertain or ignorant about their bodies. Young people are confronted with endless images of sex while at the same time they are not necessarily more comfortable about discussing sexuality. The dual images of openness and repression are projected through media, government and social institutions at the same time, leading to at best confusion and certainly to a distorted view of what sex means. In November 2004, the month that George Bush was re-elected as US president on a sexually conservative, sanctity of marriage programme, *Desperate*

Housewives was the second highest rated show on television.[83] The more we talk about and look at pictures of sex, and assume that everyone is having a good time, the harder it is for people to admit to any problems – exactly the opposite of our original aims.

This discrepancy between the images of sexuality and the sexualised nature of society, and the lack of genuine satisfaction which derives from many sexual relationships, is inherent in a society where the condition of working people denies them the right to really free relationships. The porn videos and lads' magazines, which are so widespread today, do not themselves create commodified relationships – they are its particular products in the early 21st century. Capitalism acts to destroy and distort genuine human relations, reducing them to relations between things, rather than between people. The art and literature of the past 200 years has repeatedly returned to the theme of how money and wealth, and their adulation, destroy love and human relationships. Karl Marx talks about this process as "alienation": the goods which workers produce are taken from them and confront them as something alien, as commodities on the open market. Work does not seem an intrinsic part of his or her life, but something external to it:

> The worker does not affirm himself in his work but denies himself, feels miserable and unhappy, develops no free physical and mental energy but mortifies his flesh and ruins his mind. The worker therefore feels at ease only outside work, and during work he is outside himself. He is at home when he is not working and when he is working he is not at home. [84]

Sexual relations should be one of the major releases from the world of work. But two things mean that sexuality becomes itself part of the alienation that people experience as they are denied any real control over the work process or indeed any other part of their lives. One is that the world away from work is increasingly reduced to consumption and sexual relations. Marx makes the point that:

> the worker feels that he is acting freely only in his animal functions – eating, drinking, and procreating, or at most in his shelter and finery – while in his human functions he feels only like an animal... To be sure, eating, drinking, and procreation are genuine

human functions. In abstraction, however, and separated from the remaining sphere of human activities and turned into final and sole ends, they are animal functions.[85]

The family, the central institution of life outside of work, fulfils the function both of consumption and of sexual services and procreation. Yet it does not become a release from alienation or an even an escape from it, as the demands of work, its pressures and level of remuneration follow each worker home and profoundly shape family life.

The second problem is that sexuality and personal relations themselves suffer from alienation. Sexual relations confront us as something apart, a constant aspiration which no one can live up to. Liberation sexually may have got closer in terms of openness and lack of the sorts of taboo which once dominated working class life, but it remains as distant as other forms of human liberation. This is the conundrum at the heart of the sexual revolution, which can only be resolved through a wider change in society.

The family: the best of worlds, the worst of worlds

"ALL happy families are alike but an unhappy family is unhappy after its own fashion".[1] Leo Tolstoy's introduction to *Anna Karenina* sums up the great division in our minds about the family. It offers an ideal of love and happiness, in which the family enriches the lives of every individual member; but at the same time there are so many examples which fail to live up to the ideal where the dominant feelings inside the family are unhappiness, sorrow, bitterness or despair. Unfortunately, life is a little more complicated than Tolstoy saw it, because many of the most intense and contradictory emotions occur within the same family and sometimes even within the same person.

This contradiction goes to the heart of the family itself: it is the centre of emotion and care within society, a haven from a heartless world to which people cling in times of trouble and to which they aspire very often if they are outside the family. It is a unit which protects its members from the ravages of life outside its walls, which feeds, clothes, socialises, cherishes its children and cares for its old and sick. After all, alternatives to the family in our society are pretty grim: sleeping on the streets or living in "care" as a child. Men who live outside the family, and especially older men, are likely to suffer some of the worst physical and mental health problems. It has, however, another side. The family is also an imperfect institution which cannot deliver on its promise of happiness, a place where many feelings and hopes are repressed and denied, sometimes brutally. At its most extreme is the shocking fact that the majority of murders and child abuse take place within the family.[2] It is also estimated that domestic violence accounts for 16 percent of all violent crime, and claims the lives of two women a week and 30 men a year in Britain. Domestic violence is the greatest cause of ill health worldwide for women aged between 19 and 44 – worse than cancer, car accidents or war.[3]

Indeed, for many years domestic violence was treated as an individual matter in which the police and the legal system were reluctant to intervene. Rape within marriage was not regarded as a crime, and the physical beating of children was only prohibited in the most extreme of cases. Incest or severe physical or sexual abuse is still regarded as a relatively rare and abnormal occurrence, rather than a regular outcome of an institution which is based on hierarchical relationships and sexual repression, and where children are regarded as the property of their parents. The terrible cases of fathers who kill all their children, often in response to the breakdown of a marriage, are frequently linked to forms of authoritarianism where the father feels he has failed as provider and head of the family.

So this is the extraordinary and contradictory institution into which we are all born, and in which (more or less) we pass our lives. It is at once a site of love, support, solidarity and affection, but at the same time a source of much physical or mental abuse, domestic violence, hidden shames and secrets, and the suppression of dreams and desires.

The family, but not as we know it
Why does the family endure despite these failings and despite all the pressures on it from society? The most common view is because it always has existed. But this isn't true. In early human history, before the development of classes and private property, there was no family structure.[4] And the family today bears little relation to the family of 2,000, 1,000 or even 500 years ago.

The family may have existed for several thousand years, but not as we know it. In most of its incarnations it has played an economic role which has been central to the livelihood and wellbeing of its members. The family for most of human history has been centred on agriculture. Work wasn't separated from human reproduction and childcare, but was an integral part of it. There was always a division of labour where women performed the bulk of childcare and some productive tasks in and around the home, while men performed different, often more mobile, work; but both sets of work still centred on the agricultural household.

This has all changed in the past few hundred years with the development of the capitalist system, first in small parts of Europe and North America, and then across the world. Based on commodity production in the factories, capitalism created a class of wage labourers who had to sell their labour power on the market in order to survive. The traditional family could not survive such a change. A feature of capitalism became the separation of home from work. The different members of the family could no longer produce their subsistence in and around the home, so they became part of a market in labour. The home stopped being a place of production – for example, weaving cloth, as well as cheese and lace making all ceased to be produced in the home but instead became goods which were produced through industrial manufacture, and bought with wages by people who might once have produced them.[5]

The development of the factory system was characterised initially by each member of the family selling their labour power on the market – men, women and children went out to work. This led some to conclude that the working class family itself was in the process of disintegrating as the labour market pulled the members of the family apart.[6] Older family members, those children not at work, neighbours or even professional pudding makers in the Lancashire textile areas, all carried out work to try and compensate for mothers being employed outside the home. But the situation of the working class family in industry during the first part of the 19th century was dire.

The move away from this pattern saw the re-establishment of the family on a new basis around the ideal of the male wage worker and female homemaker. Two needs came together to recreate the family as a nuclear unit organised around a male breadwinner. Firstly, the more far-sighted employers could see that it provided a long term solution to capital's need to sustain both the existing generation of workers, who needed to be fed, clothed and rested if they were to remain productive and therefore profitable over any length of time, and the need to provide for the upbringing of the next generation of workers. The alternatives for the employers were to either work the existing pool of available labour to utter exhaustion or to provide for the upkeep of workers and children at society's expense. The former was unsustainable and the latter unthinkable. The new family structure offered a cheap remedy that threw the burden onto workers themselves to provide for existing and future workers.

But the working class also looked to recreate the family on a new basis in an attempt to provide some respite from the new world of industrial production. This initially took the form of support for the call for an end to child labour in the mines and mills. Following that, it seems without much demur, came the demand for women to be protected from certain sorts of work, and legislation was eventually passed prohibiting certain industries from employing women and children. Some factory owners backed this legislation, although it was bitterly opposed by others. The whole process of excluding women from work has been the subject of much debate, with some feminists seeing this and other legislation as a conspiracy between male workers and male factory owners to push women into the home, and I return to it more fully below.[7] However it is clear that this move in part marked a conscious decision by working people to improve their living standards and to defend the family, which they too saw as under threat. The demand for women and children to be protected from certain work, and for a family wage to cover the costs of maintaining a wife and children, appealed to many working men, and no doubt to women. It was seen as part of the battle for a decent living standard for workers.[8]

So the new family was at the same time both imposed on the new factory workforce as a means of disciplining it and largely accepted by workers as offering a refuge from the harsh realities of the new industrial system. People now gathered in the family not to work but to escape from the world of work. The at least partial achievement of this aim represented the high point of the Victorian ideal of the stable happy family and the retreat of married women into the home. From around 1870 the proportion of women employed outside the home began to fall.[9]

This all tended to encourage a glorification of home life (it was in the second half of the 19th century when mottos and samplers proclaiming "East west home's best" or "There's no place like home" were seen on the walls and mantelpieces of working class houses), a rigid matrimonial system, and a hierarchical family with the father as its clear head, and the mother's place at the hearth and cradle. This view, accepted by much of the working class, had as its ideal the middle class or even upper class family, where women's and men's roles were very rigidly defined as different and where the woman's role was decreed as domestic and decorative, away from the important public affairs or industry which were the preserves of men. As one historian wrote of the position of women, "For all who could afford it – and, after all, it was they who mattered – woman's place was in the home".[10]

The retreat of women into the home was never total, and within the home itself the women often continued to work for money (doing laundry, taking in lodgers, making light goods). There were also large numbers of "spinsters" in the 19th century, women who never married, who were forced to rely on their own resources and were usually desperately poor. For married women, death, disability, or desertion by the man in their lives spelt destitution. Most of the children in orphanages in the late 19th century weren't actually orphans but children of widows or occasionally widowers.[11] In some industries, mainly Lancashire and Cheshire textiles, women continued to work after marriage with consequently quite different family lives and with a markedly different economic and social independence.[12] But all of this didn't make the new dominant family form any less real. Nor could the retreat from work into the home have been anything but a defeat for women, representing a conscious attempt to create a male breadwinner family, and therefore a blow for those married women who would have wanted to continue working. The consequences of these changes did not just affect those women directly involved, but all women, in that it set the pattern for the working class family for around 100 years.

In this respect, little changed until well into the 20th century, and the family as designed by this model withstood changes remarkably well. Women did over the course of time gain advances and opportunities which opened up in very limited ways education and wider job possibilities. But despite two world wars, and their profound effects on employment, sexuality and marriage, the patterns of family life in the 1950s appeared remarkably similar to half a century previously. The ideology of the man as breadwinner, the full time housewife or woman who worked part time for "pin money", and above all the centrality of the nuclear family, all remained. However, the new patterns of life so evident from the 1950s onwards led to often incremental but ultimately profound changes. Married women who were drawn into the workforce, at first part time then full time, changed their attitudes about whether the family could cope for even a few hours a day without them. In the early years after the Second World War women tended to work until they were mothers, when they stopped for a period, returning to work part time when their children got older. Today that's not the usual pattern, especially for women with qualifications, who tend to work full time with only a short period of maternity leave before resuming full time work again.[13]

Since the 1950s women have increasingly gone into higher education to equip themselves to participate in this world of work. Men and women, in the period of the greatest boom capitalism had ever seen, migrated as never before to find work, often on other sides of the globe. In the process, all traditional family relations were destroyed or weakened, leading to changed habits and attitudes.

The family's role and function became ever more detached from tradition, and especially from any remaining economic role. It also became a place where fewer and fewer of its members were cared for directly: hospitals and homes cared for the sick and elderly. Children spent ever longer in education and so were both financially dependent on their parents for longer and involved in a social sphere outside the family. Women's role (and earnings) outside the home meant that what little was produced in the home for domestic consumption (cakes and pies, home made clothes, some decorating) was now replaced by goods and services bought on the open market (ready meals, dishwashers, fast food).

The family has became a unit of consumption par excellence, with all of its members united in the pursuit of the most attractive consumer durables: which car, curtains, mobile phone, toys, wide screen television or washing machine to buy are the central issues to families increasingly identified by their adherence to certain brands. The younger this consumerism affects the children of the family, the sooner they are drawn into defining themselves by what they possess.

The family that shops together cannot, however, necessarily be expected to stay together. For one thing, the pressures of consumerism can exacerbate the tensions of family life as even two, three or four incomes in a family fail to match the demands on each member of the family to spend, spend, spend. One of the biggest pressures on the family is the labour market, which pulls women and men in relationships in different directions. The restructuring of industry over the past three decades has exacted an enormous toll, where for example if males want to work after a factory or mine shuts down, the logic is to move in search of new work. It also puts enormous pressures on relations between parents and children – there is little time for "quality time" with young children after long working hours.

But there is still today an outside as well as internal pressure for the family to hold itself intact. It is the same imperative that led to the creation of the modern family in the mid-19th century, as we have seen. While the family has long ceased to produce goods to sell on the open market, because industrial production can deliver those more cheaply and quickly, there remains no comparable means of caring for the existing members of the family and bringing up the next generation as healthy, socialised, educated beings. So the family remains responsible for the reproduction of the important commodity, labour power. Caring for the existing generation of workers, providing their sustenance, housing, healthcare, and leisure from work, is an essential job of the family. Even more important is the reproduction of the next generation. Children are born, cared for, socialised, partly educated, paid for and loved within the family.

Who benefits? Parents and children hopefully feel they have both achieved a fulfilling relationship. But economically the real winners are the employing class, who receive, at the ages of 18 or 21, a new generation of workers fitted to replace the older ones, equipped with knowledge, skills and socialised behaviour. The two lots of winners and the dual nature of the family help to explain how it keeps going when so many forces are lined up against it and act to weaken it.

It is common in many sociological accounts of the family to fail to see these two sides. It is seen either an institution with an economic function, or it is just about individual relationships. Both are wrong. The family does perform an extremely important role within capitalism (specifically the reproduction of the next generation of workers). However, there would not be such enthusiasm for the family if this were all that they were about. No one walks down the aisle in a white dress thinking that they are doing this for the benefit of capital or to reproduce the next generation of workers. They do so for reasons of love, family, the hope of having children, and the desire to create a space for love and happiness in their lives. However, they do so not in conditions of their own choosing, and economic constraints and social pressures are constantly knocking on the door of the family.

One textbook on the family which claims that Marxism has nothing to say to the individual and their impulses demonstrates the compartmentalised nature of so much academic writing. It argues that:

> micro-sociologists argue that all social life – including the family – is meaningful to those involved in it and that individuals do have a degree of free will and independence. We are not always passive victims of control, surveillance and ideology.[14]

Of course not, otherwise there would be no point in talking about political action or debate. However, it is also true that we cannot simply view individual family members as exercising a number of desires and choices without reference to wider society. Questions of class, race and ideology, all play a part. Facts of life as seemingly mundane as whether you are being made to work harder by your boss, whether you have to travel longer on inadequate public transport because house prices dictate that you move further away from work, whether your elderly relative can survive on his or her pension or receive a hip replacement operation, all impact in very significant ways on the family. Choice, free will and independence are all constrained by many factors, even though people may consciously try to overcome them. The one-sided view of the family cannot explain the way the family appears both as a true haven and the place where this hope is so often dashed on the rocks of material reality.

Love and marriage

"Love and marriage, love and marriage / go together like a horse and carriage" went the song. In the 1950s nobody seemed to think any differently. For those of us who grew up in those years, it seemed as though this pattern of life had existed forever. There were, of course, many skeletons in cupboards: children born out of wedlock brought up as their own by "parents" who were in fact grandparents, wartime marriages which were rarely talked about, people living as husband and wife while unmarried because one or the other could not obtain a divorce, and a considerable number of pregnant brides.[15] So practice was rather different from theory even in those years.

But, as we have seen, by the late 1960s attitudes to love and marriage had begun to undergo a profound alteration. Increasingly marriage was separated from sexual relations and even from motherhood. By the 1980s, there was once again the laissez faire attitude that pregnancy didn't need to be accompanied by marriage and that cohabitation was a valid and even respectable way of living. No doubt at least some of this was due to women's economic independence. Worrying about whether a man would "respect" you if you slept with him became less of an issue as women became more socially and geographically mobile, and as they no longer had to depend on a husband or father for financial support.

The new attitudes meant that the number of marriages fell dramatically, and there is no real sign of any revival. In 2001 there was the lowest number of annual marriages since 1897.[16] There were 271,000 marriages in England and Wales in 2004, just under 1,000 more than in 2003. First marriages fell from 340,000 in 1970 to 161,300 in 2004. The rate of first marriages has decreased for both sexes during the past ten years: for every 1,000 single men aged 16 and over, 34.3 married in 1994, but this fell to 25.5 in 2004. Similarly, for the comparable age group for women the figures were 41.6 per 1,000 marrying in 1994, compared with just 30.5 women in 2004.[17] The number of first marriages has declined by more than half since 1970. Many women now either don't marry at all, or if they do it is usually after a period of living together, and maybe partners will have had a series of two or three serious partners before they "settle down" to married life. The average age of first marriage in England and Wales has gone up considerably. In 2005 the average age for men was 32, while that for women was 29; this compared to 25 for men and 23 for women 40 years previously.[18] For many people, the decline in the number of marriages has also been accompanied by the ending of the belief that marriage is necessary before the birth of children.

While this shows a disregard for the legalities of marriage, it does not necessarily entail a rejection of the nuclear family form. Many unmarried mothers live with the fathers of their children in stable long term relationships, and the birth of the children is registered in both partners' names. But it does mark a considerably different attitude from the situation of up to half a century ago, when marriage and motherhood were regarded as mutually essential.

Alongside the relaxed attitude to marriage has gone a much more accommodating one to divorce. Up to the Second World War divorce was extremely difficult and expensive to obtain, so it tended to remain the preserve of the well off. The wartime marriages contracted hastily by couples who might not see each other again led to a spate of post-war divorces. The easing of the divorce laws in 1969 allowed a much further liberalisation and the opportunity for working class people to divorce in a way undreamt of for several generations. In 1961 there were 27,224 divorces in Britain; by 1969 this had doubled to 55,556. By 1972 it had doubled yet again to 124,991 partly as a result of the new laws.[19]

Before that there were a number of unsatisfactory options: staying together "because of the children" or for other reasons; setting up home with another partner away from the local area, usually pretending to neighbours and workmates that this was a bona fide marriage; living alone. Today legal divorce figures are among the highest ever, although the 2005 figure of 155,052 was slightly down on that of the previous year. Around a third of marriages are ending in divorce.[20] There are nearly as many divorces as first marriages, and slightly more divorces than remarriages, which are slightly down.[21] Marriage and relationships are not seen as being for life, and there must be a suspicion even at many weddings that this will be a relatively short period of conjugal bliss. While first marriages increasingly fail, that doesn't stop people engaging in second and third marriages. There were 123,000 remarriages in 2003.[22] Behind the separation of many divorced couples is clearly the desire to try to find a new ideal husband or wife. This expectation of divorce and of limited marriages has changed the face of the family. There are more complex relationships, with previous partners who parent children remaining involved, with children of different mothers or fathers making up sometimes larger families.

It is probably not coincidental that these changing customs and practices, especially on the part of women who have found sexual and social constraints lessening and who no longer feel it necessary to live in the rigidly determined way of previous generations, come at a time of profound social change involving women and men. In the 18th and 19th centuries it was the upheaval caused by people being driven off the land and into the growing towns and cities that required changed ways of living and the reshaping of family structures. The impetus for new patterns of behaviour today stems from the great social upheavals of the 1950s, 1960s and 1970s, when women's lives and expectations began to change substantially, and their personal relations followed suit.

Social attitudes, even among those who are married, have changed considerably. The pressure on the family to adapt and remake itself when faced with initially unpalatable options is obviously great. Although there are many terrible stories of children disowned by parents for being gay or for having children outside marriage, there has clearly been a much greater social acceptance of these issues among the older generations. Parents quickly learned to "forgive" children who lived as couples outside marriage, or who came out as gay or lesbian. The happiness at a new grandchild tended to override any unhappiness or shame at it being born outside marriage. So in the space of a generation the attitudes not only of the young but also even of many of the old have changed considerably.

However, there is still a gap between young and old, with those aged between 25 and 34 being nearly three times as likely as people over 65 to see nothing wrong in premarital sex.[23] While women traditionally had more conservative attitudes than men, they now tend to have more progressive ones:

> Women were more opposed to premarital and extramarital sex than men were in the early years [studied]. Since then, women's opposition to premarital sex has halved while men's opposition has changed in the same direction but to a lesser extent.[24]

By 1994 only 21 percent of women (and 27 percent of men) agreed with the view that "married people are generally happier than unmarried people".[25] By 1997 one survey reported that just under two thirds of those asked thought marriage should be forever; 39 percent said they felt it was important for couples to live together before they got married.[26] Another survey on attitudes showed 56 percent thought it was "a good idea" for couples intending to marry to live together first, and 67 percent thought it acceptable for a couple to cohabit, even where they don't intend to marry. On the other hand, only 9 percent agreed "there is no point getting married – it's only a piece of paper" and 54 percent agreed that "people who want children ought to get married".[27]

You might expect from the declining number of marriages that weddings would have declined in fashion. The opposite seems to be true. There are fewer weddings, but remarriage figures tend to track the divorce rate, suggesting a naïve but engaging belief in marriage despite particular failures. Weddings are ever more expensive – they have become increasingly elaborate celebrations of an institution to which fewer and fewer people subscribe.

White weddings are relatively new. In the 19th century only the rich wore white – everyone else who married wore their best clothes, sometimes supplemented by rented white gloves or a specially bought or made suit or dress which could be worn again.[28] This habit continued well into the 20th century, until the 1930s. Often several marriages were performed at once in city churches in places such as the East End of London. Popular wedding days were Christmas, Easter and Whitsun, and August bank holiday, because these coincided with holidays and so weddings were part of a wider celebration.[29]

However, the spectacle of white weddings has grown throughout the 20th century. The 1950s saw the development of the "big wedding" and it was claimed then that 58 percent of skilled workers and 45 percent of unskilled were married in the "grand manner".[30] That meant a white dress, often with veil and train, bridesmaids, reception outside the home, a church as opposed to register office wedding, and a honeymoon. A study of weddings in the 1970s in Swansea, south Wales, shows how committed young women were to "a proper wedding". Even when young women found themselves pregnant and having to rush the marriage, some were reluctant to abandon the trimmings of the "big day" completely by marrying quietly in a register office.[31] While the early 1970s marked the high point of marriage, and there are many more alternatives to marriage for women today than ever before, there is every sign that the "big wedding" is getting bigger and more extravagant. This is most obvious among the very richest in society. The disastrous marriage of Prince Charles and Princess Diana in 1981 did not prevent their wedding itself from becoming a benchmark in grandeur imitated by millions around the world. This marriage coincided with the high tide of Thatcherism and the turn towards a more market based consumerist society, and this only helped to accelerate the trend, as people were encouraged to buy into the family dream. Today the trend towards big celebrity weddings, complete with paparazzi, remote castles as venues, Hollywood film star guests and ever more fantastic themes, is complete. The footballer David Beckham and his wife Victoria married while sitting on giant thrones, Tom Cruise in an Italian hill town castle, and the new aristocracy takes its place alongside the old.

The rest of us don't need to hang around on street corners to catch a glimpse of the magic: mass circulation magazines like *Hello* buy the exclusive rights; the weddings and speculation about them are covered as serious news; the outfits are copied and reproduced for next year's working class weddings. Buying into the big wedding even at the lower end doesn't come cheap. The wedding dress, catering, transport, booking halls or hotels, stag night, hen night, honeymoon, will all add up to thousands of pounds even when provided on a minimalist basis. That's before each guest pays for outfits, presents and accommodation, all of which is likely to run into hundreds of pounds per person. The wedding takes an ever more elongated form, both on the day itself, where there is often a post-wedding reception followed by a much bigger evening one, but there are also the stag and hen nights, sometimes entailing groups of friends spending a weekend in European capitals; weddings abroad, where the guests all travel to exotic or picturesque destinations to celebrate with the bride and groom; and dinners and parties for families and friends in the days before the wedding.

These elaborate rituals and celebrations are planned and booked months if not years in advance, and play at least as central a part in family life as weddings have ever done. The wedding industry is large and profitable: whole racks of magazines are devoted to planning the "big day" and weddings play a big part in most women's magazines; every major store has wedding lists and wedding departments; attractive venues can charge large sums for receptions; and the church itself rakes in considerable fees from this most popular of religious ceremonies. A range of experts is on hand to advise the bride, ranging from bakers, caterers, florists and vicars, to full scale wedding planners who organise to ensure that everything goes right on the day. Custom and practice decree what the bride should or shouldn't wear, who should pay for what, who should be invited to which part of the wedding, what the bride's mother should wear, and much more.

The months before and after the event are filled for the bride and groom and their families with planning and decision making, then reminiscences, viewing the photographs and videos and hopefully happy memories. All this is no doubt a major attraction of the event: it is a major source of family involvement and memory, a shared experience on a scale of the arrival of children or grandchildren, a day which brings the whole family together in a world where regular personal contact may be erratic or difficult. Diana Leonard Barker writes of her 1970s wedding study:

> Weddings nowadays are a source of excitement and interest for women in particular and, together with births and christenings, deaths and funerals, form abiding topics of conversation in the home, factory and office. These are the main occasions on which kin may meet as a group and when husband and wife may participate jointly in social activities.[32]

Thirty years later, little has changed (although husbands and wives probably have less segregated social lives):

> Weddings are the only major ceremonials organised by most ordinary people, certainly by ordinary women. They are times of planning, saving, booking, choosing, checking details, and of endless expense.[33]

The wedding is popular in itself, a stage in the life of friends and relatives which is of profound importance to them and to those close to them. But the "big wedding" speaks to something else: a desire to fill life with something important, memorable, and lasting where for one day at least all attention focuses on the bride, and to a lesser extent the groom, and a desire to make that day as "perfect" as possible. The day and the lengthy celebration and preparation around it are seen as a relief from the alienation of everyday life, the monotony of much work, and the reality of living away from loved ones. It takes this form firstly because in capitalist society emotions are increasingly identified with commodities which can be bought and sold. So marital happiness is identified with a series of purchases of goods and services which supposedly spell happiness. Secondly, the desire for release from the fears and worries of this society often takes the form of a romantic ideal offering an alternative to "real life". That the idealised wedding has reached its height alongside record levels of divorce only demonstrates how "real life" fails to fulfil the hopes and aspirations of so many.

You have to be rich to afford the family

It's hard to think of the family without thinking of money. For a start, it costs a fortune. The poorest groups in society are either those with young children or the old. Fathers of young children are some of the hardest workers outside the home, with employment rates among men at their highest when the children are under 5. One third of fathers spend more than 50 hours at work, compared with a quarter of childless men doing equivalent jobs.[34] The cost of bringing up a child has been estimated at more than the cost of an average family house. A 2004 survey commissioned by Woolworths claimed that from birth to university parents spend about £164,000 feeding, clothing and educating a child, compared with £146,000 for a house.[35] Another survey for *Family Circle* magazine found 16 to be the most expensive age but also found that "70 percent of parents said they would help their child buy their first car and 80 percent expect to fund part of their university education. Some 44 percent will also help their child buy their first home".[36] A third survey for the Liverpool Victoria Friendly Society found the cost of the first five years of a child's life was £46,695, that parents in the UK spend on average £30,000 on their child between the ages of 19 and 21, and that the cost of three children would add up to nearly half a million pounds.[37]

The images of children and family projected by advertising, television programmes, lifestyle magazines, government and its agencies have a tacit assumption that certain commodities are affordable and available. These include a well decorated and spacious house; a new car; holidays in other well decorated and spacious houses; hobbies and interests such as playing musical instruments; computers, mobile phones and iPods for all the family, and fashionable clothes.

You don't have to be an economist to work out that the average male wage can't provide all this. Even the average male and the average female wage combined, assuming both work for wages, is likely to be hard pressed to do so, especially when the costs of working (travel, childcare, lunches and clothing) are taken into account. So this is a picture of an idealised family rich in commodities, not the picture of most working families, let alone those who have to live on benefits. Any such family will be in the top 5 or 10 percent wealthiest part of the population. This is a model beyond the attainment of most people.

Yet there is an inexorable pressure for most of us to strive to conform to such a family model. Families who do not own these commodities tend to be seen as a problem: homeless or overcrowded families are regarded less as a happy family unit and more as a set of statistics. Indeed family happiness is often equated with housing; living happily ever after with acquiring at least one dream home. So great pressure is placed on the family to achieve a home – any home at first because it is important to "get on the housing ladder". Permanent revolution then reigns in the home: there has to be a never ending process of decorating, home improvement, changing colour schemes, ripping out kitchens and bathrooms to replace them with the latest model, buying new furniture, and of course moving house because this is the way you move "up the housing ladder". Just as there is now a plethora of television programmes where rich male celebrity chefs tell people how to cook at a time when fewer people than ever cook meals from raw materials as opposed to heating ready meals, so there has been a major growth in house and home related programmes at a time when work outside the home involves lengthy hours and when people are spending less time in the home. These programmes tell people how to decorate their house, how to improve its value on the market, which areas are desirable to live in, where you can buy cheap and sell dear, how you can spread the inflationary housing market in Britain to elsewhere in Europe.

As happy families equal home, home equals ever greater consumption. Don't be satisfied until every room is newly decorated and then start again. Don't just chuck out your chintz, as the furniture superstore IKEA told us in an advertising campaign, but chuck out perfectly serviceable washing machines, cookers or fridges in the name of fashion and sparkling novelty. The effect is frightening. The family under capitalism has always been a centre of consumption, a feature that grew as it lost all remaining productive functions. But in an era where women's wages are needed as well as men's to cover the costs of running a family, where there are record levels of credit and indebtedness, where powerful images surround us with the message that the only happy families are the ones which consume together, consumption of goods by even the youngest members of the family has become one of its major features.

One of the main leisure pursuits today is shopping. Every holiday families are deluged with special offers about buying sofas, DIY and cheap electrical goods. Boxing Day and Easter Monday, once days of traditional leisure pursuits, now see record crowds in shopping centres. Sunday trading has turned the one day where traditionally little commercial trade was performed into the second busiest shopping day of the week in Britain. Families encourage other family members to spend, as do advertisers: tired from working in and outside the home? Treat yourself to a day at a spa. Or a new top, or just some chocolate.

Household debt is at record levels, both for personal debt and for secured debt on houses. The dream home is therefore often mortgaged to the hilt and under permanent threat of removal if payments cannot be maintained through unemployment, death or just over-indebtedness. Women are very susceptible to debt, because they have to provide clothing and furniture for families often from inadequate incomes, and also because they are at the receiving end of much social and advertising pressure to "improve" their homes. One of the largest groups of women prisoners in Britain today are there for debt.

This consumption does not, of course, exist in a vacuum. There has been an awful symmetry between women being drawn into the workforce and the increased commodification of the home. Technological change is harnessed to working life for women and allows them to take care of childcare and domestic duties while still putting in a full day's work. Mobile phones allow children and parents to stay in contact. It would be hard to imagine the development of mothers' full time working without the existence of videos, DVDs and home entertainment systems to entertain the children and act as a form of childcare while parents perform other household tasks. Microwave ovens, freezers and dishwashers have all become the means of rapidly preparing meals and clearing up after them.

Women's work outside the home has been closely connected with the development of commodities which have eased the burden of housework. The connecting of most households to the national grid after the First World War opened a market for electrical appliances such as irons, fires and cookers. Women largely made up the workforces of these "new industries" in a circular development which allowed greater women's economic participation partly because of labour saving devices in the home, devices which women themselves produced.[38]

So homes have become much more high tech places than 50 let alone 100 years ago, but this limits the separation of home from work. It is true that women's relationship to shopping is completely different from their parents or grandparents' – when there was no refrigeration or private transport, little cupboard space and sometimes daily payment of wages, shopping was a day to day local event.[39] A whole day was devoted to washing in the household, whereas now that process is spread across the week, carried out often at night by machinery. The traditional baking day where women made bread, cakes and pastries has disappeared, home production unable to compete with the range of pastries and cakes available at all levels of quality and price on the open market.

However, because today the much higher levels of consumption are tied to women working, they take a very different form from the traditional luxury consumption of the rich. Most commodities, especially the more costly ones in the family, are either essential to allowing women and men to work (for example a car for shift workers or those who have to take children to nursery before work) or greatly enhance the ability to work (such as washing machines or microwaves or computers). Added to this are the range of services which allow some of the tasks once done inside the family to be bought on the market, from supermarket home deliveries, carpet and curtain cleaners, ironing services, to takeaways and home delivered cooked foods. In addition, the technical appliances have "increased [the] household's dependence on the technical experts who maintain, repair and alter those gadgets. The private character of consumption is surely compromised by this dependence".[40] The computer technicians, plumbers, electricians and the like who service the gadgets all charge high rates for their expertise. Technological advance also means that "their higher turnover and the faster rate of technological obsolescence involve the consumer in more frequent trips to the showrooms".[41]

Increasingly families who can afford it (usually within the top 5 percent of incomes) are turning to paid domestic labour in the home. The growth in the number of cleaners and other domestic servants has been very great in recent years as double income professionals find they can afford some domestic help which comes relatively cheap in a low wage economy.[42] Au pairs and nannies are much more common. The vast majority of these low paid workers are women, often immigrants who find they have to accept such jobs.[43]

The ideal family is only sustained by substantial private financial outlay in these areas to ensure a smooth and commodity-rich household. These households also use their financial advantage to avail themselves of goods and services which once were available through public provision but are no longer: they pay for private health and dental care; buy tuition services to ensure their children pass exams; buy first class travel, and fast track their driving on toll roads. You have to be rich to buy into this image of the family. For everyone else the family means increasing debt which still fails to satisfy the desires and aspirations of its individual members.

The humpty dumpty family: can they put it back together again?
The transformation in the lives of families which marks the 1960s and the decades since inevitably produced a backlash in defence of "family values", and this has been at work for as long as these social changes were apparent, epitomised by Mary Whitehouse and Lord Longford in the late 1960s and early 1970s, Victoria Gillick in the 1980s and John Major's "Back to Basics" campaign in the 1990s. Ideas and values which once seemed on the extreme fringe of right wing politics are now adopted by government ministers who link family breakdown with the overall decline of society. Many of the social ills facing us today are blamed specifically on single parent families, a lack of father figures or the supposed lack of discipline in the family and the failure of families to eat together or to communicate sufficiently.

Family breakdown is the new buzzword for politicians desperate to deflect criticism from their own or their predecessors' policies. So while New Labour introduces ASBOs for children who clearly need help, not punishment, former Tory leader Iain Duncan Smith talks about the importance of marriage as an institution, implying that any parent who lives alone or divorces is somehow inadequate or uncaring.[44] While much is made of the impact of these changing families on the lives of children, we should not regard this phenomenon as belonging solely to the late 20th and early 21st centuries. These "broken" families, where only one parent is involved in the upbringing of the child, were quite normal historically if we look beyond the last century. Then families were split up by death rather than separation, but the effects in many cases were the same. Early mortality meant frequent remarriages, often involving much younger partners, resulting in sometimes unrelated siblings living in families, when the children of a dead father, for example, stayed in the stepmother's house (the recurring figure of the wicked stepmother in fairy tales testifies to how widespread this situation was).[45]

Today, however, both the natural parents of the child often play a role in the care and education of their children, even though the relationship between the couple has ended. Many children have a relationship with their natural parents, the subsequent partners of each parent, and any children of the subsequent partners. While we should not pretend that such relationships are necessarily happy or easy, they can give the opportunity for a more extended network of emotional and economic support, as well as childcare. When grandparents and other relatives are included in this network, it means that each child potentially has a number of adults involved in its upbringing.

Yet this is seen by the new ideologues of the family as a problem rather than an opportunity for several adults to participate in the child's wellbeing. Their fears increase in direct proportion to the poverty of the families involved, linking them with the tradition going back to Victorian times of distinguishing between the deserving and undeserving poor. Government ministers' use of the phrase "hard working families" sums up an attitude which assumes that everyone who has money deserves it and everyone who does not must deserve that too.

It is a remarkable retreat from the social policy of the post-war boom years to treat people who suffer social deprivation of any sort as culpable. But perhaps we shouldn't be so surprised at this. After all, it was the arch-privatiser and scourge of communities Margaret Thatcher who once said, "There is no such thing as society. There are individual men and women, and there are families. And no government can do anything except through people, and people must look to themselves".[46] Nor should we be surprised by the recent figures showing that of the top ten towns where large numbers of people thought there was a problem with anti-social behaviour, three were former mining communities and a further two were declining steel towns.[47]

The phase of neoliberal capitalism under which we live, with its fixation on free markets and global integration, has produced low wages, long hours and a much greater geographical movement of people, all of which has no doubt contributed to the breakdown of families. It has also seen the rolling back of welfare and public services which has dominated Western capitalism since the Second World War and sometimes long before that. In Britain council housing and state pensions date back to the first decade of the 20th century. Many social and welfare functions, which might once have been provided by local or national government, now fall back onto individual family members and the family collectively to provide. This is true of childcare, care for the elderly and disabled, some teaching of literacy and numeracy. Not only are the costs of bringing up children very high, but they also stretch over a longer period, as children now tend to be in full time education until 18 or 21. Today 58 percent of boys and 39 percent of girls between the ages of 20 and 24 live at home with their parents.[48] Those not able to work for whatever reason – youth, old age, disability or sickness – are thrown back onto the resources of the family in order to avoid serious deprivation. So working children will sometimes supplement the pension of older relatives in order to improve their health or diet.

This makes the family a greater defence mechanism and source of support than perhaps in times of boom. This is particularly true among the working class, where there may not be a great deal of distance between the ability to keep one's head above water when in receipt of a wage, and sinking below the surface if the wage is lost and replaced by benefits. The gap between the "respectable" working class, with its access to a limited number of the consumer goods which are deemed so vital to the family, and those sometimes called the "underclass", who live in a state of permanent poverty and are excluded from the possibilities of family prosperity, is often smaller than imagined.

Poverty is very common among families who have young children. Child poverty in Britain is worse than in most of Europe.[49] Around 3.4 million children (27 percent of the total) in Britain live in poverty, 43 percent of children who live in poverty are in one parent families[50] and the proportion of children living in poverty has doubled in the last generation.[51]

While government policies have targeted lifting children out of poverty, and 700,000 children have been between 1998 and 2005, this amounted to a reduction of 17 percent, while the target was 25 percent.[52] Some experts claim that the methods used have not only failed to meet targets, but that extra financial resources are needed if the aim of halving child poverty by 2010 is to be met. The National Children's Home (NCH) chief executive, Clare Tickell, said:

> It's an outrage that 3.4 million children in the fifth richest country in the world live in poverty. The government must act immediately if we are to save these youngsters from the cycle of deprivation and social exclusion that they face... Without extra resources – at least £4 billion – the 2010 target of halving child poverty will not be reached.[53]

Crucial to these figures is the fact that child poverty does not just exist in workless households, but is common among what is sometimes called the "working poor". Higher pay and better education and job opportunities should also be part of a strategy to end child poverty. One of the effects of the sort of low wage economy which Britain has become is the structuring of child poverty into the equation. Women's low wages exacerbate the problems of single parents, many of whom simply find that it is impossible for them to carry the costs of working (especially costs of childcare and transport) and still provide a living income for themselves and their families.[54] The problem of child poverty has all sorts of knock-on effects which cost society at a future time in different ways, and this process seems to be escalating: "Those who grew up poor in the 1980s are suffering greater disadvantage in mid-life than those who grew up poor in the 1970s".[55]

Putting the family back together in these circumstances is an impossible task. It is overwhelmed by poverty, immigration and emigration, the strains of everyday life from shift working to long distance commuting, the endless grind to earn enough to pay the bills and standing orders which represent almost daily outgoings for the model family. So the family will continue to break down, especially as much of its previous cohesion has depended on women in particular putting up with conditions and relationships which younger generations are unlikely to accept. At the same time, there will be constant attempts to try to hold it together, or at least to put sticking plaster over the worst cracks. Legal intervention into families, now a major part of British law, will continue to attempt to force parents to do their job better and to criminalise children for various acts and omissions, while school exclusions and other measures will continue to be used as a means of removing difficult problems rather than trying to deal with them. Commentators and politicians will continue to blame parents, especially the poorest working class parents, for problems at least in part created by poverty, poor housing and lack of facilities.

From their point of view, there really is no choice. To begin to look at real alternatives to the present family would mean a huge outlay of resources to allow the social provision of services at present provided within the privatised family. That might be much more popular than paying for nuclear weapons or wars, at least with most of us, but it would be at immense cost to each national capitalist class, and would put them at a competitive disadvantage compared to their rivals. So they thrust the burden of the family onto individuals, and enforce that process by scapegoating those individuals who do not or cannot carry the burden.

Yet the family can be socialised: as we shall see, it happened in wartime, when nurseries, communal restaurants and shoppers were provided for essential war workers. But we can also see today how the rich eat in restaurants most nights, have their houses cleaned, have full time carers or even overnight "hotels" for their children, send out their washing and ironing, have their shopping delivered and their children taken to and picked up from school. In richer areas of London there are private nappy services. There is only one reason why such facilities should not be available to all families, and that is the profit motive which decrees that such services are beyond our reach. A society where the wealth went into these areas and not into weapons and profits for the rich would not only be much better and easier for all members of the family. It would also allow us to begin to develop genuinely loving relationships not constrained by economic limitations and the drudgery of work, and by the ideal of a family which cannot keep its promises.

Work: all day, every day

"THE increase in female employment in the rich world has been the main driving force of growth in the past couple of decades. Those women have contributed more to global GDP growth than have either new technology or the new giants, China and India. Add the value of housework and child-rearing, and women probably account for just over half of world output".[1]

Women going out to work may have contributed more to wealth than rising economies or technological advance, but you could be forgiven for missing it if you were listening to politicians or reading the newspapers. There is little recognition of women's economic role, which has been achieved on the cheap. Low wages and lack of investment in childcare have continued despite the rise in female employment. Indeed, the rise in women working in countries such as the US and Britain has arguably held all wages lower than they would otherwise be, as women have formed a major reserve army of labour for capital to draw on. The employment of men *and women* has thus led to greater levels of exploitation.

The drop in real wages and the lengthening of working hours, both key features of the current global economy, can be partly explained by the rapid increase in female (and migrant) labour. This has contributed significantly to the rising share of national wealth going to profits rather than labour. Women workers also find themselves subject to ever greater work discipline and monitoring. Whereas once many service jobs offered some control over the pace and content of work, the new service industries have become rigidly hierarchical, supervised and geared towards maximum productivity. A comparison between domestic work in the 19th century and call centre work today shows how much the service sector is made up of wage slaves probably more exploited than their ancestors.[2]

The meaning of work

"A woman's work is never done" goes the saying. Under capitalism that work is divided into two parts – women's domestic role as wives, mothers and carers; and women's economic role as wage earners outside the home. As we have seen, until at least the middle of the 20th century, it was the domestic role that was regarded as central for married women and the aspiration for single women. Women were concentrated for a long time in two main areas of production – the textile industry and domestic service, which were the two major employers of women until after the First World War. Single women then began to enter paid work in ever larger numbers, in the newly expanding light industries, and in clerical and administrative occupations. But these jobs were expected to end when women married. In some industries there was a "marriage bar", so women had to leave work when they married, as they did in professions such as teaching. The spheres of production and reproduction were separate, where paid work was part of a man's world. Today married women work in ever increasing numbers and women equip themselves for skilled work though training and education on an unprecedented scale. Currently the number of women working outside the home is almost equal to that of men and is greater than it has ever been.[3] But women come to the labour market at a disadvantage: they earn less, have far more domestic responsibilities and still remain in female dominated jobs. That's because the revolution in working practices which has taken place over the past 60 years has not been matched by other social changes which could have alleviated women's burden in the home. But despite this women's changing position at work has been remarkable.

Wartime women

When the former mill girl turned popular singer Gracie Fields sang about the experience of war factory production, she was in tune with millions of women.[4] In fact, women in Britain had a unique experience during the Second World War compared to their counterparts in much of Europe and in the United States. They combined the immediacies of war and the suffering that ensued from it with the demands of industrial conscription on a very wide scale. Nowhere else was this the case.

In the US women did go into industry in very large numbers, as symbolised by the figure of "Rosie the Riveter", but there was no compulsion on them to do so.[5] Nor did Americans suffer the bombing, rationing, evacuation and many other features of British wartime life. In Germany, Hitler was very careful to avoid the large-scale conscription of German women. He feared that this could lead to the sort of social unrest which rocked the country after the First World War. Nazi ideology also strongly insisted women's sphere was the home. Instead Hitler relied on largely foreign conscript and slave labour from the occupied countries of Europe to expand wartime production.[6] The result was that "Germany's female labour force increased by only 1 percent from 1939 to 1944".[7] In occupied Europe women played an important role in the resistance in various countries and operated in very dangerous conditions far removed from those of Britain's factory workers. Sometimes these women were both resistance members and factory workers and showed great courage in campaigning against occupation.[8] Much of continental Europe, including Germany, suffered worse consequences of war, especially bombing and devastation, than Britain.

In Britain, while the war was very threatening at times, it did not overwhelm working class life in the way in did in occupied Europe. So the war was both extraordinary and ordinary at the same time. Fear of death and invasion was ever present, especially early in the war, and the bombing and evacuation caused great disruption to home and family life. However, as the war wore on, the disruption took another form as the lives of women went in a quite different direction from anything that might have been predicted in the late 1930s, as women became workers in the factories, the civil service offices and the armed services on a much wider scale than they ever had before:

In no country did women provide so large a part of [the] increase in employment as in the United Kingdom. Eighty percent of the total addition to the labour force in 1939 to 1943 consisted of women who had previously not been employed or had been housewives.[9]

While young single women had begun to go out to work in permanent jobs in the 1920s and 30s, before the war there was very little breakdown in the sexual division of labour, with women taking newly created jobs rather than replacing men in the more established industries. So they worked in the new motor industry, but not in the older areas of engineering where technological change was slow and craft unionism strong, such as shipbuilding and locomotive construction.[10] In addition, only a small proportion of married women worked before the war. Things changed on both fronts during the Second World War.

So married women increasingly went out to work even when they had children.[11] By 1943 there were 7.5 million women in paid employment, a massive increase on the 1931 figure of just 1.25 million, with the proportion of married women working rising from 16 to 43 percent over the same period.[12] In the period from 1939 to 1943 alone up to 1.5 million more women entered work in "essential industries".[13] It is estimated that there were now three quarters of a million women in industry with children under 14.[14] Equally, women entered jobs previously done by men because so many men were conscripted to fight. The number of women in engineering rose from 97,000 to 602,000 between 1939 and 1943, representing an increase from 10 percent of the workforce to a third (34 percent). Similar figures applied to industries such as transport, shipbuilding, metal, chemical, vehicle building, water, gas and electricity. In these industries women made up a third of employees in 1943 compared with 14 percent at the war's outbreak.[15]

It is impossible to say how many women might have worked if they had had the choice, because most of them did not. Attempts at cajoling women into work were not as successful as the government and employers wanted, so an element of coercion was introduced. Successive laws were passed to ensure that women would work in essential work or join the armed forces. This began in 1941, when all women from 19 to 40 had to register at employment exchanges; by 1943 this had risen to age 50. Some women could be directed to certain jobs.[16] Women without dependants had to work and could not leave their jobs, nor could employers refuse the employees sent from the labour exchanges.[17] Young women faced actual conscription from late 1941, although they could choose the armed services, essential occupations or civil defence. Married women were exempted from conscription and women were divided into "mobile" and "immobile" (if they had family responsibilities). "Mobile" workers could be moved to the industrial areas to work.[18] All this amounted to "considerable powers of compulsion over women"[19] where "women in certain age groups were in fact conscripted to work in war industries".[20]

While the results of this conscription were not as draconian as it might appear, young single women did often face severe penalties if they did not concur with their treatment. One woman who left her job to move to the north east of England to be with her serviceman husband lost entitlement to unemployment benefit because she would not move to a munitions factory 200 miles away, while in Coventry two young women were imprisoned in 1942 for absenteeism.[21] The effect of conscription was not just felt in the factories. During the war there were half a million women in the armed services and an extra half million clerical workers, compared with the pre-war figure.[22] While it was felt impossible to treat married women, especially those with children, in the same way as young single women, they too were subject to much pressure to work. "War Work Weeks" were held in the industrial areas to encourage women workers. At the one in Coventry in 1941 women from the big munitions factories led a procession dressed in overalls with "V for Victory" songs embroidered on them, and they sat at machines mounted on lorries to illustrate their work.[23] But family duties made it very difficult for women to work in the first place – and work conditions once they were in the factories made it very hard to care for their families. In many working class households, it was still the norm for husbands and children to come home for a cooked meal at lunchtime. The mothers of over 4 million children had responsibility for their midday meal at the beginning of the war, and there were few factory canteens.[24]

It is true that major efforts were made to recruit women and a variety of measures were put in place to make it easier for them to leave home and family. But the lot of the woman worker, especially one with family responsibilities, was very hard. Nurseries were provided in much larger numbers than ever before, but they never came close to fulfilling the needs of all working mothers. At most 25 percent of women war workers' children under five had nursery places, so there was an absolute shortage.[25] Nursery provision was created by the Ministry of Labour and was closely connected with work in war industries. The Ministry of Health resisted any notion of collective and universal provision, preferring individual childminding arrangements instead. Despite this, the number of nurseries rose from just 14 in October 1940 to 1,345 by July 1943.[26] But the nurseries were located in communities often some distance from the factories. At first the restricted hours they opened made them of limited value to many war workers, whose shifts might be from early morning till evening, or overnight. But eventually hours were extended and some residential nurseries were permitted in industrial areas. Birmingham had "children's hotels" where children stayed overnight while their mothers worked.[27] However, childcare was directly connected with work and women still had childcare responsibilities outside working hours as well as the household jobs to perform. The government and authorities alleviated some of this: factory canteens and school meals were extended so that the midday meal was very often provided outside the home. British Restaurants were established which sold cheap hot food and some factories even provided facilities for women to shop. By 1942 there was officially sanctioned leave of absence to shop.[28] However, most women found the problem substantial: rationing meant long queues and shortages of various goods. For women who worked in factories all day, this meant that all sorts of fresh food in particular weren't available. There was, in addition, the usual routine of housework, in an era where washing machines or laundrettes were not available, laundries were expensive and household equipment was basic. Washing involved heating water in boilers, having to use mangles, poor quality soap, and there were no dryers except racks inside the home.

Women's attitudes to work appeared quite different from men's. Young women in particular rebelled against the enforced discipline of factory work. They tended to be more sceptical about wartime propaganda urging them to work harder. This was also the section of the workforce who spent the most on keeping up appearances, despite the trials of wartime, and a relatively large part of many of these women's wages went on cosmetics, fashion and going out.

Government plans to prohibit cosmetics in 1942 were abandoned for reasons of morale.[29] Absenteeism was high among women in the factories. Most observers connected this with family and home commitments. Women's absenteeism was especially high at weekends, for example, when children were home from school, and there were high levels of sickness put down partly to boredom, partly to domestic commitments.[30] At one Newcastle engineering factory there was a 20 percent absence of married women in the gun shop in 1942-43, which management described as legitimate because of the women's domestic circumstances.[31]

In addition, many women found the hours exhausting and the work itself unpleasant, if not dangerous. Legislation restricting women's hours or prohibiting night work was lifted under emergency orders. Many workers lived in adverse conditions outside the factory and the strain on their nerves was very great. There were great demands on productivity throughout the war, but often women workers rebelled against these, even if in inchoate ways. One survey of factory life pointed to young women taking their time before starting to work in the mornings, talking while at their machines, and taking long cloakroom breaks. The amount of time spent not working was relatively high.[32] Another survey revealed that clock watching was not unique to peacetime work:

It is at a little before eleven that the first signs of slacking off begin to appear. People start going out to the cloakroom and hanging about there for long periods, doing their hair, talking, eating the cakes which they have bought for dinner and tea. The subject of what time it is (which by four in the afternoon...has become almost an obsession) begins to appear in conversations.[33]

Whatever the motivation to work in war industry, and as we have seen it always involved a high degree of compulsion, the reality of exploitation was felt as strongly here as in peacetime work. Grievances at work were often dealt with individually, for example through absenteeism, but women also took steps towards collective organisation. Here they came up against problems over equal pay, the right to work and provision of nurseries. On some questions they had to fight the unions as well.

Equal pay for women was an increasing issue as the war went on.

Some women saw the question as a continuation of the fight for the suffrage, so that women could achieve a level of economic as well as political equality. There had been nothing approaching equal pay for women before the war, partly because the level of job segregation meant that women's and men's work was often separate and women's work was by definition low paid. But during the war women did clearly often do exactly the same work as men had done; yet they still did not receive anything like the same wage. The trade unions and especially the skilled unions had a double-edged approach to this. They did not regard women as sufficiently skilled to earn the same as men, but neither did they want male wages undercut because this could mean either that women would be employed in favour of men or that men, when they were re-employed after the war, would be expected to work for lower wages.

The main engineering union, the AEU, regarded women "dilutees" as temporary workers who would be displaced by men after the war. In the meantime the dilutees should be organised and relatively well paid because in a sense they were guardians of the men's jobs. The Extended Employment of Women Agreement, made in 1940, explicitly stated that dilutees should be regarded as temporarily employed.[34] But the fact that the craft unions wanted to preserve wage rates even if it was women who earned them led to a number of battles over pay, and the whole argument for equal pay. This in turn led to "a growing trend towards wages militancy" by women workers.[35] One of the major wartime strikes was at Rolls Royce, Hillington, near Glasgow, in 1943, over equal pay.

Women's wages did rise in relation to men's during the war, but never became anywhere near equal overall.[36] Pressure over women's wages led to the establishment of a Royal Commission on Equal Pay in 1944. President of the AEU Jack Tanner in his evidence to the Commission summed up the contradictory attitude:

> Our stand upon [equal pay] is first in regard to equality that as a union we maintain that women are entitled to the same wages for doing the same work as men; and secondly there is and has been the fear that if women do not receive the same wages, the same rate for the job, as men then that is a danger to the men, and it would lead to trouble…within the ranks of the trade unions and among the working class generally, if there was a need

to take a stand against the employment of women, even though that stand was being taken because women were receiving a lower rate of pay than the men were.[37]

By the time the commission reported two years later most women were out of the war industries, so its findings were somewhat hypothetical. One and a quarter million women left industry between 1943 and 1948.[38] Many did not want to leave their old jobs, according to an AEU survey. Out of 1,000 women surveyed in engineering jobs, 663 wanted to stay in the industry – a third who wanted to stay were married women.[39]

The new workers

The loss of their jobs in the war industries was a blow to women – conscripted into the work, they had found a level of income and independence which could not be matched elsewhere, and many needed to work out of necessity. The narrowness of the craft unions, the role of the state – which insisted that men who had fought could get their old jobs back – and an ideology that still decreed women were homemakers all played their part in pushing women out of the war industries. So too, of course, did the closure of the nurseries and the British Restaurants. Even before the war ended, there were signs that the nurseries were to be closed down, and after the war the Treasury withdrew funding for them.[40] This did not mean women stayed in the home. Chronic labour shortages meant the government was soon advertising for women workers to fill gaps and the 1950s boom created millions of female jobs. But the post-war settlement in industry ensured the re-establishment of the pre-war rigid sexual division of labour and the reinforcement of women's status as low paid part time workers. Such an outcome was colluded in by the post-war Labour government, which regarded equal pay as too expensive and likely to displace men.[41] The government also emphasised the conventional family which in turn reinforced unequal pay, lesser hours and unpaid childcare. So the post-war generation of women workers still lacked access to apprenticeships or to higher education, except for a tiny few. Training was confined to typing and shorthand, comptometer and punch card operating, and hairdressing. All this only began to change in the 1960s. Until then women's work was seen as a secondary occupation.

One of the reasons why it did change was the increasingly high number of married women who were working. The shortages of labour created by the long post-war boom and relatively full employment meant that married women became a major labour reserve for capital. Conditions were created where married women found it relatively easy and desirable to work, and they entered the workforce in large numbers. Even just after the war, in 1947, there were 683,000 more women in industry than there were in 1939, and increasingly the number of married women was making up the difference. By 1951, 20 percent of married women were employed, double the proportion of only 20 years earlier. By 1960 married women formed a slightly greater proportion of the female workforce than single women.[42] Pearl Jephcott, author of a fascinating study of married women at work, wrote in 1962 that "at least half of today's female factory workers are married; so are more than a third of full time women teachers, and perhaps a quarter of the nursing profession".[43] At the Peek Frean biscuit factory in Bermondsey, which was the subject of her study, 82 percent of the factory women employees were married, and 46 percent of all operatives were women part timers.[44]

What allowed the changes in married women's work patterns? Firstly, the years spent in pregnancy, giving birth and full time childcare were much reduced compared with previous generations. It was estimated that "in the 1890s the typical working class mother spent about fifteen years in a state of pregnancy and in nursing a baby for the first year of its life, as compared with four years or so" (in the 1950s).[45] Women could now expect a long life ahead of them after their children had grown up. Technological change had also significantly reduced the amount of housework that was needed to maintain a decent standard of living. Gas and oil fired central heating, washing machines, gas and electric cookers, vacuum cleaners, fridges, ready meals and fast food outlets all reduced the amount of time spent on household chores. In fact, there was a circular process at work here: women felt more able to work because of these devices, but they also worked to help pay for household goods which could ease their burden. Usually the cost of these goods fell on the individual family, so capitalism created the demand for more commodities from which it made a profit; it also created a new workforce from which it also made a profit.[46]

The experience of wartime had also marked a watershed –

women now felt it was much more acceptable to work and they had become much more used to working as well as being mothers. It was a watershed too for the marriage bar which was lifted in the civil service and most local government after the war.[47] In industry it was finally eradicated with the labour shortages of the long boom.

However, women did not obtain much help in going to work from government or state in the post-war period. Little progress was made on equal pay, and nurseries remained a distant dream for most women. Even the best intentions were thwarted by other financial priorities, which did not include aiding women's equality. Often the intentions were far from favourable in the first place.[48] There was little commitment to real childcare provision. A joint circular sent out in 1945 from the ministries of health and education argued that "the proper place for a child under two is at home with his mother".[49]

Working mothers

It is hardly surprising then, in the absence of the kinds of measures that had been undertaken during the war, that so many of the married women who went out to work in the post-war period did so on a part time basis. Women were encouraged to work twilight shifts, hours that fitted in with their families, as a means of supplementing husbands' incomes without disrupting the domestic role which was still seen as predominant for most women. Between 1951 and 1981 the number of part time employees increased by over 4 million. The vast majority of these were women, many of them with dependent children. A study in the early 1980s demonstrated that whereas 70 percent of working mothers worked part time, only 26 percent of women without children worked part time,[50] while mothers of under-5s were the least likely to work.[51] An extensive survey carried out in 1980 by Jean Martin and Ceridwen Roberts, *Women and Employment*, showed that women in their teens had the highest rates of economic activity of all women, followed by women in their 40s. The lowest rates were for women in their late 20s.[52] So married women with children still had the least likelihood of working and when they did work they were much more likely to do so part time.

But the picture of the part time woman worker fulfilling her housewifely duties as well began to look outdated as the 1980s progressed and as more and more mothers began to return to work full time, thus creating an even bigger workforce with new patterns of work. The dip in women's employment as they took time out for childbirth and childcare evened out. Between 1975 and 1998 the employment rate for 28 year old women, for example, increased from 42 percent to 69 percent.[53] In 1961 only 11.5 percent of married women with dependent children under five were economically active, whereas by 1981 a quarter of those with one child under two were, and over a third of those with three to four year olds. The majority of mothers with school age children were economically active, even where they had three or more dependent children.[54] The overall proportion of first time mothers returning to work within six months of the birth nearly doubled between the late 1940s and late 1970s, but this was mostly through women returning to work part time. But this changed by the late 1980s when "a woman who had been working full time when she became pregnant was just as likely to return to full time as to part time work."[55]

Today women are workers outside the home in greater numbers than they have ever been in history. Around the turn of the 21st century, there were 12.5 million women in the labour market, nearly one million more than a decade previously, with 65 percent of women with dependent children working, including a majority of those with children under five.[56] By the 1990s young women could expect to work for a decade longer than women who were born early in the 20th century.[57] The number of women working continues to increase, while the number of men working continues to decrease. Around 70 percent of all women are now in employment compared with 56 percent in 1971.[58] The maintenance of full time work patterns for large numbers of mothers is one of the biggest changes that have taken place. "The number of women who work during pregnancy and return to work within nine to eleven months of the birth of their child has increased dramatically in recent years": in 1979 24 percent of such women returned to work; by 1988 this stood at 45 percent and in 1996 was at 67 percent, of which 24 percent were full time and 42 percent part time.[59]

Women with children are also working longer hours than previously, and the rate of increase for those with children has grown faster than for those without. Mothers of children under five increased their average weekly work by four hours between 1984 and 1994, whereas women without children increased theirs by only 0.4 hours.[60] There is no single reason why this change – and it shows absolutely no sign of reversing – came about. The greater availability and acceptance by employers of maternity leave, women's desire or need for continuous employment especially in certain competitive work and the desire to return for personal and social reasons, all played a part. However, the main reason that mothers go out to work is to help maintain the family income – in other words, because of economic necessity. The importance of women's earnings to the family income increased markedly in the post-war boom. Overall women's earnings made up 7.9 percent of household income in 1965 and 11.3 percent in 1983. In households where a married woman was working, her income made up 19.5 percent or 27.4 percent of household income, depending on whether there were children or not.[61]

This growing dependence on the female wage partly explains the increase in full time working for mothers. There is also some evidence that women in lower income groups have increasingly been pushed out to work to compensate for the low and sometimes falling wages of many working class men. Whereas before the 1980s it was the wives of higher income men who saw their employment increase most rapidly, from the 1980s onwards it was those of lower income men that increased fastest. The share of family income contributed by women grew fastest among families where men had low or median earnings. It is estimated that without women's pay the rate of poverty among married or cohabiting couples by the early 1990s would have been 50 percent higher than it actually was (at 13.1 percent against the actual 8.1 percent).[62]

So women were often under intense economic pressure to work, but the conditions in which they did so were by and large much worse than in the 1950s and 1960s. The decades of the 1980s and 1990s, in particular, saw two very deep recessions where men often lost their jobs, especially in industries such as steel, engineering and mining, but where the growth of service and administrative sectors continued apace, thus providing many "women's jobs". The pressure on women to work outside the home was greater given the growing insecurity of the male wage.

The 1980s and 90s also saw a marked increase in the rate of exploitation for very large numbers of working people. Whereas for much of the long boom there had been real increases in living standards and a major expansion of welfare provision, the era of Thatcher and her US counterpart Ronald Reagan saw that process go into reverse. Conditions worsened dramatically in some areas: people worked longer hours or were forced to accept split shifts which took up a great deal of what should have been leisure time in the working day. The introduction of greater "flexibility" in the workplace led to the abolition of certain rights such as tea breaks. In some industries wages were actually cut – for example as a result of privatisation, where public sector jobs were reassigned at lower rates of pay, or in industries such as printing and journalism where union busting led to a general lowering of wages and worsening of conditions across the whole sector. Women were moving into work at precisely the time when unions were being weakened and established conditions and agreements were being torn up. At the same time the welfare state was under attack, with more of the burden of welfare pushed back onto the individual family. The prospect of universal and affordable childcare together with decent conditions and real improvements in women's lives appeared even more remote than it had done one or two decades previously. Now women were being told that they had to work and that childcare while they worked was their responsibility – and that it was also their responsibility to equip themselves to enter the labour market by acquiring the right education and skills. On top of all this women still had their family responsibility. The "double burden" doesn't begin to describe this situation.

Childcare

If the health service was run on the same basis as childcare in Britain, people would be lying bleeding to death in the streets and the vast majority of patients would have to rely on relatives or paid volunteers who already had to care for other sick people. Yet we expect millions of children of working mothers to be cared for by grandparents and other relatives, friends and other unpaid carers. The bulk of paid childcare is performed by registered childminders, often themselves mothers who cannot work outside the home. Only a small minority of children are cared for in nurseries or other childcare institutions.

The post-war retreat on nursery provision and the ease with which part time work could be fitted in with childcare meant that publicly funded childcare provision never seriously accompanied the post-war boom. Since the mid-1970s persistent attempts to cut back on public spending have also meant that any universal and publicly provided childcare system has been denied to the millions of working women who could benefit from it. There is much evidence to show that a major reason for mothers not working is the lack of affordable childcare. One study showed that a third of women who did not return to work after having a baby said they could not earn enough to pay for childcare. Among mothers who did not work, nearly a quarter said they would work full time with the childcare of their choice and a further 55 percent said they would work part time. Only 19 percent of non-working mothers said they would not work even with the childcare of their choice.[63] The gap between supply and demand has been calculated by the Day-Care Trust as one registered childcare place for every 7.5 children under eight in England.[64] Although the vast majority of three and four year olds now have some form of nursery education, this is mostly only part time. The market rules in childcare, with miserly levels of full time state provision and the onus placed on parents to find the resources – both family and financial – to pay for it.

Childcare costs in Britain are the highest in Europe. The funding of childcare falls overwhelmingly on the individual family. Overall £190 million comes from private companies; £50 million from miscellaneous sources, £150 million from the government directly but a gigantic £1,655 million is from private individuals (of which £110 million is from government indirect subsidies).[65] Childcare thus inevitably becomes a tax on working men and women, which is simply often too onerous for them to afford. So by the mid-1990s it was estimated that the cost of childcare for two children, one preschool and one older, had reached £6,000 a year.[66] By 2006 the typical nursery place cost £7,300 a year, a rise of 27 percent in five years. In London and the south east it is estimated at over £10,000 a year, making it a struggle even for many professionals.[67] Live-in childcare is increasingly concentrated among the rich. "The scarcity of nannies has driven up salaries and perks, making them the preserve of the very wealthy".[68] The director of a charity, earning with her partner more than the £58,000 a year which would allow them tax credits, was quoted in the *Financial Times* as paying her nanny £250 a week to look after her two children full time. It is estimated that parents living in London have to set aside £35,000 gross income to pay for a professional nanny – as much as or more than the combined income of many working couples.[69]

Promises by the New Labour government to dramatically increase the amount and quality of childcare have not materialised. A report by the Institute for Fiscal Studies found that the shortfall in childcare was worse than in any other EU country, and that the expense of the available provision put a heavy burden on working mothers, with some spending a quarter of their salary on care. There are just eight day nursery places for every 100 children under five and after-school clubs are available for only one in 14 of under-16s.[70]

One of the consequences of the failure to provide affordable childcare has been the much lower level of workforce participation of single mothers compared with mothers in relationships. So the dramatic increase in work participation by mothers in couples has not been matched by single mothers, who often find that unless they can command an above average salary, paid work is barely worth doing once the extra childcare costs are taken into account. So 61 percent of single mothers do not work, and the problem barely changes when children first attend school, since mothers are still responsible for childcare before and after the school day and cannot work full time.[71] It is especially acute for mothers of under-fives, with less than a third of these single mothers in paid work.[72]

The exorbitant costs of childcare mean that income plays a central role in determining the type and extent of the childcare provision available to many women and this in turn has a large impact on the nature of the work that many women are able to do. Commuting and long hours are obviously much more difficult for women with young children unless they have sufficient income to pay for professional care over a long period of the day. The most extensive childcare is also the most expensive. So nannies tend to care for pre-school children for the longest hours in any particular day, followed by registered childminders. Nannies were more likely to start early, finish late and work five days a week. Lack of such childcare means either turning to limited state provision or often relying on unpaid sources. Parents used informal childcare by neighbours, friends and relatives for 62 percent of pre-school children and 77 percent of school age children.[73] But such "informal" (or unpaid) childcare with neighbours or friends is much more likely to be for shorter hours during the day and for one or two days a week which in turn means having to working relatively near to home and often part time.[74]

However, for many working class families unpaid childcare is often the only option, mainly by fathers and grandmothers, when the mother is not there. The use of fathers and grandparents is much higher among manual workers than among professionals and managers. While 29 percent of professionals' and 27 percent of managers' children are cared for by fathers, the figures rise to 45 percent for children of skilled manual and 50 percent for children from semi-skilled manual families. Grandparents are the carers for 18 percent of children of professionals and 25 percent of children of managers and employers, but this rises rapidly among intermediate and junior non-manual families to 44 percent, the same proportion as the children of skilled manual workers.[75]

So the availability, cost and extent of childcare continue to profoundly shape the position of women entering the labour market and leave many working class women at a significant disadvantage with regard to the type of work they can do and the wage they can command.

The rate for the job?
The popular image of the working woman is of a high paid, well educated professional able to cope with a demanding career, a home and family, and challenging social life. These women exist in far greater numbers than even 20 years ago, but they don't even make up half the story. Despite half a century of increasing recognition that women have the right to equal pay they still don't have anything like that in Britain. While as early as the Treaty of Rome in 1956 the European Economic Community (forerunner of the EU) adopted the International Labour Organisation (ILO) Convention 100 calling for "equal pay for work of equal value", Britain still lagged behind in granting equal pay. During the 1950s and 1960s there were campaigns for equal pay, especially among public sector employees, and which tended to be led by women in the unions. The union leaderships were sometimes hostile and usually disinclined to do very much. Very little happened, and it was only at the tail end of the 1964-70 Labour administration that Barbara Castle introduced legislation on equal pay. She did so against a background of increasing militancy by women workers, epitomised by the women machinists at Ford Dagenham who struck for equality with men in a certain grade. The years of endlessly passing resolutions and appealing to the better nature of governments and employers were over. As Sarah Boston has written in her book on women and trade unions:

The approach of "relying on male colleagues", waiting "for social attitudes to change", or leaving it to collective bargaining to grind its way towards equal pay over several more decades was rejected. The new approach was much more aggressive.[76]

Women needed all the aggression they could muster to win equal pay. The Equal Pay Act was eventually passed in 1970 but was given until 1975 to be implemented, giving the employers several years to plan schemes for regrading which would avoid substantially increasing most women's wages. The definition of equal pay under the act was much narrower than the ILO convention, calling only for equal pay for the same or "like" work as men. In a labour market as segregated sexually as that in Britain, this allowed many employers to claim that there was no direct comparison with men and so women could be kept at lower rates.

There was some effect on women's wages as a proportion of men's and the impetus of the new law led to some improvements. However, in the early and mid-1970s a number of strikes, especially in the engineering industry, were also instrumental in helping secure equal pay. In 1983 the Equal Pay Act was amended to allow studies of "equal pay for work of equal value" if the workforce wanted them. Despite some initial gains from the act, progress towards equal pay went flat in the second half of the 1970s, although renewed progress was made in the second half of the 1980s.[77] But if the pay gap has narrowed since the mid-1970s it is very far from disappearing. The pay gap is now 17.2 percent compared with 31 percent when the act was first passed over 30 years ago.[78] Women's earnings stand at 82 percent of men's.[79] The improvements in narrowing the gap in the 1970s and 1980s once again stopped in the 1990s, and can be said to have barely affected part time workers whose hourly pay is still only 60 percent of men's.[80]

One of the major reasons why women's pay has not advanced further is the occupational segregation of men and women. This operates both at the level of all women or mainly women's industries and occupations ("horizontal" segregation) and through women being clustered in the lowest grades and on the bottom rungs of mixed occupations ("vertical" segregation). Women account for 93 percent of secretaries, typists and personal assistants, and 61 percent of teaching professionals. A full 10 percent of women workers are sales assistants, 6 percent are secretaries and 5 percent are nurses.[81] A quarter of women are employed in administration and secretarial work compared with 6 percent of men. While 17 percent of men are employed in skilled trades, only 2 percent of women are. With personal service jobs it is the other way round, with 2 percent of men and 13 percent of women being employed in this sector. Similarly with sales and customer services (5 percent men and 13 percent women) and process, plant and machine operatives (13 percent men and 3 percent women).[82] The highest paid occupations included some of the most male dominated – treasurers and company financial managers, underwriters, brokers, police officers above inspector, business analysts and work-study managers. The lowest paid occupations include many of the female dominated jobs – retail checkout workers, educational assistants and other childcare workers, hairdressers, counter-hands and catering.[83]

But for a significant minority of women it is now possible to earn as much as or even more than men. A fifth of women now earn more than their working partners, compared with one in 14 in the 1970s.[84] But it is not the main picture. Even by the mid-1990s, 20 percent of women earned less than or equal to the bottom 10 percent of men and only 3 percent of women earned equal to the top 10 percent of earners. In fact, around three quarters of women fall into the bottom half of male pay distribution.[85]

Poles apart

Many women now see their life as defined by their relationship to the labour market, but they don't all come to the labour market in the same way. It is commonly assumed that there is a polarisation in work between those in full time careers and those in casualised, low paid and part time work. In reality, there has been a different division taking place in women's work over the past two decades; between the minority of women who have done extremely well from the 1980s and 1990s – who command salaries beyond the wildest dreams of most working class men as well as most working class women – and the mass of working women who have found the pressure of work intensified as they enter the labour market in ever greater numbers. There has been the growth in numbers of women in managerial, professional and administrative careers, whose earnings and control over the labour process make them part of a managerial and sometimes governing elite; and then there are the mass of women in routine clerical and administrative jobs, as well as the public sector "professionals" like teachers whose conditions increasingly resemble the former; and there are those, heavily concentrated in personal services, who often work part time, are in the lowest paid work and often see little future in their work. Those in routine full time work are closer to those in part time and low paid work than they are to those in the higher managerial or professional jobs. This is true in terms of wages and conditions as well as the fact that many women will move between full time and part time work in the course of their working lives.

These developments were becoming obvious by the 1980s. Jill Rubery and Roger Tarling wrote of the double edged nature of women's employment in 1988:

> Women's employment has been protected and expanded not because women are progressively overcoming their relative disadvantage in the labour market, but because of the continued existence of these disadvantages which causes them to be an attractive source of labour supply to employers for particular types of jobs.

They argue that women were beginning to secure their position in the labour market "by becoming more stable and continuous participants in the labour force and by actively increasing their levels of qualifications pre and post entry to the labour market". But they also warn that this will benefit only a minority, "with the employment conditions for the majority deteriorating while an increasing minority acquire more of the characteristics…traditionally reserved for male labour".[86]

These predictions have been borne out. Women who can rise to the top of society have done very well from the 1980s onwards. The very limited commitment to equality which has opened up at the top of society has been of great service to these women. A minority of women have thus been able to enter traditional male bastions and gain substantial rewards in terms of income, status, and the ability to pay for others to perform personal domestic services such as childcare and cleaning. Women made up 52 percent of new solicitors in 1997, 32 percent of managers and administrators, 27 percent of buyers, brokers and sales reps and 34 percent of health professionals.[87] The percentage of women in management positions rose from 6.9 percent in 1989 to 14 percent in 1998. By March 2007, 19 percent of senior management jobs were held by women.[88] These positions were far from equal with men at the very top of society (the proportion of women directors grew from 2 percent in 1989 to 7 percent in 1998) but they were significant changes in a world where only 18 percent of MPs were women, 10 percent of judges or magistrates and 4 percent of police officers at or above the rank of inspector.[89]

However, these women have tended to accept the idea that they cannot take into account any of the aspects of being a woman that might put them at a disadvantage. A survey of executive women throughout Europe demonstrated that childcare benefits were their lowest priorities because "they simply want to earn good money and make their own decisions about how to solve their childcare issues".[90] Whatever their disadvantages with regard to men of their class, the relationship of these women to most working class women is managerial and often adversarial. The women in designer suits who drive expensive cars have become a part of working life – and most working class women are discovering that they get no special favours from this new breed of women managers.

Then there are the other women in suits – this time the cheaper mass-produced ones from Next or BHS – or in uniforms. These are the mass of office workers, the uniformed bank and building society clerks, the nurses, the workers in Sainsbury's or Tesco. Add to them the teachers, childcare and welfare workers, the very young and female workforce in the call centres, and you have much of the female working class today. There are over 867,000 workers in call centres, 56 percent of them women.[91] The fastest growing occupations since the 1990s have tended to contain disproportionately high numbers of women: sales assistants, data input clerks, storekeepers and receptionists; education and health service workers; and the caring jobs of care assistants, welfare and community workers and nursery nurses.

These women in their majority are low paid, often engaged in routine and repetitive work, and are subject to many of the traditional controls over work which were once confined to manual workers. The introduction of machinery into office work has transformed the nature of work, with photocopiers playing the role of printers and nearly all work being tied to a machine. Computerisation means that the machine monitors work, so managers know exactly what a worker is doing at any one time. In shops the checkouts measure speed of throughput, and act as stock takers, placing new orders as they mark what is being sold. Even work which was once considered part of the professions – such as nursing, lecturing or teaching – is now subject to much greater managerial control, with many of the disciplines of the traditional factory job.

There is no fundamental difference between these workers and those who work part time. As we have seen, increasing numbers of women work full time when they are able to do so, but there are real barriers towards them doing so all the time. These barriers include low pay, childcare and other caring responsibilities which mean that for at least part of their working lives many women will work part time. The sociologist Catherine Hakim has argued that most women are not interested in careers and prefer to centre their lives round childcare and home responsibilities. Only a minority of women, she says, want to work full time in high powered jobs.[92] This argument only serves to justify the status quo with its existing gap between high paid women and those part timers who are presumably happy in their low wage, low status jobs. But the connection between part time working and family responsibilities is overwhelming. While care in the home remains privatised, millions of women will continue to work part time regardless of their aspirations, because they have no alternative.

The *Women and Employment* survey showed that women part timers were more likely to be in "women only" jobs; a majority of them worked between 16 and 31 hours; while the average length of the working day for full time women was 8.8 hours (including meal breaks and travelling), for part timers it was 5.2 hours. Over half of women part time workers finished work by 4pm to pick up the kids from school.[93] Women in couples with children who worked part time were more likely to work evenings than women working full time (12 percent compared to 8 percent) and nearly one in 20 women part timers with children also worked nights. This suggests mothers take part time work when fathers or other members of the family can care for the children.[94] Satisfaction with part time jobs is clearly relative: a 1990s study showed that women part timers were over-qualified for their jobs. Over half of women part timers, given their qualifications and experience, felt they could expect a better job. They were less likely than full timers to say their current job was the one they liked best.[95] There have been increases in recent years in the number of part timers who would prefer a full time job.[96] Much has been made of the satisfaction which women part timers feel in their jobs, and undoubtedly many do. But as the authors of the *Women and Employment* survey commented:

> In some ways it is not surprising that such a high proportion of part time workers were happy with their hours of work; unless they can find a job with suitable hours they are unlikely to be able to work at all.[97]

Hard times

The right to work has been an important slogan for women at different times in history. It was raised in the 19th century, when legislation excluded women from certain work (in the mines and other industries, and from night work). It was raised in the 1930s and 1940s, as women came up against the marriage bar. And it was one of the key demands raised by the women's liberation movement from the late 1960s onwards. Many of the demands have since been realised, but at a cost. Women have not been made unemployed in times of recession or economic contraction, as was so widely predicted by feminists in the 1970s, but they have become a workforce noted for low pay and whose part time component tends to fare worse than full time workers.

However, it is notable that conditions at work today are not especially gender specific in many instances, with the working conditions of men and women, part time and full time, noticeably worsening during the 1990s. The average British household with two adults was working seven hours a week more at the end of the 1990s than in the early 1980s. Work rates have intensified more for women than for men. Speed up, greater "flexibility", wages cuts in many industries (especially those which have been contracted out from the public sector to private industry) are all responsible, as is more aggressive management which has eliminated many breaks and "interruptions where people could slack off a bit".[98] The most common length of working week for men is 40 hours, followed by 60 hours as the second most common. Nearly 1.5 million men work over 60 hours a week. The most common female working week is 38 hours, the second most common 40 hours.[99] Fathers tend to work longer than they did, around two hours a week more than in the late 1980s. They work an average 47 hours a week, and a third of men with children in the household work over 50 hours a week. But mothers are also working longer hours – between 1988 and 1998 average working hours for mothers increased from 27 hours to 33 hours, an increase of six hours a week compared to the four hours increase from 35 hours to 39 hours for women without children. In households with children, both men and women are more likely to work nights or evenings than in households without children, and one in four households has at least one parent who regularly works in the evening. While the number of women working the shortest hours actually fell during 1988 to 1999, those working the longest hours grew sharply. The number of women, both with and without children, working under 20 hours a week fell by around half in the course of the decade. The number working more than 40 hours went up sharply, from 28.4 percent of women without children to 42.1 percent. The number of women without children working over 50 hours went from 4.8 percent to 12 percent. Although women with children were less likely to work as long, those working between 40 and 50 hours also increased from 15.9 percent to 25.3 percent. By 1998 women were around as likely to work overtime as men, although their overtime was much more likely to be unpaid, while women who work nights are twice as likely to be low paid as those working days.[100]

Various trends here are not difficult to discern. Everyone is working considerably longer hours, and despite the large number of women who work part time, many are finding that their work patterns are becoming increasingly similar to those of men, both the length of hours worked and the increased demand for overtime. Part time workers tend to be working longer hours, even though they remain part time. This marks a bigger change for women than for men. Secondly, family life is under greater pressure from the increase in working hours, with parents finding that they are working more unsocial hours than those without children. Thirdly, while the largest groups working evenings and nights in 1998 were either in personal services or worked as plant and machinery operatives, the biggest increase in those working evenings and nights was in sales and professional occupations.[101] This suggests that new groups of shift workers are joining the more traditional ones. Nurses, some service and catering workers, transport workers and many factory workers have always worked shifts. Now this is extending to shop workers and the large numbers of sales and advice staff working from call centres. Women are therefore likely to be making up a greater proportion of shift workers as time goes on.

All this hardly represents an opening up of new and interesting career paths for women or a challenge to men's roles. The better paid factory shift work is often not open to women. Wages and conditions in areas such as call centres and supermarkets are some of the worst. After 20 years of deregulation, weakening of unions and increasing shift work, women and men are being pushed towards a growing discontent and sometimes resistance in order to assert some control over an ever worsening situation.

Can women organise at work?

Women's entry into work in large numbers has coincided with worsening conditions for the working class as a whole. All the worst aspects of Thatcherism – attacks on rights at work, the weakening of unions, the decline of welfare and public services, and the intensification of work – marked the 1980s and 1990s. These policies have been continued under ten years of New Labour. So many women, alongside men, have found their rights under attack. Whereas the fight over equal pay coincided with the growth of the women's movement and the rise of working class militancy from the late 1960s onwards, there has been no comparable movement which could give working class women the confidence to fight back against the worsening of their conditions. Despite this, a remarkably large number of women are in unions, and there are signs that women join unions today at a faster rate than men. Women's concentration in the public sector also makes unionisation more of a possibility, since public sector unionism has survived much better than it has in the private sector. However, it is also true that women's domestic responsibilities together with ideological conditioning often make it hard for women to be activists at any level inside the union. Traditionally it was regarded as exceptional in most unions for leading activists to be women and the dominant view of many male trade unionists was that women are hard to organise and not really interested in unions.

In fact, women have always organised where they thought there was an issue they could fight over and where they found the union relevant to them. This was true as far back as the Match Girls' strike in London's East End in 1888, which was the first of the big strikes that created the "new unions" in the late 1880s which started to organise female and unskilled labour. It was true of the women from the Bermondsey jam and pickle factories who organised flying pickets dressed in the feather boas of their "Sunday best" in the hot summer of 1911, when a strike wave shook the country. It was true of the women who carried on the fight for equal pay from the 1930s right through to the 1960s. But it was also true that the structural divisions inside the working class, with the low numbers of married women working and the development of part time work from the 1950s onwards, all made women's organisation harder and often made women's trade unionism "invisible". It was only from the late 1960s on that this began to change. The Leeds clothing workers in 1970 followed the Ford women. Night cleaners in London struck and campaigned for better conditions in 1971. Teachers, nurses, civil servants and council workers all began to see themselves as workers rather than non-striking "professionals" expected to work for very little, and took strike action for the first time. The Winter of Discontent, when large numbers of public sector workers struck in 1979 in protest at worsening conditions and pay, is often portrayed as a series of strikes by bullying male workers which brought down a Labour government. This is false – it was a movement of both men and women, where very large numbers of women struck, picketed and demonstrated for their rights – all of which were under attack from James Callaghan's Labour government.

The policies undertaken by that government, continued and expanded by Margaret Thatcher from 1979 onwards, served to weaken unions and take back many of the gains won by working class people in the period after the Second World War. Welfare was under sustained attack, representing a double blow for women. They worked in large numbers in the public services, especially health and education, and they carried the burden of welfare cutbacks in the family. Perhaps more importantly, the concerted assault on different groups of workers by the Thatcher government working with the employers led to a worsening of conditions throughout the working class. The lengthening of hours throughout the working class during the late 1980s and 1990s has its roots in the spectacular successes scored by the employers against the British working class during the 1980s. The two most notable were the miners' strike of 1984-85 and the dispute at Wapping, where Rupert Murdoch had moved his newspaper titles to a union busting plant.

These two pivotal disputes had a significant effect on women at work and in the unions, despite the fact that the attacks were launched at male dominated unions with very strong organisation and traditions. One was to weaken all union organisation, including that of women. The argument that the traditional old unions had little to offer women might have had some truth. After all, some of the craft print unions excluded women for many years and were very reluctant to allow them in as new printing technology developed from the 1970s onwards. The miners, meanwhile, still had a "page 3" pin up in their union magazine, despite much feminist protest, right up to the eve of the great strike in 1984. But the weakening of these unions did nothing to help the position of women. Whereas in the late 1960s and early 70s women's position had improved as workers won important victories, the converse was also true. Women were among some of the most vulnerable workers and this took its toll in making them work harder, for longer, and often for less pay.

Another dimension of these strikes, however, was the emergence of women's support movements. The movement of miners' wives created a new generation of women militants, who picketed, travelled round the country speaking and organised community support networks in the mining areas. Many of the women later went on to study at university; some broke up with their husbands, and most felt this was a new departure. Although the print workers' wives and families did not have the same impact or cohesion, they too organised picketing, speaking and support in the face of vicious police attacks.

The class response of the wives was incredibly important in signalling that working class women and men saw their interests as connected. Throughout the years of defeat from the late 1970s onwards, the level of strikes fell and both men and women found it hard to take any action in defence of their interests. This has begun to change in recent years, as a new militancy begins to make itself felt among teachers, journalists, post office workers, medical secretaries and council workers. Many strikes now are notable for the involvement of women, if for no other reason than that many of the big unions have very large female memberships. Unison has 72 percent women members, the shop workers' union USDAW has 60 percent, NUT 76 percent, and the GMB 38 percent.[102] Any look at strikes today shows women participating in what was once seen as a male activity, and often showing the men the way in terms of militancy. In these disputes they are as likely to find themselves up against women employers and managers as they are against men. Despite the highly male dominated structures of the unions today, by 2005 women were more likely to be members of unions in Britain than men.[103] They are beginning to play a role in the unions, including standing for the highest positions, that they did not do a generation ago. And much of the traditional "women's work" in jobs such as caring for the young old and sick are now much more highly unionised than in the past.

Women do, however, face a crisis of representation in the unions. The "glass ceiling" is as much a feature here as in higher management. Although women are the majority in many unions, they are under-represented at workplace level as lay reps and shop stewards. This pales into insignificance compared with the structures of the union full time bureaucracy, however. There are very few women in senior officials' positions. So by the early part of this century out of 62 TUC affiliated unions, 47 had male general secretaries or chairs, while 15 had women. At the level of full time officers, women tend to be badly under-represented.[104] There will have to be a fight within the unions as well as with the employers to change this.

Despite this, the involvement of women in organising and fighting back demonstrates that work has become a central part of their lives and they are acting accordingly. It is now impossible to talk about the working class and not mean women as well as men. This leaves women with much greater potential social power too, a transformation from the era of the isolated housewife.

Men: how Mr Right became Mr Wrong

TALK of male crisis is everywhere. We are inundated with stories of sexually predatory women, men who are losing all self-worth because they cannot be breadwinners and boys who are "failing" at school. In the 1990s Hollywood films such as *Falling Down* or *Disclosure* started appearing which painted a picture of a world where the old masculine values no longer apply and where women are taking cruel advantage over men at work. They portray a world where men lose jobs to women, and find themselves sexually harassed and discriminated against by women. All this makes men neurotic and ill (supposedly once the preserve of women). It was reported that in the US "movies featuring muscular men such as Russell Crowe and Brad Pitt were giving males an inferiority complex". As record numbers of male subscribers to gyms were noted, US psychotherapist Roberto Olivardia commented that "men tie their self-esteem to their physical appearance, it's a huge problem".[1] Men now are much closer to women in their attitudes to physical appearance. They are more likely to follow fashion, to buy personal toiletries and to worry about their figure and looks: "Approximately 10 percent of people with eating disorders are male, though among school children this may be as high as 25 percent".[2] Men are, however, more likely to become seriously ill than women, and on average die younger than women and have a higher rate of suicide. Nothing seems to be going right for men: increasingly they seem threatened by "career women", frightened by their own failings as men and with a terrible sense of loss for a past golden age when men and women both knew their place.

We should, of course, put this into perspective. In many areas of life it is still a man's world. The more powerful and prestigious the institution in our society, the more heavily male dominated it tends to be. This discrimination exists throughout society. As we have seen, working people's jobs are still highly segregated on the basis of sex, and sexist images in advertising and the media are still overwhelmingly of women.

But there is one very important truth in the general view. The feeling of male crisis reflects a society where men's and women's positions have changed dramatically in the past half century and where neither sex fully understands what these social changes represent. As the generations live out these changes – and continue to experience further changes – they incorporate new ways of looking at the world and living without necessarily viewing the total picture. In addition, the uncertainties about the roles of men and women are very closely overlaid with another set of changes which has been going on – the restructuring of industry and the working class in recent decades. This is intimately connected with the "male crisis", along with the rise and fall of working class security and welfare in the years since the Second World War. The losses in these areas are intuitively connected in the minds of millions with a decline in "manhood".

What is to be done about this sense of sweeping change and the loss of past values which so permeates the present debate? The cry from conservatives is to go back to the good old days when men headed the household. Melanie Phillips has written that "the so-called 'crisis of masculinity' [is] a crisis invented by those who wish to claim that the distinctive role of fathers is redundant".[3] If only men still had their traditional role as the head of the families, everything would be all right. It would certainly restore the "natural" order of things, according to one man interviewed in a study of men and the family: "It makes most sense really for me to be the one who puts most effort into my job and bringing in the family wages. I think she prefers it really that way too".[4]

Unfortunately for those with such views, there is no going back to the old way of doing things. Women are now permanently part of the workforce and therefore the sex roles ascribed to them and to men are bound to change. Reasserting the "traditional family" is to try and force human relationships back into a mould in which it no longer fits. Nor do many people want to go back completely to the old ways. Most women value the degree of limited choice they now have about when and where they work, whether they marry and have children, and the chance to develop their ideas and talents through education. Most men accept and probably like the fact that women are not totally financially or socially dependent on them. However, we are at a challenging but also frightening moment in history: the old ways of living are changing rapidly, but whose values will dominate the new ways of living?

Male order: the post-war settlement

Millions had suffered the misery of the 1930s, fascism, war and the depression. Men had fought in the Second World War, as had an unprecedented number of women. Civilians had been as much a part of this war as official combatants. Now people wanted a better life, a home for themselves and their families, children who would be healthy and who would have chances which their parents never had. A home centred family, with the male as provider and the woman returning from her war work to look after the children was the aspiration. Alongside this ideal model the idea of the family wage was resurrected and with it the idea that women "shouldn't have to" work. A former bricklayer from Liverpool's Scotland Road, recalling his life and attitudes as a young man before and during the Second World War said of the time:

> The man was the king pin, he was the breadwinner, he was the provider, but you were always told that a gentleman should always behave properly to a lady. You opened the door. You protected her. You walked on the outside of her.[5]

Care of children was still seen by many as unmanly: one clerical worker with a young baby in the 1930s recalled that "the idea of a man pushing a pram, that was almost unheard of. I remember once saying, 'I'm not going to push that bloody pram.' I think that was embarrassment".[6] In Lancashire those men who did push prams were known as Mary Annes.[7] If the father often shied away from overt roles in infant care, that pattern tended to continue as the children got older when the father's role was as provider and figure of authority, as a 1940s Salford father said:

> I'd get in from work and my wife would tell me a list of things to deal with…and you'd have to dish out the punishments… It was like a Shakespearean part you played. Dad was the bad guy.[8]

This still seemed perfectly natural to most men and women, despite the upheavals and changes caused by wartime. Men were the pinnacle of the family – as the breadwinner and provider. Work and the entry into work were perhaps the most important events in working class life. Steve Humphries and Pamela Gordon, in their oral history of men's lives, say, "If there was one defining moment when our interviewees felt they grew up and began to be treated like adults, it was when they started a full time job." This usually happened at 14 for men, when they could dress in long trousers, be allocated more food than their younger siblings at home, and receive various privileges in return for their pay packet being handed over to their mum. In particular they drank, smoked and wore fashionable clothes – all traits which marked them out as adult men – and they enjoyed a status in the family which took them away from childhood. Growing up was having paid work.[9]

The promise of the post-war boom initially reinforced values of masculinity: full employment and the expansion of the welfare state meant real material improvements in living standards and the opening up of greater opportunities in everything from education to domestic consumption. In return working people had to keep their side of the bargain: they would work hard at their jobs for these higher wages and they would build stable family units. This required a continuation at least in principle of the sexual division of labour as established in the 19th century – despite the increasing changes in women's lives. But, as Susan Faludi writes of the contradiction that greeted the GIs who came back from the war to the US and which could equally well have applied to Britain:

> The promise was that wartime masculinity, with its common mission, common enemy, and clear frontier, would continue in

peacetime… World War II, however, would prove not the coronation of this sort of masculinity but its last gasp.[10]

Full employment meant, of course, full male employment. But as we have seen, very soon women were also working, and even the part time woman's wage quickly became a very important factor in the rising living standards which many working people were coming to expect. Women's awareness of the limitations of their position as homemakers was also becoming more apparent. Even in the 1950s this frustration and discontent was expressing itself in all sorts of different ways. There were the lucid if limited demands for women's liberation from Betty Friedan or Simone de Beauvoir and the brilliant novels of Doris Lessing which expressed the dilemma of intelligent women who wanted independence and often rejected marriage and motherhood.[11] There were male writers too, who expressed some of the frustration of post-war middle class men with the ideology of the suburban home and nuclear family, and who saw women as constraints on their freedom and creativity.[12] These artistic expressions were symptomatic of a society which seemed calm on the surface but whose certainties were being undermined.

Within 20 years of the boom beginning in the late 1940s, young women were expecting a much higher level of education than their mothers, and wanted to work after marriage; young people were rebelling against the values of the post-war boom societies, with their comfortable but stifling atmosphere. The young Americans who went to fight in Vietnam in the 1960s and early 1970s found a very different response from the GIs of 1945 when they returned from the war. This time:

He was greeted on his return by women not blowing kisses but indifferent or even hostile to his efforts. These women did not leave their jobs upon his arrival; many of them didn't accept or accepted only resentfully a renewed dependency upon him… The loved one whom the man imagined himself supporting and protecting was often doing just fine on her own, and she didn't much appreciate his efforts to assert his authority. In fact, sometimes his wife now saw *him* as the oppressor.[13]

The old ideas began to break down very fast. Women no longer wanted to live in subordinate relationships, and many men also wanted more equal relationships too. So in the US, by 1990, sole male breadwinner households (consisting of a married couple dependent on a man's wage) accounted for only 14 percent of all households, down from almost 60 percent in 1950.[14] Whereas in 1957, 53 percent of the American public believed unmarried people were "sick", "immoral" or "neurotic", by 1976 only 33 percent had negative attitudes towards the unmarried – with 51 percent viewing them neutrally, and 15 percent looking approvingly on people who remained single.[15] "Alternative lifestyles" developed in the 1960s and challenged not only conventional heterosexual relationships but also the whole basis of the nuclear family.

In the 1970s the post-war boom came to an abrupt end, "male" jobs were lost in very large numbers and women's changing role began to make itself felt. Perhaps this marked the beginning of the notions of "male crisis" which are so prevalent today. The loss of manufacturing capacity was the key to the change in jobs. All the Western post-war economies had seen the continuation of an earlier trend for service jobs to displace manufacturing ones. Technological advance coupled with a greater productivity of labour led to more goods being produced by fewer workers. The proportion of manufacturing workers therefore was bound to fall as they became more productive and as the demand grew for workers in industries which serviced manufacturing – from transport and finance to catering.

But the 1970s also marked another qualitative change, at least for the post-war generation: the end of the long boom brought the return of high unemployment, the worst attacks on welfare since the 1930s and a series of major recessions which heralded the restructuring of very large parts of manufacturing industry. This meant the loss of many manufacturing jobs which hit men disproportionately hard. In Britain engineering, cars and steel all saw jobs go in large numbers in the late 1970s and early 1980s. Steel production in 1975 was below the 1970 level. Motor vehicle production stood at 1.6 million in 1975, down from 2.1 million in 1970.[16] Unemployment, which had been at 2 percent or less during the post-war boom, rose sharply, from 1.27 million in 1979 to nearly 2.5 million in 1981, and was up to over 3 million by 1983, where it stayed for several years, and was around 2.5 million in 1991.[17]

Overall employment in UK industry and manufacturing fell from 47.8 percent in 1961 to 37.5 percent in 1981 and 30.6 percent in 1987.

MATERIAL GIRLS

During the same period the growth of commerce and services over-took manufacturing to account for the majority of jobs. The total of all male manual workers as a proportion of occupied males in 1971 stood at 61.79 percent; by 1979 the percentage of male manual workers was 57.6 percent, but the proportion of skilled manual workers fell much more, from 29.08 percent of occupied males in 1971 to 19.2 percent in 1979.[18]

These changes had all sorts of implications beyond the actual loss of employment for the (mainly male) workers affected. Losing skilled jobs meant a loss of status, often a status which had existed through several generations of a family. It meant the loss of any power in the workplace for people who had been traditionally among the best organised workers in the unions. It had effects on the whole of the family whose patterns of life were based on the idea of the male breadwinner. More than anything, it contributed to a sense of lack of worth – a notion that these men had nothing to contribute now they no longer received a pay packet, but were instead dependent on the state or on other members of the family. This despondency and sense of worthlessness was felt most strongly among the men themselves, and is repeated time and again in the anecdotal stories of life without the "respectable" work that they had come to expect.

Two other major changes were taking place at the same time. Men in manual service industries – for example dockers, who had built up similar traditions and strong organisation during the long boom, also found themselves under threat in similar ways to their counterparts in manufacturing. At the same time, the boom in other forms of service, especially in finance and high-tech industry, contin-ued to draw in increasing numbers of women workers. Women didn't usually directly take men's jobs, and many women in manu-facturing also lost jobs, with the number of women employed in manufacturing falling in the 1970s.[19] But women's loss of employ-ment in manufacturing was more than replaced by new jobs in the expanding areas. Many of the men made redundant were older work-ers who were ill equipped for the new jobs and were either unwilling or unable to enter this new work. Older men, more than any other group, felt themselves to be on the scrapheap.

But changes in the pattern of men's and women's employment did not result in women now coming out on top. Women were still stuck in the low wage jobs. They were still more likely to work part time and, although the rate of unemployment for men is around double that of women,[20] there are still more male full time workers than there are women.[21] As recently as 1999, 23 percent of male employee jobs were still in the manufacturing industries – obviously a minority of male jobs, but at nearly a quarter, sufficiently sizeable to be noticed.[22] Women did enter new jobs, it is true, especially in the managerial and professional areas. But overall they still tended to be ghettoised in women's jobs.

Housewife's choice?

Are men superfluous to women and the family? The question would not even have arisen 30 or 40 years ago. Its starting point is the very great changes to the family and women's ability or desire to head a household. Once women go out to work, gain some independent income and have fewer children, they are much less likely to have to or want to have a man about the house than was once the case, as we saw in chapter 1, with the number of lone mothers tripling since the early 1970s. However, three quarters of children are still brought up in two-parent families. In addition, the idea that men have little or no role within the home hardly matches their increased participation in childcare and housework. Most fathers who do not live with their children are not the "deadbeat dads" of tabloid mythology. The majority remain in contact with them: 70 percent of non-resident fathers have some contact with their children and 50 percent see their children every week.[23] Most children are therefore either living with fathers or in regular contact with them – hardly the basis for a mass crisis of men feeling that they do not fulfil the needs of women and children.

One of the notable features of the change in men's behaviour has been the increase in male work around the home. This is a strongly contested issue: different surveys show different results, and surveys of who does housework are notoriously subjective. But there is general agreement that, as women have ceased to be full time housewives, they have reduced the amount of work that they do in the home. As women move into full time work, the gap between the amount of housework that they do and the amount done by their male partners narrows. The number of hours devoted by men to household chores stood at an average of 17 minutes per day in 1961; by 1985 it had risen to 40 minutes a day.[24] During the same period the time spent by British women on routine housework fell by 55 minutes a day or 6.5 hours per week. In the initial part of this period the amount of housework done by men also fell, suggesting that domestic appliances made affordable by the long boom had some impact on curtailing the overall time spent on domestic labour. But that changed from the 1970s when the work of all men went up from 15 minutes to 40 minutes a day and that of full time employed men from 13 minutes a day to 35 minutes. This "probably therefore reflects ideological changes as well as the practical pressures associated with married women's move into paid employment".[25] While the total number of hours spent on housework has fallen for all women, it has not done so proportionately, with full time workers gaining least and with those without employment benefiting most.[26]

On the other hand, working parents of both sexes spend more time devoted to childcare – especially to childcare for the under-fives. Employed men spent an average 44 minutes a day mainly on childcare in 1985 compared with 11 minutes in 1961 – far less than the 107 minutes spent on the same childcare by women in 1985, but a substantial increase nonetheless.[27] Many men tell researchers that they would like to play more of a role in their children's lives than their own fathers did during their childhood.[28] However, the sexual division of labour is still one which sees women doing the bulk of domestic labour, despite the very great changes over the past few decades. A study in the mid-1990s showed that mothers spent much more time doing cooking and housework than men (2.59 hours per day as opposed to 0.41 hours) and more time caring for children and adults (1.56 hours against 0.54). Men did more paid work (5.31 hours per day compared with 2.06 hours for women) and spent an hour a day on travel, compared with half an hour for women. Women did, however, spend more time than men sleeping and socialising.[29]

The amount of work done outside the home by either or both partners has a decisive effect on the amount of domestic work carried out by parents. The responses of young mothers and fathers to questions about the division of labour in the home bear this out. Even when both partners worked full time, mothers still took responsibility for the majority of household chores, but here 27 percent of men said they shared preparing and cooking the meal, 40 percent shared shopping equally and 35 percent shared cleaning equally. When the woman worked part time the participation of men fell (to 15 percent, 28 percent and 16 percent respectively). Where the wife was at home full time, only 10 percent shared cooking the main meal and only 11 percent shared cleaning. Mothers' responses to the same questions showed some differences but not massive discrepancies. In general women were slightly more likely to answer that they did most of these chores and slightly less likely to believe they were shared equally.[30]

The overwhelming conclusion is that where both men and women work full time they are most likely to share chores, but even then chores are far from being equally shared. The traditional division of labour still applies, and men do most DIY and repairs. Marrying or living together doesn't seem to help the division of labour. A study of gender balance in marriage or cohabitation showed that single women spend an average of ten hours a week on housework, while single men spend seven; if they form a union, she spends 15 hours a week while the man spends only five.[31]

Even so, where the wife works and the man stays at home, the man's share increases, although not sufficiently to reverse roles. This is also the area of greatest discrepancy between men and women, so 28 percent of men believe they do most cooking of the main meal when only the women works, while only 6 percent of wives think their husbands do this.[32] Some commentators have even suggested that men in full time work actually do more domestic chores than unemployed men with working partners.[33] So where the sex roles are most obviously reversed – where the woman works and the man stays at home – there are signs that the man has particular difficulty fitting into the "housewife" role, while the woman both works outside the home and has to shoulder a substantial domestic burden as well. If this is the case, it suggests an ideological as well as a practical reluctance by some men in the home to take on this role, itself a product of the low esteem in which housework is held, which in turn comes from the nature of housework as repetitive and unpaid work inside capitalist society.

It is hardly surprising that those men who are forced from the labour market feel disoriented and without social value. This, after all, was how many housewives felt, and still do feel – but the men lack their social conditioning to be able to cope, hence their inability to even become "good housewives". Unemployed men who are responsible for childcare see themselves mostly as "failed providers" rather than successful childcarers.[34] Susan Faludi reports an American transportation manager laid off and now working as a secretary writing of himself, "I was *someone*... Now I'm nothing, just a temp".[35]

Miners at Yorkshire's Grimethorpe colliery, which shut in 1993, describe the feelings of men in this situation. One says, "My day? I get up and do the washing, hang it on the line, get the kids to school, do some shopping, get the tea for when she gets home... The government talks about training, education. What for?"[36] Another says, "We had pride in our work, we made a contribution to the world, we had a place, a proper purpose. Gone. Now I'm a housewife".[37]

How did men respond?

In a sense this is the wrong question. Men respond in all sorts of different ways. They are divided by class, ideology and social orientation. The same can be said of those who comment on male behaviour: they reflect opinions from across the whole class and political spectrum. These opinions may be highly ideologically loaded in favour of a certain pattern of behaviour and a certain sort of family.

A common view of men's responses to the changes in their lives is that it has led to more aggression, with more overt macho behaviour, with claims that violent behaviour is increasingly the definition of maleness: "The most tangible form of maleness these days is its association with violence".[38] So being a man means rejecting feminine attributes and adopting traits which women supposedly don't have. If women work, gain educational qualifications and access to areas of society which were once closed to them, then men have to hold onto their areas of speciality – in this case violent behaviour. But this does not correspond with the actual development of men's behaviour. Men are more likely to commit crime but also to be its victims. They are twice as likely as women to be victims of violent crime. "Young men are particularly vulnerable: 53 percent of victims of violent street crime are men in their twenties, and males aged between ten and twenty are twice as likely as girls to be attacked".[39] Among young men aged 16 to 24, 12.6 percent of them experienced violent crime in 2005-6, compared to a 3.4 percent national average.[40]

A number of what could be called aggressively pro-men's organisations have developed, whose premise is that women have all the advantages and that men have to band together in order to stop themselves being taken to the cleaners by predatory ex-wives or bosses. "Families Need Fathers" or "Fathers for Justice" in Britain or the evangelical "Promise Keepers" in the US base their appeal on the return to traditional male/female roles within the family, with the assumption being that men need to take back what has been lost to them by "uppity" women, who do not "know their place". But it would be wrong to see these organisations or the views they express as dominant. The increase in the number of men who care for children, who accept ideas of women's equality or who reject traditional roles shows that many men have little time for such ideas. The number of out gay men has also increased, suggesting a greater willingness among men to come to terms with their sexuality. A minority of men clearly welcome the end of traditional "masculinity" and have fitted quite easily into new and different ways of living. But the picture for the majority is probably a lot more contradictory. Many can see the advantages of a world where they are more able to express themselves emotionally, where there is no stigma in a man being seen to care for children, and where men are able to pursue careers or interests which might have been once seen as "feminine". However, in a world where few alternatives are on offer, having a "real man's job" or being "head of the household", or bonding with other men in a "masculine" environment, can take on a key importance.

One of the reasons why many men's attitudes are so contradictory is because the signals sent to them by society are also contradictory. Much of the dominant ideology in countries like Britain is egalitarian in tone. The received opinion among the majority of the establishment and the bulk of the media is that men and women are both expected to work (indeed the stay at home mother who expects an income from the state is now regarded with disapproval). Men and women are also expected to share housework and childcare where practically possible and families are deemed to operate as contented units of consumption where a degree of democratic choice is allowed to all its members. Men who behave as authoritarian father figures are regarded as both rare and wrongheaded. Dads like Tony Blair or David Beckham demonstrate that caring comes naturally to fathers. No one could call them Mary Annes when they push the pram (not that they do it very often, since this is the nanny's job). But even while men are being encouraged to show their emotions, there are much less pleasant developments which also have an ideological effect on men's attitudes to themselves. So we see the reassertion of traditional male values, at least among a layer of men: lap dancing clubs, lad magazines, an insidious campaign against the notion of "date rape", a resurgence of sexist language, and continuing high levels of violence against individual women.

While it is commonly assumed that the worst sexist attitudes and most gross sexual behaviour exist in the manual working class, and that the educated middle classes are somehow immune from such behaviour, a glance at social and business practices in the City of London, or a profile of the readers of "men's magazines", tells a different story. Many of the most revered and respected institutions of capitalist society encourage and disseminate ideas of male domination. Big business, the judiciary, the Stock Exchange and the armed forces are all very heavily male dominated. However, since the 1980s this male chauvinism has been explicit rather than implicit. The New Lads with their old attitudes about women were a phenomenon described thus by Simon Nye, writer of the television series *Men Behaving Badly*:

The Lad was created by the meritocracy (or new plutocracy, depending on your political allegiance) unleashed by Margaret Thatcher in 1979. The shouty young men that crowded London's trading markets and exchanges, earning fortunes and scaring away cupboardsful of sniffy Guildford stockbrokers, were the Trojan Lads, hidden in the bellies of financial institutions and wheeled inside the walls of the establishment. And it was okay to swear and be a bit of a sexist because they worked *bloody* hard.[41]

The main expression of the "lads" has been the rise of the "men's magazines" – glossy and upmarket, filled with expensive advertising – and by the late 1990s they were selling 1.5 million copies a month between them.[42] The titles range in sophistication and presentation but there is no doubting their selling point: the covers always have women in various states of undress. The inside is little different, containing vast amounts about sex, a lot of football, and a very strong interest in conspicuous consumption. These magazines possess a general assumption that "foreigners" are inferior, being both strange and stupid, that women really "want it" according to the most stereotyped male fantasy, and that any real man will only be interested in beer, sport and "shagging". But these are aspirational men behaving badly. The editor of *GQ Active* described his average reader as between 25 and 35 and likely to be "cruising down the motorway in an Audi with a mountain bike on the roof".[43] Advertising is aimed at 20 and 30-somethings with large amounts of disposable income, focusing on cars, clothes and army recruitment.

Some have argued that the lad phenomenon and the men's magazines have a positive effect, that they are "an attempt by straight men to come to terms with their new position in the world, with the second wave of feminism and the undermining of traditional forms of gender identity".[44] But any inspection of these magazines shows little understanding of coming to terms with the second wave of feminism – or even the first. Features in *Loaded* include "Do It Before They Ban It with a round up of naughty activities and where you can still legally participate in them; the Sex Hunter goes to Prague to Czech out (arf) the world's first fully-filmed brothel and participate in some action; and the Top 10 crisps of all time".[45] In *FHM*, which is supposed to be more sophisticated, items include "85 Man Skills…you can master in a day (if you're a really quick learner)"; "Keeley! Britain's hottest woman annexes our trousers". Again "Oh God – The Bed's On Fire! The secret sex zones even she didn't know she had"; "MI6 Left Me To Rot! The SAS spy deserted in an Afghan jail".[46] International analysis is at the boys' comic level. The Taliban "spend a great deal of time bossing women around. This may sound like a pretty good idea, especially if your girlfriend nags you a lot, but trust me, these guys get it all wrong". The Germans start wars. The French don't wash, eat snails, and are ungrateful: "twice in the last 80 years we've had to go over there and kick the Germans out for them, but have we ever had a word of thanks." Mexicans "sell their sisters to any passing gringo with $2 in his wallet".[47] The more down-market *Nuts* does a 21st century version of "readers' wives":

> *Nuts* is always the place to come for the sexiest Real Girls and this week we're really on top of our game. Tracy invites us into her bedroom in Real Girls! Real Places! While lovely Lianne from Wimbledon demonstrates how easily the fine female form distracts us blokes. In Real Girls Talk Sex the topic of the week is seduction, and as usual Ladies Confess makes us come over all unnecessary.[48]

And so it goes tediously on. In fact the lad magazines are full of old sexism, racism, nationalism and homophobia masquerading as witty, playful and ironic. This is Benny Hill humour dressed up for the 21st century. Underlying it is a deeply conservative set of values and in this they resemble the 1950s too. Women who complain about such images, who don't find the sexist jokes funny, or who in any other way break from the norm, are regarded as humourless, too unattractive to get a man, or lesbians.

We love women, is the cry of the new lads, but they don't love women at all. They love a particular stylised and objectified image of women because they believe this enhances their masculinity and status:

> In the case of lad mags there is not only nostalgia for images of women in the mode of *Playboy* at its heyday, but also the desire to utter all the offences known to man, freed from the imagined tut-tutting of "ardent" feminists. Men's magazines celebrate images which three decades ago feminists would have denounced without hesitation; but these contemporary images are set in a context which attempts to deny us the right to have any opinion at all.[49]

The US *Playboy* magazine, founded in 1953, saw its role as being about "reclaiming the indoors" and was about a male rebellion against the conventional middle class female dependency of the 1950s.[50] Now women are outside the home and the level of openness about sexuality is much greater, the message of the magazines is that men can still celebrate their domination in the face of the threat of liberated women – and who can dare to complain? The dichotomy between the image of the submissive, domesticated housewife and that of the sexually aggressive whore is matched by contrast between the touchy feely new dad and the aggressive and sexist New Lad.

The various institutions of capitalist society play a very important role in projecting a view of masculinity which reinforces sexual divisions and which asserts a very traditional pattern of life. This is probably truer of the military than any other area of life. Military values have gained an increasingly weighty position in a world racked by war: Troops in wars such as those with Afghanistan or Iraq are encouraged to display the worst macho traits, while trashy memoirs of SAS exploits top the best-seller lists. Women who are allowed to join the armed services are expected to deny any conventionally "feminine" traits and become proxy men for the purposes of the military. The culture of violence which is the army's whole rationale tends to permeate throughout wider social and family life of soldiers. Susan Faludi describes the Citadel, the military academy in the southern US state of Georgia where the first woman cadet was forced out after a hideously male chauvinist campaign against her. Examples of male violence towards other men included a member of the cycling team forced to hang by his fingers over a sword poised two inches below his testicles, a noose over the bed of a black freshman who had refused to sing "Dixie" and the torture of a racoon stabbed and mutilated to chants of "Kill the bitch".[51] One cadet, who contemplated suicide as a result of constant attack, saw many of the assaults as a gender battle, although carried out by men, where those attacked were "women":

> Virtually every taunt hurled in his direction, he recalled, equated him with a woman: whenever he showed fear, they would say, "Bryant, you look like you're having an abortion", or, "Bryant, are you menstruating this month?"[52]

The arrival of a real woman at the military college was just more than they could stand.

The social institutions which instil supposedly timeless masculine values are themselves ideologically and materially shaped not by centuries of tradition but by relatively modern capitalist development. The supposedly traditional military values are those of modern, highly technologically sophisticated warfare. In many ways these values conflict with the changing lives of men and women today. But there are several reasons why they have such a purchase. Wars can create a feeling of heightened interest, something out of the ordinary compared with the day to day boredom of work. They can therefore appear as a challenging alternative to the routine world of work and family, somewhere that a man can affirm his masculinity by protecting his country, his family, the weak and powerless. Such ideas dovetail with some of the right wing ideas about men, women and the family, which aim at reinforcing men's role as protector and provider, and women's subordinate position. However, there are limits to this glorification of war and this can be seen by contrasting contemporary images of war and those from the aftermath of the Second World War. Today these images are much more negative, reflecting disenchantment with war following Vietnam and the subsequent wars in the Middle East and south Asia.

Professional sporting events also foster high degrees of male bonding and cults of masculine strength and courage. At the same time these events encourage cheerleaders and the appearances of glamorous wives and girlfriends, in case anyone might think that looking at all these muscular male bodies might encourage anything other than red-blooded heterosexuality. The close connection between male work and sport has not necessarily disappeared with the change in male work patterns. It can even take on a greater importance when there is less certainty in other areas of life. Male boredom and disorientation can mean a greater investment in sport or other leisure pursuits.[53]

Sport grew in an organised fashion as part of the growth of 19th century capitalism, and its development has very much mirrored that of the mass media, from the mass circulation newspapers of the late 19th century to satellite television today. The mass media has created glamorous male images to do with sporting achievement. These assume dedication, single-mindedness, a certain ruthlessness, and a high level of physical endurance and training. These are seen as male characteristics, and success in them is rewarded with hero status and the devotion of beautiful women. Sporting events also produce a sense of excitement, a break from the routine of life – usually fairly harmlessly, although much nationalist, sexist and racist sentiment is generated.

Part of the debate about men is about the attempt by conservatives to shore up the old set of family values in the face of an increasing unwillingness on the part of many people to live in the conventional nuclear family. Melanie Phillips's aim is quite transparent – forcing men to work would solve many of the social problems that confront those who run our society at present:

Male breadwinning…is neither arbitrary nor anachronistic. It is important both to cement masculine identity and to civilise aggressive male characteristics. That's why unemployment has played havoc with young boys' socialisation and shattered their fathers' emotional and physical health. Employment is an instrumental, goal driven activity which permits men to serve their families through competition. In that way it directs male aggression into pro-social purposes.[54]

The Phillips view of men is the modern equivalent of those who in the 1960s decried the absence of a war or national service into which young men could be conscripted. Men who were not provided with this external discipline were bound to grow their hair long, take illegal drugs and play loud music. Today those who are excluded from work are accused of a propensity to violence and – even worse – allowing the state to take responsibility for their families. Men have to know their place, and it is to work, the only means, in Phillips's chilling phrase, of "civilising" them. If this authoritarian picture of an orderly world where men are breadwinners and women accept a role as mothers and wives suggests that men have a built in tendency to violence and bad behaviour, it is by no means unique. The idea that men can only be redeemed and civilised by the family is quite widely held, and not just by those like Melanie Phillips who are on the radical right of the political spectrum.

Boys will be boys?

There is a strong element of class prejudice in the current fear of untamed and marauding young men. Young men are held to be particularly scary because they commit so much crime and violent attacks. But older working class people also come under attack for not bringing up their children properly, a view permeated by a sense of fatalist acceptance that the new generations are bound to replicate the social problems of their parents. The remark by a manager of a youth offending team to Beatrix Campbell captures this:

> These boys have watched their mothers being beaten to hell by their fathers. They're all misogynists. We try to deal with these gender issues in an ongoing way but you can't undo the effect of 16 years of doctrine in a child's life very easily.[55]

Campbell sees mothers as the thin red line, the only element of civilisation preventing teenage boys from turning into complete barbarians: "Some of the women dread the challenge to their relationships with men for whom no one but these women takes responsibility".[56]

Young men are accused by feminist Angela Philips of a high level of criminality, connected to the Y chromosome: "Perhaps it's time we considered the possibility that in our society...there is something pathological about the way boys are raised".[57]

It may be convenient to explain young boys' behaviour by reference to their gender, but it is much more complicated than that. Firstly, the critique is not aimed at boys in general, but at working class boys in particular and especially (at least in code) at young blacks. When the prime minister's son Euan Blair was found drunk in Leicester Square after receiving his GCSE results, no one saw this as symptomatic of wider social problems. Blair attended one of the top London schools and his educational and social background prepared him for becoming one of the elite. The fear about boys in Brixton or Handsworth is that they have a very different future in store. They lack the financial support available to middle or upper class children and have little prospect of creative or well remunerated work. Their under-age drinking or drug taking is likely to be regarded very differently from that of richer children who live in respectable areas. As we saw above with the military cadets in the Citadel, often hideous levels of institutionalised violence are acceptable within certain establishments. High levels of violence take place between boys in public schools, but this is regarded as acceptable inside the institution and is anyway enclosed within four walls, deliberately separated from wider society.

The common picture of working class boys identifies them with violence and criminality and links this to a sense of inadequacy, a product in particular of boys' growing social inferiority to their female counterparts. This inferiority is particularly heightened in education, where recent figures show girls regularly outperforming boys in exam results. But in both areas perception does not always match reality. It is true that the vast number of those carrying out muggings, battering, burglary, joyriding and rioting are men, but juvenile crime is "overwhelmingly non-violent".[58] Between the mid-1980s and mid-1990s the proportion of male juveniles found guilty or cautioned fell.[59] Crime is connected with unemployment and the gender unemployment gap is high, with males much more likely to be unemployed than females. A survey by senior probation officers in 1993 found that 70 percent of serious offences were committed by the unemployed.[60] Recession and crime seem to have a special connection in the inner city areas, where deprivation is higher and the young are more likely to be marginalised. Crimes against property tend to increase as personal consumption falls, and so are connected to poverty and unemployment. This is not true, however, about crimes against the person, which are mostly carried out by young men and which tend to increase as personal consumption rises.[61] The most disadvantaged 5 percent of society are 100 times more likely to have multiple problems than the most advantaged 50 percent, including conduct disorders, police contact, cannabis use, mood disorders and alcohol abuse; 63 percent of young people in prison were unemployed at the time of arrest.[62]

Sandy Ruxton argues that the explanation of the link between masculinity and criminality lies in the sex roles which men and women adopt when they become adults. The contradiction between the male child and the adult is greater than that between the female child and adult:

> The dominant view of masculinity is that a man should be tough, strong, aggressive, independent, rational, intelligent, and so on. But the dominant image of children is that they are vulnerable, weak, immature, passive and dependent. This creates a particular contradiction for boys, which is heightened as adulthood gets nearer, simply because, within the construction of childhood, being a man cannot be achieved.[63]

If this is true, then becoming a man means rejecting all the traits most closely associated with childhood – and which all too often are also associated with "femininity" – and instead adopting behaviour and practices regarded as manly. Gangs, a degree of criminal behaviour, fighting, and scorning certain forms of learning which are seen as childish, are all part of this process, as is the adulation of sporting heroes. There is a class element to this: high status schools tend to foster a liberal version of the old public school ethos – individual excellence in sport, but also a sense of purpose in learning, providing an expectation for all concerned in these enterprises that their pupils will fulfil an important place in society. The middle and upper classes place much store on individual development, to a certain extent apart from the mass of people, with the aim of creating the ambition to succeed in a career later. Teenage boys from these sorts of background will see themselves as preparing for such a future. Working class boys take their adolescent development much more from the streets and from popular culture: collective praise for individual sporting or musical expertise is highly valued and practical and physical attributes attract a higher status than academic ability. It is this sort of masculinity which is so objected to by the commentators, yet in itself it represents a threat not to the mass of people but to the dominant ideology which tries to put working class kids in their place. Why should ability at break dancing not be valued as highly as playing golf? Or the ability to memorise song lyrics not be as valuable as knowing multiplication tables? The fashion for streetwise clothes, the customisation of school uniforms, the refusal to accept the narrow middle class ideology that is now imposed with such a straitjacket on the schools, are all a form of rebellion which often stresses aggression as a means of asserting some sort of control and status in life.

Even here we should hold on to some perspective. Most boys are not extremely violent and are not habitual criminals. Some of the most common crimes may be more "feminine" than "masculine". Home Office figures confirm that an eighth of all recorded offences are for shoplifting and that more women than men are cautioned for this crime. It is especially common among young women and 7,528 girls between the age of 13 and 15 are cautioned each year. This compares with 6,370 boys.[64] Women made up 41.3 percent of all shoplifting offenders at Xmas 2006.[65] One survey found that 89 percent of 16 year old working class girls had been involved in at least one physical fight.[66] Nor are boys illiterate morons who want to learn nothing at school. It would be hard to deduce from recent furores over some of these questions that juvenile crime was not pandemic. Nor would one conclude that – as is the truth – more boys pass exams than in the past and there is less illiteracy among the young than among the old. It is true that in many areas of education girls do better than boys, and that their improvement rate tends to be much faster than boys. But this is hardly surprising, given that the expectations about work and education for women have been transformed in the past few decades. Back in the 1950s and 60s, when girls tended to do worse in education than boys, this was put down to girls having low expectations of a career and their internalisation of their oppression. Today, especially when educational qualifications have taken on such heightened importance in the labour market for workers of both sexes, it is hardly surprising that girls attempt to equip themselves for competition in that market alongside boys. It may be as well that the preponderance of girls in clerical and white collar jobs may encourage them slightly more than boys to gain qualifications.

This is a process of equalisation between the sexes. It can lead to boys feeling that they are doing relatively worse and that they feel a lack of self-esteem as a result. However, the fact remains that the position of boys in education is improving too, but at a much slower rate. The proportion of young women in the UK achieving two or more A levels has doubled since the mid-1970s, whereas the number of men doing so has risen by just under a half in the same period. Even so the number gaining A levels has risen substantially.[67] Whereas 173,000 women were full time undergraduates in 1970/71, by 2004/05 there were 680,000. Comparable figures for men were 241,000 and 549,000.[68] The big increase in women's participation and rise in qualifications seems to have stemmed from the 1980s, perhaps the most decisive decade in marking the idea that women had to take responsibility for their own self-advancement, and this advance has certainly continued through the 1990s and the first years of the 21st century. Whether it will continue – marking an ever growing widening gap between the sexes – or whether it will stabilise with broad levels of equality but with women at a slight advantage is too early to say.

What is indisputable, however, is the role of class in education and this appears to have a much greater influence on performance than gender. Pupils in comprehensive schools in the poorest urban areas achieve half the success rate at GCSE of those in better off urban areas.[69] In 1991/92, 55 percent from families of professionals went into higher education aged under 21; by 1998/99, 72 percent did. In 1991/92 only 6 percent of those from unskilled working class backgrounds went into higher education. By the end of the decade this had risen to only 13 percent. Professionals were more than twice as likely as the national average to see their children in higher education, while unskilled workers were only half as likely as the average to do so.[70] The sense of worthlessness and bitterness at what the future holds must surely be connected in the minds of working class girls and boys with this lack of access to the sort of education that holds out the promise of financial and social benefits. For when we

MATERIAL GIRLS

look at those children who gain no qualifications, there is not a massive discrepancy between boys and girls. So 8 percent of boys and 5 percent of girls gained no graded GCSEs in 1997/98, while 26 percent of boys and 33 percent of girls gained 2 or more A levels.[71] Seeing the educational divide as a boy/girl question only obscures the much greater division of class, something right wing commentators are so keen to deny.

What sort of a society sees women as a threat?

Now men know what it's like to be a woman, is the common response from many of women who find themselves regaled with stories of male crisis. Women can't help thinking that we've always had to put up with this – why is it different when it happens to a man? Time and again the experience of men who have lost work or are doing lower grade work than they have been used to is compared to women's traditional malaise at being in the home. Bill Costas, an unemployed meatpacker aged 34 in the US moans, "I don't see anybody anymore. The guys I worked with were my buddies... We'd go out after work and have a beer and shoot the bull. Now I don't even know what they're doing anymore".[72] Some believe men's problem is precisely because they are in the traditional "female" role.

But of course they are not in the traditional female role. Men still go out to work in very large numbers, they still hang on to nearly all the really powerful jobs in capitalist society, and they still leave women holding the baby most of the time, whether these women do it for love or for a paid wage. Men are not full-time housewives very often – and those who claim to be are often working at home part time in an occupation which has a high degree of autonomy and is relatively well rewarded. This is a very long way from the low status work, isolation, and tendency to depression, boredom and nervous illness that housewives have suffered. Those men who most closely approximate to such a role are the long-term unemployed, usually without direct childcare responsibilities, and often older, who sense their worthlessness in their inability to sell their labour power.

The real transformation here is that men and women are moving closer together in terms of their work and their domestic life, but they are struggling to do so in conditions not of their own choosing. They do so against a background of continuing women's oppression and intensified exploitation for both men and women. No wonder so many feel in crisis. No wonder as well that increasing numbers are beginning to question a society which treats men and women in this way. The experience of capitalist society potentially acts as a unifier of working class people: the very process of exploitation brings large numbers of people together as workers. They face similar experiences of low wages, petty rules at work, the tyranny of timekeeping, and being constantly tied to machinery. They perceive a common enemy in the form of the employer. But there are also other forces at work: most importantly, capitalist society also acts to divide working class people. This is done in a thousand small and large ways, and through a combination of ideological and material factors. Women's material disadvantage in terms of wages, for example, is underpinned by the view which still prevails that women are either primarily mothers or sex objects. Racist and nationalist arguments feed on the fact that in capitalist society there is scarcity amid plenty and that workers have to compete for limited resources. So competition between workers for jobs or housing or education can act to reinforce racist ideas. Society tries to pit men against women, blacks against whites, even Catholics against Protestants. When an oppressed group gains anything at the expense of those they are supposed to be competing with, this is enough to cause a crisis. Instead of seeing the real source of problems as lying in the wider social system, working people all too often see the problem as lying within the immediate division of these scarce resources.

There are two points to be made here in relation to men and women. Women have not benefited at the expense of men. They still work in the home and in paid work. Both sexes are under increased pressure, with the lives of working men and women unrecognisable compared with one or two generations ago. Both now have to work to provide an adequate family income; both are pressurised to ensure that their children gain the education and qualifications to equip them for the labour market as it is today; both struggle to fit the tasks of childcare and housework into their busy lives. As the family becomes a centre of enhanced consumption, so individual men and women are sold an image of themselves that goes well beyond the old roles of breadwinner and homemaker. Now they are meant to successfully transcend these past roles and adopt at least some of the roles once seen as the property of the other sex. Fitting into these new roles may be more rewarding or enjoyable in some cases, but it is usually hard work. So women work for less than equal wages, while men are expected to participate in unpaid childcare.

The second point about male/female relations is that the discomfort which men feel at the new situation they find themselves in only demonstrates how artificial the old circumstances were. In *The Condition of the Working Class in England* Frederick Engels wrote of the unease felt among men as they lost their work in textiles and saw their wives or daughters earning more money than they could.[73] Engels wrote of how insane this system was and how degrading it was to both sexes, since it "unsexes the man and takes from the woman all womanliness without being able to bestow upon the man true womanliness or the woman true manliness".[74] There was nothing natural about gender roles or about the attitudes and status which were attributed to them. Instead:

So total a reversal of the position of the sexes can have come to pass only because the sexes have been placed in a false position from the beginning. If the reign of the wife over the husband, as inevitably brought about by the factory system, is inhuman, the pristine rule of the husband over the wife must have been inhuman too.[75]

Or as Shere Hite, the US author who has written groundbreaking books on the relations between the sexes, puts it in her latest work:

Today's subtle changes in millions of individuals are aiming toward a new social order, one filled with more love, warmth and caring than we know at present, yet no longer based on the antiquated family system with its hegemony requiring that women submit to male authority or that men feel they are "in charge" and "responsible" for everyone, not able to interact equally with the others but required to act "better than the others, and prove it". A democratisation of private life. For the better.[76]

In an unequal society, there must always be someone on top – but there is nothing natural or fair about this. This is the basis of Engels' argument, developed elsewhere, that the family and gender roles within it are artificial constructions.[77] The male crisis is a product of a society incapable of treating its members as equal human beings, but which instead robs them of any control over their lives. The response to this among men in particular is twofold. Men often cling onto a sense of identity or pride in supposedly masculine values or traits, which they think set them apart from women (or indeed from men who are regarded as being "feminine"). But at the same time they feel a sense of unease and of powerlessness in controlling what happens in their world. This explains much of the seemingly contradictory behaviour of men today and also points to a possibly frightening but potentially exhilarating future, as an understanding of the shallowness and inequity of the old relationships leads to a wider questioning of how the world is run.

War: liberation, like it or not

On 17 November 17 Laura Bush took over her husband's weekly radio broadcast to deliver a message. The First Lady of the United States, who doesn't like public speaking and who is not known to have spoken up for women's liberation before, made a plea in support of the war being waged by her husband in Afghanistan, on the grounds that it would help the women and children there:

> The brutal oppression of women is a central goal of the terrorists... One in every four children won't live past the age of five because healthcare is not available. Women have been denied access to doctors when they're sick. Life under the Taliban is so hard and repressive, even small displays of joy are outlawed – children aren't allowed to fly kites; their mothers face beatings for laughing out loud.

Warming to her theme, she continued:

> Only the terrorists and the Taliban forbid education to women. Only the terrorists and the Taliban threaten to pull out women's fingernails for wearing nail polish.[1]

The same weekend she was joined by Tony Blair's wife, Cherie (using her married name rather than her professional name of Booth), who launched a campaign to improve Afghan women's rights and education. Downing Street said Mrs Blair wanted to "lend her support" after seeing and reading how women had been oppressed under the Taliban. A spokesman said:

> Their human rights have been denied, people have been executed in football stadiums in front of cheering crowds, girls have had to be educated in secret. There is a story that we have to keep telling.[2]

Keep telling it they did. Hillary Clinton, the former First Lady, joined in. Together with other senators she hosted a press conference for Afghan women's rights activists on Capitol Hill, and wrote in *Time* magazine, "We, as the liberators, have an interest in what follows the Taliban".[3] This was a change: despite his administration being lobbied by US feminists to pressurise the Taliban over women's rights years earlier, Clinton's husband had shown no concern for the situation of women in Afghanistan before the war. Nor had Bush.[4]

But who could now resist a war of liberation which also meant women's liberation? Images of polished fingernails being torn out, beatings as punishment for laughter and the banning of flying kites sent shudders down the spine and only underlined the superiority of Western values. The argument was calculated. When George Bush launched his war on terror in September 2001 his language was militaristic and masculine: Bin Laden wanted dead or alive, bring it on, smoke 'em out. But however horrified people were by the events of 11 September 2001, they were not too keen on the world's only superpower bombing one of the world's poorest countries, Afghanistan, because its Islamic fundamentalist government was supposedly harbouring Osama Bin Laden and Al Qaida.

The argument about women's liberation was a vital one for the US and British governments, putting "a feminist glow on some of the most brutal bombing of the 2001 campaign".[5] Some feminists were all too happy to oblige. Eleanor Smeal, leader of the Feminist Majority, said after meeting a group of US generals, "They went off about the role of women in this effort and how imperative it was that women were now in every level of the Air Force and Navy." The involvement of women in bombing an estimated 10,000 Afghan civilians who died during the war in 2001 gave Smeal no qualms, since "it's a different kind of war".[6]

The spin was dutifully repeated by liberal media: women in the White House were "not only making the strategy, their gender is part of the strategy…a weapon to attack the Taliban's treatment of Afghan women".[7] The Taliban's treatment was summed up by one image – women in the burqa, the full-length head covering and gown worn by many women in Afghanistan. Much news coverage focused on this issue:

> Reporting on the burqa far out-numbered reports on women's struggle for fundamental rights – to education, health, personal safety, political participation – perhaps because the people the US had chosen as allies had rotten records on granting any of those.[8]

The Taliban regime was a terrible one and few people mourned its demise. However, it grew from the horrors of invasion, war and civil war that had faced Afghanistan in the two decades before it came to power. It was seen by some as a force for stability, despite its repressive and anti-women policies. Many of the practices followed by the Taliban were also followed by the allies of the US in the Afghan war, who then became part of the government. The Northern Alliance, its main ally, was a notoriously violent and corrupt organisation of warlords, as committed to Sharia law as the Taliban. An Afghan judge told Agence France Presse in December 2001 that public executions and amputations would continue, although they would display the victim's body in public for less time than the Taliban! According to a spokesman for Amnesty International USA in November 2001, "There are even more documented cases of women raped by the Northern Alliance than there are by the Taliban".[9]

However, these warlords were now on the side of modernity versus backwardness and were part of a coalition bringing liberation, not just to the Afghan people in general, but to its women in particular. The terms of debate were, of course, highly ideologically loaded, with backwardness represented by women who covered up while modernity was about women uncovering themselves. The day that US networks broadcast images of women throwing off the burqa in

Afghanistan coincided with the first episode of a television fashion show from the Victoria's Secret chain, known for its erotic underwear.[10] As Zillah Eisenstein writes, "I wonder why the rape camps of Bosnia or the sexual slavery of women by the Japanese military during World War Two were never called traditionalist and 'backward'."[11]

By early 2002 George Bush could say in his State of the Union address:

> The last time we met in this chamber the mothers and daughters of Afghanistan were captives in their own homes, forbidden from working or going to school. Today women are free, and are part of Afghanistan's new government.[12]

Well, the last bit was true anyway. The occupiers ensured that a system of positive discrimination in the electoral system led to a certain quota of women representatives. But little has changed for the better in the lives of Afghans in five or more years since the war ended and Bush made his speech, and sometimes it has changed for the worse.

Guardian journalist Natasha Walter visited the country on the fifth anniversary of the war. In a piece headlined "We Are Just Watching Things Get Worse" she agreed that some things had improved since an earlier visit just after the end of the war:

> You can now see women moving around Kabul in a way they could not five years ago; the majority do not wear the burqa, sporting instead a variety of Islamic dress from shalwar kameez to a short coat with a bright headscarf.

However, she also reported Human Rights Watch saying a third of districts are without girls' schools and traditional practices like child marriage still continue. Many of her interviewees were fearful for the future.[13]

An even bleaker picture is painted by an October 2006 report on the position of women five years after the war. While it records that Afghanistan's new parliament in 2005 exceeded its 25 percent quota system for women, these rights on paper have not been matched in practice. In some provinces security for women is worse than in 2001, honour killings are on the rise, and:

the last two years have witnessed the murder of women aid workers, attacks on women elections workers, the continuation of severe forms of domestic abuse, trafficking and prostitution of women, an astronomical rise in cases of self-immolation, high rates of child marriage, the kidnapping of young women, and minimal protection from rape and assault.[14]

Promised funding for reconstruction has not been there and the availability of clean water, education, healthcare and means of making a livelihood are all inadequate. Insecurity and poverty go hand in hand. Perhaps most tellingly, "Military spending currently exceeds development and reconstruction spending by 900 percent".[15] By 2007 the Taliban was growing again and thousands of civilians were dying, many as a result of US air strikes that claimed to be targeting the Taliban but were hitting the local population.

The human consequences of humanitarian war

It was much harder to make a similar case when it came to the war on Iraq. Women in Saddam Hussein's Iraq had the highest level of political participation anywhere in the Middle East and an advanced level of education. Iraq was a much more developed and secular society. Therefore the pro-war message focused much more on breaches of human rights. Before the first Gulf War in 1991 a notorious story gained currency, that after invading Kuwait Iraqi troops had torn newborn babies from incubators in a Kuwait City hospital. It was false.[16] This story was nonetheless recycled in the run up to the 2003 war.

The importance of human rights stories was not lost on the Bush administration and its supporters in Britain. While they tried to scare their populations with stories of weapons of mass destruction, they also appealed to humanitarian instincts, especially by claiming that Saddam Hussein was a dictator who "killed his own people". Saddam was indeed guilty of this, although the 2 million Iraqi deaths attributed to him include the deaths in the Iran-Iraq and Gulf wars, during the first of which he was backed by the US. One atrocity committed by Saddam was used repeatedly in the run up to war in 2003: the massacre of 5,000 Kurds in Halabja in 1988. The massacre was barely mentioned in the run up to war in 1991, because of the proximity and the complicity of the US. Between the invasion of Kuwait in August 1990 and the end of the first Gulf War in February 1991, it was mentioned in only 39 US news stories. In 2003, by contrast, the story was mentioned 57 times in February and 145 times in March, the month war began.[17]

Launched on 20 March 20, the invasion was over within a month. The occupation was, however, always contested. Resistance grew up in different parts of the country; the occupiers responded with mass arrests, smashing into houses, treating women with contempt and sometimes arresting them along with the men. This treatment only helped to fuel wider resistance, as did the failure to repair the infrastructure or improve the lives of Iraqis. Electricity and water were only sporadically available, schools and hospitals were crumbling and ill equipped, while millions of dollars went to the big Western reconstruction companies.[18]

Women's position deteriorated. As in Afghanistan, there was a paper commitment to women's rights – UN Security Council Resolution 1483, passed on 22 May 2003, gave a commitment to a "rule of law that affords equal rights and justice to all Iraqi citizens without regard to ethnicity, religion, or gender".[19] Here as well it made virtually no difference to most women. In the course of the invasion and immediately afterwards Human Rights Watch estimated at least 400 women and girls had been raped and thought that this was an underestimate because many rapes were not reported due the stigma, so the real figure was much higher.[20] There were many cases of kidnap or killing by criminal gangs. A number of women were taken hostage, including the British woman Margaret Hassan, who was killed, and the Italians Simona Toretta and Simona Pari. Women detainees of the occupying forces have also been subject to torture and ill treatment, especially at the notorious Abu Ghraib prison. Among the "intentional abuse of detainees by military police [MP] personnel" were "a male MP guard having sex with a female detainee" and "videotaping and photographing naked male and female detainees". A woman's rights activist and political scientist, Huda Shaker Neimi, described a US troop checkpoint in Baghdad in 2004 where she had objected to her handbag being searched. A soldier pointed a gun at her, then pointed to his penis and said, "Come here, bitch, I'm going to fuck you".[21]

There was also an attempt to alter laws to weaken women's civil rights and force them to rely on religious institutions to deal with issues such as marriage and divorce. However, this resolution,

MATERIAL GIRLS

introduced by the US-installed Iraqi Governing Council, was defeated after protests and lobbying by women's organisations.[22] The effects of war on health and well being have also been stark. One particular danger is the effects of depleted uranium weapons, dating back to the first Gulf War in 1991. Doctors in Iraq estimate that birth defects have increased by two to six times, and three to 12 times as many children have developed cancer and leukaemia since 1991. There are many miscarriages.[23]

A poll conducted among Iraqis on the fourth anniversary of the war showed 67 percent thought reconstruction efforts in Iraq had not been effective. Just 38 percent said the situation in the country was better than before the war, while 50 percent said it was worse.[24] Insecurity and the general collapse of society have greatly worsened the position of women, who have to carry the burden of caring for the family in such appalling conditions. Many young women and girls are denied an education because the situation is too dangerous. In some areas women feel that they have to wear the veil either because they are made to do so or because they judge it prudent to do so. The Iraqi writer Haifa Zangana, long exiled in Britain because of her political activities in opposition to Saddam Hussein, marked International Women's Day 2007, four years after the war began, with a scathing critique:

> The regime in Baghdad's Green Zone is busy organising a cele-bration of a different kind for this year's International Women's Day on 8 March. Among its highlights will be the execution of four Iraqi women. This follows on from its decision to honour four of its Iraqi officers accused of raping a young woman... Long gone are the colourful parades of Iraqi women celebrating their achievements. Now we only have parades of death, where the "liberated" and "empowered" Iraqi women and girls, covered head to toe with hijabs and abayas, will queue at police stations, prisons, detention camps, hospital "fridges" and crowded morgues looking for the disappeared, kidnapped or their assassi-nated loved ones.[25]

She concludes that "women's basic rights are being eroded in Iraq", a state of affairs presided over by occupying powers whose rhetoric on human rights is contradicted by its actions.

Western feminism and Muslim women

If the situation of women in Afghanistan and Iraq were not bad enough, they also have to deal with the condescension of many Western feminists. Modern feminism in the West came out of the movement against imperialism, the movement against the Vietnam War; and while many feminists continue to hold to those ideals, there are others who have allowed the rich and powerful in the West to co-opt feminism for their own ends of war and colonialism. For at least some of these feminists one gets the distinct impression that there is nothing worse than religion and nowhere better in the world than the West. So war, repression and colonial rule can be justified in the name of overcoming "backwardness"; and the inherent superiority of countries with easy access to women's studies courses, and the freedom for women to wear heels as high as they like or skirts as short as they like, should be obvious.

While such feminists describe themselves as secular, it is one religion, Islam, rather than all religions, for which they reserve their greatest antipathy. Here they concur with much of dominant media and political coverage in the West, which infers that Islam is a uniquely backward and repressive religion. While such a view is clearly connected with late 20th century and early 21st century issues of war and imperialism, the issue of women's dress has particular resonance for these feminists.

One Afghan woman described how:

> in the late 1990s we tried to explain the sufferings of Afghan women to American feminists. We worked with the Feminist Majority, but soon we realised that they had their own agenda which was not in the interest of Afghan women. For them the issue of burqa was the most important issue. For us, the issue was women's access to education, health and employment. After the fall of Taliban, they brought large numbers of burqas from Afghanistan, they cut the parts that covers the face and sold them to raise money. We were offended and objected. They responded by refusing to include us on their platforms.[26]

The obsession with this question alone, at the expense of much more fundamental economic and social questions, has become widespread since the beginning of the "war on terror" in 2001, but it has echoes from the colonial period of the 19th century when the British in India and Egypt, and the French in Algeria attacked the veil as an emblem of women's oppression and the inferiority of Muslim societies.[27] Lord Cromer, the British consul general in Egypt from 1883 to 1907, railed against Islam's treatment of women, believing that veiling and seclusion were the "fatal obstacle" to the Egyptians' "attainment of that elevation of thought and character which should accompany the introduction of Western civilisation".[28] Cromer's commitment to women's rights only went so far though; he raised school fees in Egypt, so preventing girls' education, and discouraged the training of women doctors. Back in Britain he founded the Men's League for Opposing Women's Suffrage, with an effrontery of which George Bush would be proud.[29]

The assumption today by some in the West that Muslim women in the former colonial countries are passive and oppressed objects who need to be protected from their oppressors is connected to a colonial or imperialist view of the world which suggests that these women cannot act in their own interests and that their adherence to certain cultures or religious beliefs must inherently make them oppressed. These weak women need to be protected by the strong. Whatever the good intentions of such people, they are allowing their values to be co-opted by a project which presides over inequality at home and cannot bring equality to those it conquers:

> Sometimes feminists may identify with the stance of the masculine protector in relation to vulnerable and victimised women. The protector-protected relation is no more egalitarian, however, when between women than between men and women.[30]

Why should Muslim women in countries such as Afghanistan, Iraq or Iran be singled out for special help in the name of opposition to religious bigotry? For example, abortion has been either illegal or severely restricted in European countries as diverse as Poland, Portugal and Ireland, due largely to the influence of the Catholic church in those countries. There is little outcry about the oppressive nature of these states or campaigning for abortion rights in these countries outside the countries themselves. Western feminists do not see their counterparts in those countries as being incapable of fighting for their rights, nor do they feel that they have to intervene to show Irish or Polish women how to campaign. Why therefore do they adopt a different attitude to women in Indonesia or Pakistan? To take another example, repression of gays has been on the increase in Poland in 2006-7, largely as a result of government policy, and fuelled by right wing thugs. Yet Poland is a member of the EU, therefore little is said on these questions. One doesn't have to think too hard to see how this would be portrayed if it were happening in a majority Muslim country.

These attitudes also ignore the differences within Islam and the political challenges mounted within Muslim countries from women themselves and their male supporters. As Elaheh Rostami-Povey points out, "Historically feminism in Muslim majority societies has been diverse." She continues:

There is a rich literature by Muslim and secular feminists who identify with Islamic culture. For decades they have discussed the positive side of Islamic culture and history. Haleh Afshar, Leila Ahmed, Riffat Hassan and Fatema Mernissi, amongst others, have discussed the history of powerful and respected women in Islam from Khadija, the first wife of the prophet Mohammed and first convert to Islam; to Aisha, the youngest and last wife of the prophet who is considered to convey the most reliable source of Islamic law. They see Islamic marriage as a contract in which women's work is paid, valued and not invisible... They have criticised the conservative and patriarchal tradition in Islam which has taken away women's rights and continues to subject women to unequal treatment. At the same time they have challenged the perception of Muslim women in the West. They have argued that the West's simplistic views of women's place in Islam are part of the context of narratives of inferiority and otherness.[31]

The ignoring of such progressive views and wide political differences is particularly marked in feminist attitudes to Iran, an Islamic republic widely tipped as the next country to receive the attentions of George Bush in the war on terror. Iran is a very different country from its much poorer and undeveloped neighbour, Afghanistan, or from devastated post-war Iraq, with a large and very young population and a growing economy. It is also developing as a major regional power. The laws of the Islamic republic are in some cases restrictive and oppressive towards women. Women have to cover their heads in public and are subjected to much discrimination. But the contradiction between the ideology of the Islamic state and the changing position of women since the revolution in 1979 has pushed women's issues onto the political agenda. There are women's trade associations, women's NGOs, and other organisations which are part of the democracy movement. Women's literacy rate has risen from 52 percent in 1986-87 to 94 percent in 2004, and 62 percent of university students are women. Contraceptive usage is at 74 percent. Women have the vote and more gender balanced family and employment laws exist.[32]

There are many debates within feminism in Iran, and many women who play or have played a prominent role in politics. The Nobel Peace Prize winner Shirin Ebadi, a Tehran lawyer who has campaigned for human rights and been imprisoned by the regime, is one such notable woman. She spoke in London at a meeting organised by Action Iran in 2006 where she argued against an attack on Iran.[33] A letter to the *Financial Times* signed by Iranian, Iraqi and British women stated that the women's movement in Iran "grows daily: something only a war could stop".[34]

It is hardly surprising that women attracted to ideas of women's liberation in non-Western countries are not necessarily attracted to feminism as espoused by some women in the West. They have the right to ask why Western women and men are still trying to impose their values on the women of the Middle East, Africa and Asia when colonialism is supposed to be a thing of the past. They also have the right to see some forms of feminism as connected with an imperialist agenda, and to see it as ignoring race and class.

Some writers have called the view that portrays the West as the best place for women, and the Muslim East as a backward place where women are passive victims, Orientalist feminism. Roksana Bahramitash describes its popular appeal in North America: "Orientalist feminism is popularised through novels and films, and it has become a 'boom industry' that has created huge problems for Muslims".[35]

It does not seem to occur to those who want changes in women's lives in Muslim countries that allying feminist ideology with Western values, which have such negative associations in many Muslim majority countries, may be counter-productive.

British politics and Muslim women

Britain's imperial past means that debates over Muslim women and oppression are not confined to what happens in Kabul, Baghdad or Tehran, but are a central question for women and men in Britain as well. Britain is home to an estimated 1.5 to 2 million Muslims mainly from south Asia. The majority of the younger Muslims were either born here or have lived most of their lives here. Their parents first came in large numbers during the long boom of the 1950s and 60s, settling in east London, Birmingham, and in the textile towns and cities of West Yorkshire, Lancashire and the Midlands. When they first came, they tended to be identified by their geographical origin – Indian, Pakistani, Bangladeshi (after 1971) or East African Asian. It was only much later that these ethnic minorities came to be identified primarily through their religion.

Most British Muslims were poor when they came here and they and their descendants by and large remain so, even after decades of hard work. Muslims (especially from the Pakistani and Bangladeshi communities) remain the poorest. They are the most likely to be unemployed and have some of the worst housing, education and health of any group in British society.[36] Pakistani and Bangladeshi women are 30 percent less likely to be employed outside the home compared to white men and women.[37]

The vast majority of Muslims in Britain are working class, and therefore historically gave support to Labour and often joined trade unions. They have been, and despite small improvements remain, under-represented in British politics, either in parliament or in the trade union machine. However, in recent years the Muslim community in Britain has become much more politicised, over a range of issues: Salman Rushdie's book *The Satanic Verses* in the late 1980s, the wars in Bosnia and Chechnya during the 1990s, the ongoing situation in Palestine, and most recently the war on terror and the attacks on Afghanistan and Iraq.

The war on terror has brought the question of Islam and Muslims to the fore. It is posed by some as a clash of civilisations, by others as a war with an implacable enemy, Al Qaida, which spreads everywhere, headed by a fanatic, Osama Bin Laden, who is out to destroy the West and who incites his co-religionists to commit acts of terror to bring this about. Most Muslims would not recognise themselves in this description, but they might point out that Bin Laden was a

Western creation, funded to fight the Russians in Afghanistan in the last years of the Cold War. It is Western policies which have built his support. Even today the vast majority of Muslims in Britain would reject any political identification with Bin Laden, stressing their desire to be part of British society and for their children to have a better future here than many of them have done.

A government with two wars and occupations in Muslim countries under its belt, and sights on future wars, has found it impossible to leave it there, however, and has put increasing pressure on the Muslim community. Foreign office minister Denis MacShane said in 2003 that it was "time for the elected and community leaders of British Muslims to make a choice"[38] between being British and being Muslim. All too often this choice leads to a focus once again on the question of what women wear in the Muslim community.

Jack Straw, former foreign secretary and therefore a main player in the war on terror, consciously created a public argument in October 2006. He told his local paper, the *Lancashire Evening Telegraph*, that he felt "uncomfortable" when women wearing the face veil or niqab came to see him in his MP's surgery, and that he asked them to remove their veils while in his office. Straw said that he wanted to open a debate about the veil.[39] To put this in context, Straw had been MP in Blackburn, a Lancashire town with a very large Muslim population, for 27 years. His discomfort had never publicly surfaced before, despite presumably many surgeries and many elections where he was happy for veiled women to vote for him, not to mention his trips to Saudi Arabia where women have to wear the veil and where he does not appear to have made his discomfort known to his hosts.

Now, however, with the war on terror going badly, with the government pushing through yet more restrictions on civil liberties, and with the Muslim community still disaffected with the Labour government over the war and related questions,[40] Straw fixed on the clothing of a tiny number of Muslim women to launch a debate. All this put the Muslim community on the defensive and led to an increase in racism in public life and debate, in the process giving publicity to views formerly held by a far right fringe.

Hijab or not hijab

The debate over women's dress in the Muslim community didn't begin in Britain. In France the hijab was banned for schoolgirls in 2004 on the grounds that French education had to be secular and that ostentatious religious symbols could not be worn. Although this affected other religions, it was clearly aimed at the 6 million strong largely North African Muslim community.[41] In the Dutch elections of 2006 the government party talked of banning the burqa even though only perhaps as few as 50 women in the whole of the Netherlands wear the garment.[42]

The whole approach taken to the wearing of the hijab or other forms of dress has been to somehow accept that the problem is Muslim women themselves, rather than to look at the wider context. Far from the wearers of the hijab refusing to integrate such women are increasingly likely to face abuse and racial attacks. As the Islamic Human Rights Commission has reported, an increasing number of women wearing hijab report discrimination, harassment and abuse:

> It appears that the general attitude towards them has become negative as there is a noticeable rise of hatred, assault, nasty looks, insults and slurs towards Muslim looking women. Even children have been reported to have behaved violently towards women wearing hijab.[43]

There are reports of girls being refused permission to wear the hijab in school and even one of a private school refusing the right of a Muslim girl to wear it outside school![44]

Before Jack Straw spoke out there was discussion about the hijab and the niqab in Britain, but when the French ban was implemented, most politicians and commentators in Britain opposed such a move here. In the aftermath of the London tube and bus bombings of 7 July 2005 the atmosphere began to change, with the government and media putting increasing pressure on Muslims to "put their house in order" and "integrate" into British society. The reality of the racism faced by many Muslims is again being ignored, with Muslim women repeatedly being painted as extreme for wanting to dress in the way that they do. Television personality Ulrika Jonsson opposed the right to wear the jilbab at school, saying, "Of course we must be sensitive to people's beliefs and traditions, and be flexible in catering for them but *the line really has to be drawn* somewhere".[45] The implication is clear: Muslim women are testing the patience of most moderate and reasonable people, of which Ulrika Jonsson is clearly an example, by insisting on wearing such traditional clothes.

The feminist argument about women covering themselves also emerged. The *Independent* columnist Deborah Orr, in an article headlined "Why This Picture Offends Me" and with the picture in question showing two women with niqabs in a London street, described a woman she saw taking her children to school "dressed outlandishly in an outfit that proclaimed her adherence to an ancient religious code that contradicts the law of this land in its denial of equality of opportunity to women and men." She continues, "The values these outfits imply are repulsive and insulting to me. I find these clothes to be physical manifestations of outdated traditional practices…that oppress and victimise women, sometimes in the most degrading, cruel and barbaric of ways".[46]

This seems rather a lot of ideology to invest in one piece of cloth, however offensive it is. It is also rather insulting to Muslim women to believe that their dress automatically says something about them, in a way that any form of Western dress would not do. It may come as a shock, but how Muslim women dress does not necessarily tell you about their politics or relations with men. There are women who cover themselves because their husband tells them to or because they believe that women should be subordinate to men. There are also women who choose to wear the niqab or hijab because they want to make a religious or social statement. Take, for example, Sarah Hussein, a 19 year old married student from Acton in west London:

> I have had abuse thrown at me so many times [for wearing the veil]. When I was growing up I didn't wear a veil and then I made a spiritual decision to wear one… I am not doing anything wrong. I am interacting with society and studying society.[47]

There are differences among Muslims themselves about the Koran on this question, with the vast majority of Muslim women in Britain rejecting the need to cover their faces and their whole bodies. Many wear the hijab or headscarf, others a loose scarf, others no head covering at all. As in any religion, there is scope for interpretation. However, while Sarah Hussein talks about her spiritual decision to cover her face, there are clearly cultural and political reasons why women in Western societies decide to wear the hijab or niqab which go beyond a simple question of religion. There is much anecdotal evidence that more Muslim women are choosing to cover their heads, including women who took this decision in adulthood after a period of sometimes years where they did not wear a hijab most of the time. A study by academics at York and Leeds universities, which involved interviews with a number of Muslim women living in Britain across the generations, argues that:

> in the post 9/11 climate of Islamophobia women wearing the scarf, the mohajebehs, are making a political choice. They are publicly branding themselves as Muslims at a time when such a label carries the potential fear of making them vulnerable to open hostility.[48]

The study describes a new form of Islam among the children of immigrants which is clearly connected to questions of identity and marks an element of politicisation in the community from the 1990s onwards. Dress has become part of a Muslim identity in Britain rather than any simple continuation of the traditional attire of the "old country", as it was for the first generation immigrants:

> Frequently women who chose to wear the veil do not come from families who practise seclusion or insist on wearing the hijab; their mothers and grandmothers may dress modestly, and if from the Indian subcontinent they often wore the "traditional" sari or shalwar kameez, but not the hijab. The head cover, worn by young women, particularly in the West, is very much the product of the late 20th century. It is a reconstructed emblem that allows them to combine jeans and jackets and the latest style in kitten heel shoes with the hijab.[49]

Two points stand out from these and other examples. Firstly, the way in which Muslims dress and practise their religion in Britain is at least partly both a response to racism and a way of dealing with it. Secondly, there is an ideological battle within the Muslim community about what being a British Muslim means, where women in hijabs and their male supporters are fighting against a conservative agenda. Both of these arguments seem to be lost on those feminists in Britain who find any form of Muslim dress offensive. It would be particularly hard to understand women's oppression among ethnic minorities in Britain without taking racism into account as a major feature of their lives and one which distorts moves towards integration and multi-culturalism. Institutional racism means integration does not occur on a level playing field because of discrimination towards ethnic minorities in schools, housing, policing and employment. It goes side by side with Islamophobia, surely the last respectable racism in Europe, which finds its expression in racist abuse, physical attacks and murders, but also in the constant portrayal of Muslims as "outsiders", "fanatics" or "backward".

When the columnist Joan Smith writes:

> But if I loathe the niqab and the burqa when I see women wearing them in Iraq or Afghanistan, it would be hypocritical to pretend I don't find them equally offensive on my local high street.[50]

she is in danger of objectifying Muslim women in a way that she would be unlikely to do with another group of women. Indeed, some of the feminist debate seems to be suffering from double standards. For example, are we "offended" by a man being acquitted on a rape charge or when a women's refuge is closed because of council cuts? Do we "loathe" the sight of some Orthodox Jewish women who wear wigs (for similar religious reasons that Muslim women cover their heads); or the sight of Christian nuns, covered from head to toe and cut off from men by their religious vows? Most of us could perhaps think of much worse sights on our local high streets, however much we might disagree with these women's religious beliefs or practice.

The hijab or any other form of clothing should not be seen as inherently repressive, and Western politicians and feminists should stop telling Muslim women what not to wear. We should oppose the forced covering of women that takes place in countries such as Iran or Saudi Arabia. It is not the business of state or religion to make women wear particular clothes. We should also oppose the prejudice and discrimination that are demanding women take off their veils or scarves. Women themselves have the right to choose what they wear and when they wear it.

The anti-war movement
The Stop the War Coalition was formed in September 2001 and quickly became a mass movement, organising first against the war in

Afghanistan and then against the threat to Iraq. It was noticeable for the large number of women involved, including the convenor of Stop the War and the chair of CND. There were always large numbers of Muslim women active as campaigners, speakers and stewards, and in every other capacity. Right from the beginning it involved sections of the Muslim community and at its first organising meeting a Muslim group, Just Peace, was set up. Not only was Stop the War the biggest mass movement in British history, it was and is the most diverse and most integrated, all on the basis of genuine equality. One of its founders, Shahed Saleem, wrote of it:

> Muslims were participating in this campaign as free and equal citizens in a plural society making a common, shared, collaborative stand against injustice. This is one legacy of the Stop the War Coalition – that it enabled people who had otherwise been kept segregated through the dominant social order, to share values and ideals and to work together, and for the first time to glimpse a common future.[51]

This unity was marked on all the demonstrations, most movingly on 18 November 2001 when the demonstration against war in Afghanistan coincided with Ramadan and the call to prayer to end the fast was called over a "packed and silent Trafalgar Square to resound in the heart of empire, so inscribing another line in the post-colonial history of Britain".[52]

There was much controversy about working with Muslims among the left, with sections of the traditional left showing themselves incapable of relating to a genuinely mass movement.[53] Stop the War was always a secular movement but was always open to those of any religion or none, and did much more to break down barriers and win Muslim women and men towards mass campaigning and sometimes socialist politics. This was in itself part of the socialist tradition.[54] It is one of which any socialist should be proud, and campaigning among Muslim women should be part of reclaiming the ideas of women's liberation from middle class white feminists, and making them the property of the most oppressed.

Feminism:
the limits of liberation

"I MYSELF have never been able to find out precisely what feminism is: I only know that people call me a feminist whenever I express sentiments that differentiate me from a doormat." So wrote the Irish novelist Rebecca West nearly 100 years ago.[1] The confusion is much less today, with feminism an accepted label for many women in the arts, media and politics. Newscaster Samira Ahmed says, "Feminist is the first word I'd use to describe myself", while the highly successful lesbian novelist Sarah Waters asks "Surely the real question should be not 'Why are you a feminist?' but 'Why aren't you one?'."[2]

A survey of Girl Guides found that among their older members – aged 16 to 25 – a full 65 percent said they would not be embarrassed to be called feminists.[3] The survey seemed to show accurately the dominant ideas of young women today: 81 percent of 16 to 25 year olds and 90 percent of ten to 15 year olds believe women can do any job they choose these days. The vast majority (94 percent of 16 to 25 year olds and 88 percent of ten to 15 year olds) said they would go back to work after having children.[4] At the same time, two thirds of the older age group say they are not treated with respect by boys their own age and over half say the media make them feel the most important thing is to be pretty and thin.[5]

Feminism and its adherents have won many battles in the past quarter century. Perhaps most important from the point of view of many feminists is the widespread acceptance of the idea of women's equality, at least at the level of rhetoric. But this becomes the assumption that women's equality has more or less been achieved and that the tactics of the suffragettes or the anger of the women's liberation movement are of historical interest only. So women's continuing oppression, one of the major features of our society – and one of the major sources of inequality in the richest capitalist countries – is simply airbrushed out of the current discourse. The success of what is sometimes called post-feminism has been to implant in the minds of the media and politicians the idea that equality has been achieved. What goes wrong between men and women now is no longer about oppression, but about difference. There is silence about the deep wells of inequality that still exist.

It is the time of the token woman. We have had a woman prime minister, women judges, baronesses and businesswomen. The media have embraced women as editors, presenters, heads of television channels; the professions too are much more open to women. Paradoxically, the triumph of the rhetoric of equality has taken place exactly at a time when the actual conditions of women's lives have worsened, and this rhetoric has then been used to justify policies which will harm women. As we have seen, in the name of equality war is justified on the grounds of its benefit to women, but so too are policies designed to cut welfare and force women out to work, or plans to make men pay more for their childcare. Equality has been turned on its head in some cases. Dianne Feinstein, a US feminist who became mayor of San Francisco and then a Democratic Party Senator for California, praised a court ruling which overturned a state law requiring the reinstatement of women workers returning to jobs from maternity leave. Feinstein said, "What we women have been saying all along is we want to be treated equally. Now we have to put our money where our mouth is".[6] The consequences of such policies have been to encourage the majority of women and men to accept the same or even worsened conditions while being exhorted to look to a small number of aspirational role models, all of who experience far easier and more privileged economic and social conditions. The same process has gone on among black people in the US and Britain, where a form of racial equality is promoted, but stripped of any the radical content that informed the black movements of the 1960s. This is all rather a long way from the aspirations of those who began the women's movement four decades ago.

An idea whose time had come

Women's liberation was the product of a very specific time and a very specific place. It came out of the 1960s movements in the US campaigning for civil rights for blacks and against the Vietnam War. The very term "women's liberation" was informed by those great struggles against colonialism and for equality. One of the first theoretical statements on women's liberation from a workshop at a student conference in 1967 said, "Women are in a colonial relationship to men and we recognise ourselves as part of the Third World".[7]

The women who helped to form the women's liberation movement came from a remarkable generation. They and their male student counterparts often came from the north of the US and travelled south in the early 1960s to help campaign for civil rights. Women played a leading role in the campaign and displayed levels of commitment, principle and courage that were repeatedly put to the test. The academic Lise Vogel, from a middle class Jewish Communist family whose parents' main worries when she was growing up were "money and McCarthyism",[8] describes her involvement in the civil rights movement and her time in Mississippi as the formative period of her life. "I got far more out of being in Mississippi than I ever was able to give back," she says, concluding that "in the end I knew that I had participated in history, that what we did made a difference, and that I had been tried and not found wanting".[9] However, she, like many of her sisters, turned towards socialist feminism by the late 1960s, feeling that women's oppression was not taken into account by the other movements. This feeling did not arise by accident but was a product of these women's direct experience.

The background to the emergence of the women's movement in the US in the late 1960s was a level of sexism and indifference to the question of women's equality that is quite shocking to look back on. Women were told that their oppression was of the least importance, and told so in the most contemptuous and elitist way. At the National Conference for the New Politics held in August 1967, where a radical minority of women tried to formulate demands on women's liberation, drawing on the politics of black power and anti-colonialism, they were derided by most of the men at the conference. Shulamith Firestone was patted on the head by one of the male leaders and told to "move on little girl; we have more important issues to talk about here than women's liberation".[10] Nor was this an isolated instance. One slogan of the movement against the US draft was "Girls say yes to guys who say no".[11] When asked about the position of women in the movement, the black leader Stokely Carmichael infamously answered that "the only position for women in SNCC is prone".[12] A derisive cartoon of a woman in a mini skirt with earrings and visible panties holding a sign saying "We want our rights and we want them now" appeared in *New Left Notes*.[13] Such experiences shaped the early women's movement, which defined itself as dissatisfied with the behaviour of the male left – and who could blame anyone for feeling like that?

But the politics of the US student left in the 1960s was particularly lacking in roots or theory. By the time the women's movement was born in the late 1960s, the socialist tradition in the US was very weak, partly submerged by the lack of continuity between the old left and the new. In the US the Communist tradition had never been particularly strong compared with many other parts of the world; nonetheless it had played an important part in the big industrial struggles of the 1930s and 1940s, and in black movements, especially in the 1930s. The defeats of those industrial battles and the impact of McCarthyism were to destroy a generation of socialists and Communists across the US, and to break the continuity from one generation to the next. So when big movements emerged again in the 1960s, the activists in them were able to make little reference to the similar history of previous generations, despite the fact that many of these young participants in the civil rights, student and anti-war movements were, like Lise Vogel, from left wing or Communist backgrounds.[14] The student movement in particular was quite disconnected from the old left, and it was this that placed its stamp on the character of the new movements.

The politics of the traditional non-student left were also highly limited. If women's equality meant anything at all, it tended to be equated with the images from Stalin's Russia of women working in "men's jobs". Many socialists could see little connection between a fairly limited view of the class struggle and women's oppression. The distortion of socialism as a theory of human emancipation into its

Stalinist or social democratic versions left little room for ideas of women's liberation. Socialists too were prisoners of past history and ideology, sometimes even accepting ideas of eugenics or social engineering as the main underpinning for women's rights.

By the 1960s women's liberation was an idea whose time had come. Limiting the movement to concepts of equal rights and of gradual change seemed just too timid and slow for a generation of women who were discovering their independence in every area of life. It is not surprising that those who first embraced women's liberation were women who had become politicised through campaigning for civil rights, against racism and against war. They rightly wanted the principles governing these campaigns to be extended to the question of women as well. That they were so badly rebuffed helped to shape the women's movement in particular ways that did not always help the movement or the left. It meant that those who might otherwise look to socialists as their natural allies did not do so, and for most feminists organisation came to mean organising separately from men. It also meant that women's liberation adopted or developed theories that led away from realising human emancipation and up a series of dead ends.

Why liberation took the wrong road: 1. Theory
A whole range of theories developed in the women's liberation movement of the late 1960s, mainly in the US. Many of the seminal works date from the late 1960s and early 70s, including *The Dialectic of Sex* by Shulamith Firestone, *The Myth of the Vaginal Orgasm* by Anne Koedt, *Sexual Politics* by Kate Millett, and *Psychoanalysis and Feminism* by Juliet Mitchell.[15] Some participants in the movement, such as Sara Evans and Jo Freeman, wrote about their very valuable experiences.[16] Others, notably Sheila Rowbotham, took the ideas of women's liberation and applied them to understanding the history of women.[17] Much of feminist theory tried, correctly in my view, to locate women's oppression in the existence of the sexual division of labour, the role of the family and the separation of home and work, but it had two crucial weaknesses. It could not integrate the theory of women's liberation with an understanding of class. Partly as a result of this, it also often failed to deal with the concrete reality of women's lives. The model put forward by many feminists was still based on the idea of women in the home and men in the factory,

with little connection between the two. Yet this picture has failed to make much sense for the past half century in countries such as Britain and the US.

This mistaken model led many theorists to pose issues in a way that cannot explain the changing position of women. The "domestic labour debate" of the early 1970s attempted to place women's domestic role in the overall context of capitalist society. This development, carried out by Marxists who were trying to locate women's oppression within their role in the home, led to many important insights. They pointed out that domestic labour was hidden labour, carried out privately, and with very little status because it was not waged. Yet it had a central economic role in the continuation of capitalist society.

One assumption in much of the debate was that women were full time housewives and men were full time workers, yet even by the early 1970s women were also very often workers, at least part time, as well as being responsible for most of the housework and childcare in the home. Equally mistaken was a second assumption, that domestic labour was totally separate from capitalist production itself. The conclusion was either that housewives were a separate class who should be organised in the home, and then ally with (male) wage workers against the mutual enemy, capital, or, worse, that women were simply servants of their husbands and children.[18]

However, domestic labour takes the form that it does precisely because of its *connection* with capitalist production, with the reproduction of labour power taking place within the privatised family. Domestic labour carried out in the home is responsible for rearing the next generation of workers and looking after the existing generation of workers all at little outlay to the capitalist class. It directly produces this labour power, which can then be sold on the labour market. So indirectly the unpaid labour in the home makes a major contribution to ensuring the profits of the employers. It is therefore of crucial importance to the very existence of capitalism itself.[19]

Over the past few decades the balance of women's lives between the reproduction of labour power and their participation as paid workers themselves has changed radically. The capitalist class has managed to draw far more women into the workforce, increasing their production of surplus value and so enhancing profits. At the same time, the reproduction of labour power continues to be carried out at very little cost to the capitalist class which no longer needs to rely on an army of full time housewives to provide its next generation of workers. Instead substantial parts of the wages earned by women and men in the labour market now contribute towards paying for commodities which substitute for the role of a full time wife and mother. In addition, men play more of a role in domestic work, although much less than the woman, and are more central to childcare than they were in the past.

The change in women's role in the family has challenged the traditional view of the work/family male/female division. Two arguments that were commonplace until the 1980s have also been weakened. One of the assumptions of the "domestic labour" debate was that full time domestic labour within the family is essential to the continuing existence of capitalist production itself. This argument can no longer be sustained: it is so obviously contradicted by the facts. Secondly, women can no longer be seen as a disposable reserve army of labour to be pulled into work when times are booming but then to be sent back to the home in times of economic recession. Women are now a permanent part of the workforce.

What the past decades have shown is the ability of capitalism to adapt: the family has been able to change to meet the needs and wishes of women to participate economically and socially in society. This has challenged some feminist views which saw in employment patterns and the sexual division of labour a male conspiracy where employers and workers united to preserve their positions to the disadvantage of women. In fact, capitalism shows itself to be increasingly "sex-blind" in that it wants the most effective and cheapest workers, regardless of gender (or indeed race or nationality). However, it is prepared to use the existing structures and ideologies of oppression to ensure that those workers do not compete on a level playing field, and this in turn helps to maintain these inequalities.

By the late 1970s much feminist theory had come to explain women's oppression in terms of a system of male domination, patriarchy, distinct from the economic mode of production in class society.[20] Patriarchy theory posed a division between the interests of working class men and working class women. It has become the accepted wisdom to assert that the sexual division of labour under capitalism arose because men consciously acted to exclude women from certain forms of work which would have given them equal status and security and a higher wage, and that the establishment of the family wage represented a bargain struck by working class men and the employers at the expense of women. As a result the male sphere became the world of work while the family and domesticity became the female sphere. This argument is best articulated by Heidi Hartmann, whose essay "The Unhappy Marriage of Marxism and Feminism: Towards a More Progressive Union", had a profound effect on women's movement theory and marked an important move away from considering men and women workers as allies, if unequal ones, and towards considering them, if not as enemies, at least as rivals whose interests did not coincide.[21]

This general theory arose at least in part as an attempt to bridge questions of class and women's oppression. It was also an implicit criticism of the domestic labour debate. But perhaps more importantly, it also marked a turn away from seeing the rule of capital as the main barrier to women's liberation. The argument once again hinged on the relationship between work and the home. It was pointed out that it could not be said categorically that domestic labour was essential to capitalism – in theory at least there were other ways of organising the reproduction of labour power. It could not even be proved that the family was the cheapest way for capital to reproduce its next generation of workers. But the critique led away from any class analysis of oppression. Instead there was an increasing insistence that women's oppression lay in the sphere of patriarchy, not class, and that therefore working class men's and women's interests did not coincide. The Hartmann thesis posed as a materialist analysis which could link class and patriarchy. Except it was not a materialist explanation at all, but an extremely partial reading of the sexual division of labour based on one relatively small part of women's history, which did not take into account wider social or historical forces. Its widespread acceptance was also a retreat from those who wanted a class analysis of women's oppression.

In this section I draw heavily on the analysis of the US socialist feminist Johanna Brenner, who with Maria Ramas wrote an important essay, "Rethinking Women's Oppression", in 1984.[22] She argues that the sexual division of labour cannot be understood with reference to protective legislation or trade union exclusiveness. Protective legislation barely existed in the US until well into the 20th century, long after the "male breadwinner" sexual division of labour came into being. The example of Britain is different, of course, but even here Brenner argues that the Ten Hours Bill of 1847 and the Mines Regulation Act of 1842 had little effect on the sexual division of labour:

> To the extent that the Ten Hours Bill was effective, it appears to have limited men's as well as women's labour hours... Nor does this legislation appear to have resulted in any significant replacement of male for female labour, either within the [textile] industry as a whole or within particular sectors. In fact, the proportion of women to men in the textile industry continued to increase during the latter part of the nineteenth century.[23]

The trade unions were craftist, elitist and exclusive of women, immigrants and the unskilled workers in general. But their writ did not run throughout the working class; indeed they organised a very small proportion of workers. Whatever impact their narrow views had on general working class consciousness, they could not have shaped the whole of the capitalist sexual division of labour.

Much of the opposition to women in particular industries lay in the very well founded fear that the employment of women would act to pull down men's wages and organisation. The strike of the London Journeymen Tailors' Union against home working in 1833 was to preserve the male tailors' position. Its failure worsened the wages and conditions throughout the industry:

> That competition, rather than ideology, was the crucial determinant of male exclusivism is underscored by the fact that in cases where women were not competing with men, or where women were in the industry from the start, unions tended to include women and even gave substantial support to their attempts at organisation and strike activity.[24]

Even within the working class different strategies emerged. So around the beginning of the 19th century the Spitalfields weavers sought to organise women and enable them to serve full apprenticeships, while the Scottish weavers tried to exclude women from apprenticeships completely.[25] When the employers tried to break the union of calico printers near Glasgow in 1833 by introducing women and children as cheap labour, a strike broke out. Local women workers supported the strikers and helped to throw stones at the scab labour, and refused to cook for them in acts of class solidarity.[26] As Johanna Brenner explains:

> It is entirely unnecessary to resort to ideology to explain why trade unions were particularly adamant in their opposition to female entry into their trades. It is quite clear that when unions were unable to exclude women, a rapid depression of wages and general degradation of work resulted.[27]

In the attitude that men took towards women workers who might potentially undercut them, the need to defend working class conditions was obviously very important. But it is by no means the whole story. There is little question that women as well as men welcomed many of the changes in work that led to the shortening of hours and the removal from some of the worst aspects of the satanic mills. They certainly welcomed the ability of their children to grow up safe from the injuries which they were in danger of sustaining in paid work. The shorter hours worked in the mills after 1847 gave women more time to care for their families: "The extra hour's freedom from the mill...seems to have been almost exclusively devoted to the better care of their homes and families".[28] Before the 1842 legislation on mining there were many petitions from the Lancashire and Yorkshire towns calling for women's work to be limited.[29]

The commission's report on the mining industry described pregnant women miscarrying, women and children crawling like animals in the dark wet tunnels, and women having to return to this only a few days after childbirth. The working class saw living conditions worsening with industrialisation and they wanted to find some ways of protecting themselves. Many looked to kinship networks within the working class to provide a source of protection. The working class could control these networks and provide for those who otherwise would suffer terrible conditions of labour or the perils of the workhouse. Or, as Jane Humphries argues, "the endurance of the family reflects a struggle by the working class for popular ways of meeting the needs of non labouring comrades within a capitalist environment". She goes on:

Thus, the family, as an institution, has been shaped by the aspiration of people for personalised non-market methods of distribution and social interaction. To ignore the role that these aspirations and beliefs have played in guiding human contact and in shaping the class struggle is to fail to understand the working class family and its persistence.[30]

This is the crucial element missing from those who accept the collusion of employers and male workers. Women's role in the home reflected in part a desire of working class men and women for a better life – and they saw women's withdrawal from work as a crucial part of this. Johanna Brenner explains how the low level of wages throughout the working class even in the second half of the 19th century meant that workers could not afford to purchase services to substitute for their household work and childcare. A large amount of domestic work therefore had to be performed inside the home somehow – not an easy task, given the long hours men and women worked and given the primitive nature of household technology. So:

> a division of labour in which one person undertook domestic labour along with supplementary wage work, while another earned wages full time, was preferable to a division of labour in which two adults worked long factory hours and then returned home to do additional labour.[31]

Pregnancy, childbirth and the care of young children were particularly onerous for 19th century working class women. The inability to nurse newborn children led to terrible consequences. Hygienic bottle-feeding was non-existent, wet-nursing not a viable option, and infant mortality was high. This increased the "logic of the sexual division of labour"[32] where women, who were likely to undergo large numbers of pregnancies in the 19th century, tended to be the ones who stayed at home if the family could possibly afford it in order to care for themselves and their children.

This sexual division of labour shaped the working class family for decades to come, to the detriment of women who found themselves largely dependent on a male wage and tied to a role of domesticity whether they wanted it or not. But this path was followed by men and women who could not envisage a more egalitarian outcome, or who felt that such an outcome was simply not possible. Hartmann's attempt to develop a materialist explanation for patriarchy fails because her desire to justify patriarchy theory leads her to fitting the facts to the theory rather than the other way round. The working class family was an expression of a class on the defensive following the defeat of Chartism, not a male conspiracy to keep women in the home. The oppression of women and the continued existence of the family today can be explained in terms of class and the demands of a capitalist system hoping that it can push many of its costs onto individual families. Widespread notions of male dominance stem not from an abstract concept of patriarchy, nor from a coincidence of class interests between all capitalists and the male half of the working class, but from an ideology that constantly seeks ways to justify continued oppression and class exploitation.

Why liberation took the wrong road: 2. Class and politics

There was a connection between the early women's movement both in the US and Britain and radical and left wing politics. The movement was much smaller in Britain than in the US but had a stronger socialist and trade union orientation, influenced by the rising level of class struggle in Britain during the late 1960s and early 1970s.

However, there was a contradiction within the women's liberation movement even in its early days: while its ideas were extremely influential, it encompassed only a relatively small number of activists. So in the US by 1971 there were over 100 women's liberation publications and by 1973 the mainstream feminist *Ms* had a circulation of 350,000. Equally, there were a large number of women's studies courses by the early 1970s.[33] However, only 150 women from across New York attended the Women's Liberation Coalition each week, and only 200 came to the 1969 Congress to Unite Women. Even the more respectable mainstream National Organisation of Women (NOW) had only 30,000 members nationally.[34] So women's liberation never approached becoming a mass movement, even in the US, let alone in Britain. Its members tended to be middle class ex-students or professional women, and their emphasis was on consciousness raising among small groups, rather than mass activity. There was much fragmentation and splintering of these groups. Jo Freeman explained that:

One reason for the movement's dissolution is that it had been limited by its own origins. A product of the counterculture and New Left, it had within a few short years expanded to the boundaries of that culture, transformed and/or integrated most of its organisations and institutions, and then turned in on itself as it had no place else to go.[35]

Freeman added that "the average life of most movement activists is about two years".[36]

There was a political ferment over women's position in society in Britain during the 1970s, much of it driven by two distinct but connected changes: the liberalisation of legislation affecting women, and the radical ideas of women's liberation which were finding their way into the unions, workplaces and colleges. The Equal Pay Act, introduced by Labour minister Barbara Castle, was hailed as a great step forward. Laws on divorce and abortion passed in the 1960s heralded a new era. The first half of the 1970s saw the development of the women's liberation magazine *Spare Rib* as a riposte to the plethora of women's magazines which highlighted home and beauty in women's lives, and the beginning of women's liberation conferences and marches.

The succession of attacks on the 1967 Abortion Act that took place in the second half of the 1970s galvanised one of the biggest movements of women in defence of the law. The campaigns against the White, Benyon and Corrie Bills were led by socialist women and brought together different strands of the women's movement and the left and mobilised mass demonstrations and large public meetings, culminating in 1979 in a TUC backed demonstration in Hyde Park. The abortion campaigns helped establish women's demands as important in their own right, and as issues to be taken up by male trade unionists.[37]

But two developments prevented these achievements from being built on. The first was the defeat of the highly organised and successful workers' movement of the early 1970s, with the many practical and ideological reverses that this entailed. Even before the election of Margaret Thatcher in 1979 many of the ideas and policies now associated with "Thatcherism" were gaining ground: attacks on women and gay rights, privatisation and an increasingly conservative ideological atmosphere in debates over education and social policy.

The second development was the split between what could loosely be called radical feminism and socialist feminism. Radical feminism had been growing in Britain in the latter half of the 1970s; its uncompromising separatist strategy and refusal to engage with men either personally or politically as a means of achieving women's liberation had an appeal to those increasingly frustrated by the slowness of change and by attempts at compromise and reform which many felt did not go far enough. The focus of activity and demands of the movement began to change too: it had four original demands – equal pay, equal education and job opportunities, contraception and abortion, and nurseries. A demand for full legal and financial independence was added in 1975. By 1978 the movement had further added demands for an end to discrimination against lesbians and an end to male violence. While these were demands which rightly should have been taken up centrally by the movement, the approach of many radical feminists was to see them solely as campaigns against men. The emphasis shifted from campaigns that could involve men and women towards separatism. This was reflected in campaigns such as Reclaim the Night against pornography, and campaigns against rape and male violence. These tended to identify the enemy much more directly as men rather than target more general social and class problems.

This growing political and organisational split crystallised at the 1978 women's conference which divided acrimoniously along these lines. Held in Birmingham, it attracted 3,000 women. A group called the Revolutionary Feminists totally rejected collaboration with men. Its leader, Sheila Jeffreys, had attracted 200 women to a workshop at the previous year's conference. She explicitly rejected Marxism and socialism.[38] The conference blew up. It was split on virtually every issue, especially over the phrasing of the new demand on male violence. The fallout from the conference was disastrous, with anguish in the letters pages of *Spare Rib*.[39] The women's movement in Britain has never met as a single body since. It could be argued that this split was connected to the defeat of the workers' movement, as many of those radicalised by the 1960s failed to achieve their original hopes and reached an impasse. Rather than focusing on a clear goal, as in the early years of the movement, they turned on each other. This was an international phenomenon, most spectacularly in Italy where both the left and the women's movement imploded.[40] It marked the defeat of socialist feminism in the movement, a defeat partly brought about by socialist women's retreat on many of the issues which separated them from radical feminists. As Elizabeth Wilson wrote:

> Socialist feminism in proportion as it has distanced itself from Marxism and emphasised its critique rather than its affirmation of the socialist project, has approximated to a pale version of radical feminism without the latter's strengths. What began as an attempt to forge a Marxist analysis of women's subordination and/or an attempt to integrate Marxism and feminism has ended as simply a feminist critique of the left – a largely negative project.[41]

It resulted in people voting with their feet and abandoning the structures of the women's movement as too frustrating and incapable of effecting change. You do not have to accept Rosalind Coward's view that "people who were very damaged by personal experiences found a place to be powerful"[42] in the movement to see that the polarised nature of the discussion coupled with the impasse which was created by radical feminist politics led to division and retreat.

The effective defeat of socialist feminists in the movement led to a continued withdrawal from socialist politics. The victory of Margaret Thatcher in 1979 and her increasing attacks on the working class in the 1980s worsened the demoralisation on the left. Socialists debated the relationship between Marxism and feminism, but in this context such debate only led to crises on the left. In 1979 three influential 1960s feminists, Sheila Rowbotham, Lynne Segal and Hilary Wainwright, produced *Beyond the Fragments*, an explicit attack on Leninist organisation, which many women socialists had espoused in the previous decade.[43] The conclusion drawn by many of the 1960s generation was to join the Labour Party and seek to change it from within – a path many had explicitly rejected ten or 15 years earlier. This too marked a break from the goal of radical social change in favour of a commitment to greater representation of women within existing society. The early years of Thatcherism saw the attempt to set up women's committees and special bodies, for example in the Labour Party, some trade unions and parts of local government influenced by the left, which could bring change through the existing institutions. There were two major grassroots women's campaigns which had a real impact in the 1980s: the fight to stop cruise missiles being sited at the Greenham Common base, and the organisation of the miners' wives during the strike of 1984-85. Despite great courage and determination, neither was strong enough to roll back the attacks, and both ended in defeat.

The race to the top and the race to the bottom

For a minority of women the changes heralded by the 1980s worked very well. They were able to gain positions in work, politics and society that gave them greater salaries, status and influence than their mothers or grandmothers could have imagined. They could also keep some of their ideas about women's equality. Indeed, such ideas helped them to carve a place for women in previously male dominated institutions. So broadcasting and media, parliament and local government, the legal profession and many other areas all felt the demand for change, and acceded to it, although usually only to a very limited extent, in the sense that women, as in most professions, tended to be concentrated at the lower levels and pay rates. A very limited sort of feminism is quite compatible with the individual progress of some women up the social ladder, regardless of the wider divisions within society. But it has little to do with the radical or socialist politics that can bring about wider social change. It is also a great retreat from the founding principles of the women's liberation movement, which had regarded liberation as involving a transformation in the lives of the mass of ordinary women.[44] While women in the professions still face discrimination, as can be deduced from the considerable number of high profile cases of sex discrimination brought by potential high flying women in the City of London, the women who clean their houses or look after their children for low wages could be forgiven for feeling that lack of parity for female City workers with the six figure bonuses paid to the top men in this work may be a problem. It is hardly in the same league as the real social and economic problems which most women face. Or, to put it another way, "hitting your head on a glass ceiling is not the same as falling into the basement".[45]

The widening gap between the classes in the period of neoliberal globalisation has also deepened the contradiction between the different strands of thought about women's liberation. In particular it has highlighted the limits of liberation within a society based on class exploitation and private property. Feminism's first wave achieved women's rights as citizens through the fight for the suffrage. Its second wave in the 1960s and early 70s made women fully free sellers of their labour power, lifting many of the economic, legal and social restrictions that had prevented or at least limited women's total participation in work and society. But this gave women rights long available to men without confronting the basis of the exploitative system of capital itself. The failure of second wave feminism has been its inability to confront these wider questions. By the late 1970s the movements for radical change had been defeated, and this meant that feminism increasingly became a much more individual question, dependent on particular women's ability to equip themselves to succeed in an increasingly competitive market. That in turn meant settling for rights for a minority of women and hitching feminism's star to the Labour Party or the US Democratic Party as the least bad option for women's rights.

However, these defeats have not left women back in their old position. Women cannot be pushed back into the home because the structural changes in their employment have been too great and far-reaching. It is extremely hard in such a situation, where women have a degree of financial and legal independence, to impose the draconian standards of morality which once held sway. So the impact of the 1960s and 70s has remained and many of the changes affecting women have become permanent. Indeed even in the US where the rabid anti-abortion right wing have many friends in government and have succeeded in pressurising the Bush government to cut contraceptive spending to less than other developed countries, it is impossible to imagine abortion rights being completely rolled back. There have been important protests in recent years in defence of abortion and reproductive rights in the US, including mass demonstrations in Washington. But the pressure from the anti-abortionists acts to curtail rights in many individual states, to harass workers and users of abortion clinics, and to cut state funding, all of which make it harder to get abortion, especially for poor and working class women. There has also been resistance over other attacks on women's rights, issues about sexual exploitation, and over gay and lesbian rights.

If feminism has hit a dead end, it is a reflection of its theoretical and practical inadequacies, rather than there being nothing left to fight for. Instead the ideas of women's equality are going to have to link up with wider struggles if they are to be successful. Here there has been a major change even since the height of the women's liberation movement: women today are publicly involved in political struggles in a way that was exceptional 30 years ago. Major movements for change have been created in the 21st century – the strikes, street protests, occupations and organisations at the bottom of society that have sprung up from Venezuela to Bolivia, from India to Indonesia. Women are at the forefront of many of these protests, as they usually are when the working class movement is on the rise. Women such as Dita Sari in Indonesia or Arundhati Roy in India have become symbols of resistance throughout the world. Women's organisation exists much more deeply and extensively among women of colour and working class women than was the case during the height of the women's movement.[46] The organisation of miners' wives which grew into such a formidable part of the strike in 1984-85 was echoed when the London print workers struck two years later and then by the Liverpool dockers' wives again in the 1990s when they formed Women of the Waterfront. The one-day strike over pensions by public sector workers in March 2006 was the biggest day of strike action by women in Britain ever.[47] As we have seen earlier, women are becoming ever more central to trade unions.[48]

But if this is the future, what is left of the women's movement, in the sense of the historically specific movement that arose in the late 1960s and reached its peak only shortly afterwards? Here the record is much less favourable. The movement achieved a great deal in creating awareness about women's oppression and in campaigning for equality. Campaigns over beauty contests or abortion heightened consciousness over issues which women took up, many of which had previously not even been thought of as political. The politics of personal relationships, for example over rape and domestic violence, helped to bring legal and social changes in countries like Britain. But they also often led to political limitations as personal questions became reduced simply to questions of individual behaviour rather than being located in the social relations that gave rise to the individual behaviour.

When the unity of the early years splintered, different strands of the movement went in different directions. Writing in the mid-1980s, Rosalind Delmar recognised a "sort of sclerosis of the movement":

Instead of internal dialogue there is a naming of parts: there are radical feminists, socialist feminists, Marxist feminists, lesbian separatists, women of colour, and so on, each group with its own carefully preserved sense of identity. Each for itself is the only worthwhile feminism: others are ignored except to be criticised.[49]

This retreat into identity politics led to further fragmentation. The anti-globalisation writer Naomi Klein describes the consequences of such politics by the 1990s:

> The basic demands of identity politics assumed an atmosphere of plenty. In the seventies and eighties, that plenty had existed and women and non-whites were able to battle over how the collective pie would be divided: would white men learn to share, or would they keep hogging it? In the representational politics of the New Economy nineties, however, women as well as men, and whites as well as people of colour, were now fighting their battles over a single, shrinking piece of pie – and consistently failing to ask what was happening to the rest of it.[50]

One of the major retreats from the original ideas of women's liberation has been the failure to fit those ideas into a more general social context. The socialist feminists are the ones who today embody many of the original ideas of women's liberation, and who have an understanding of this wider context, that, in the words of Juliet Mitchell:

> feminism is an ideological offspring of certain economic and social conditions. Its radicalism reflects the fact that it comes to prominence at points of critical change. It both abets that change and envisages it with an imagination that goes beyond it.[51]

But the political weakness of many socialist feminists lies in their acceptance of patriarchy theory which sees women's oppression as existing separately from class relations, and therefore their inability to explain the reality of women's oppression today, which increasingly operates in class differentiated patterns.

The women's movement was galvanised and in part created by the rapid changes in women's lives since the Second World War and the opportunities opened up by the long boom of the 1950s and 1960s. The huge increase in women working, the expansion of higher education and the dramatic expansion in women's control over their fertility were decisive in producing the movement and the ideological challenge that accompanied it. The radicalisation of a generation of young women students in the 1960s in the US over issues of race and war led to the creation of a force for political action about these questions. This development of feminist ideas would not have happened in the way that it did were it not for the convergence of these two forces.

However, feminism was a limited political programme in which to embody those ideas. It was able to express the discontent which millions of women felt as their lived experience failed to meet their growing aspirations, but it was unable to develop fully beyond that discontent and map out a path to equality for all women. This failure was both a theoretical failure to see class division as the most fundamental in capitalist society and, connected to this, the growing practical failure to organise in a way that could bring change about. The second wave of feminism provided a very important flowering of ideas, but ones which very quickly had little left to contribute in practice. By the mid-1970s questions of class power, whether working class and socialist movements would advance or be defeated, were to decide the issues of women's liberation for the coming decades.

The period of neoliberalism has made these issues more acute and polarised. Women around the world have been drawn into industrial production, join unions and play a role in public life much more centrally than one or two generations ago. But those women in low paid work, running the houses or caring for the children of much richer professional women, working in the sweatshops of East Asia to produce designer clothes for Western markets, staffing the checkouts and filling the shelves of the big supermarkets, find that the gap between them and the richest in society is growing. The feminist managers, government ministers, barristers and civil servants find their class interests influence their feminism. So it tends to remain at the level of personal identity and rights.

This helps explain the retreat from women's liberation towards identity politics, power feminism and post-feminism which have dominated since the 1980s. Empowerment, role models and identity were promoted as the only means by which women (or blacks and other ethnic minorities) could advance. The idea that a female or black celebrity millionaire could actually serve as a model for young working class women showed how far the ideologies of equality had moved from the collective to the (pushy) individual – and in the process toned down the message. The US feminist Naomi Wolf put it like this:

> In the white heat of the mass media, saying something as obvious as "Rape is bad" can position a woman as a fanatical outsider [sic]. But power feminism means learning from Madonna, Spike Lee and Bill Cosby: if you don't like your group's image in the media, decide on another image and seize control of the means of producing it.[52]

Token support for women's equal rights goes alongside these politics and is now espoused by government, media and much of civil society, while the actual reality of women's lives is ignored.

The dream of women's liberation has not been fulfilled. There needs to be a marriage between the socialist tradition of organising women with the vast amount of practical experience of social change which women have achieved in the past few decades. New generations will have to fight many of the past battles all over again. In the words of the 19th century artist and socialist William Morris:

> While I pondered on all these things, and how men [and women] fight and lose the battle, and the thing that they fought for comes about in spite of their defeat, and when it comes turns out not to be what they meant and so other men [and women] have to fight for what they meant under another name.[53]

If being a feminist means a comfortable life and good career then it is bound to exclude millions of women. It has to be about more than changing lifestyles; it has to encompass social changes which can affect many lifestyles. If history shows anything, it is that the fate of women cannot be separated from that of society as a whole, and that women's liberation – its ideas, its activity and its commitment – has to be tied to wider change.

Socialism:
the rising of the women[1]

HERE are some little remembered facts: International Women's Day, March 8th, was established by socialist women, meeting at a conference in Copenhagen in 1910. They chose the date to commemorate a demonstration in New York in 1908 by female needle trade workers demanding suffrage and a union. These textile workers from the Lower East Side were subsequently involved in major strikes and became a symbol of resistance for the socialist movement internationally.[2] Karl Marx's youngest daughter, Eleanor, was elected to serve on the executive of the gas workers' union from 1890 to 1895 in recognition of her organising Irish immigrants, unskilled workers and women into the New Unions in Britain;[3] or that two of the best known theoretical works on women's oppression remain Frederick Engels' *Origin of the Family, Private Property and the State* and August Bebel's *Women and Socialism* – both by Marxists.[3] The women's movement, which gathered pace in Britain from the late 1960s onwards, was accompanied by a series of strikes supported enthusiastically by those campaigning for women's liberation. Rose Boland, a sewing machinist from Ford's car factory in Dagenham, who was campaigning for equal pay;[5] and May Hobbs, an office cleaner by night who led a major strike of the night cleaners, became vibrant symbols of the movement.[6]

That these facts are largely unknown today shows how the connection between women's liberation and socialism has been all but lost over the past two decades. Only now, against a background of growing movements against the ravages of neo-liberalism and war, are the ideas of women's liberation beginning to reconnect with questions about class and how a genuinely equal society can be created. In fact, the fate of women's emancipation and freedom has always been connected with wider social progress and change. Indeed, Frederick Engels could write in the 1880s, a period of rising radical ideas:

> It is a curious fact that with every great revolutionary movement the question of "free love" comes into the foreground. With one set of people as a revolutionary progress, as a shaking off of old traditional fetters, no longer necessary; with others as a welcome doctrine, comfortably covering all sorts of free and easy practices between man and woman.[7]

In every period of growing confidence and militancy the ideas of women's emancipation and liberation have come onto the political agenda. When these movements fail to break through, demoralisation and retreat follow and conservative and pro-family ideas come to dominate.

A hidden history

When capitalism developed from the heart of feudal society it did so as an economic system based on the free market and the free exchange of labour. This meant opposition to the old feudal order with its tariffs, tithes and restraints on trade, and where the church, aristocracy and monarchy dominated politically. This economic revolution was accompanied by the emergence of new ideas, which stressed the freedom of the individual, freedom of religion and freedom of thought in general. The transition from one economic system to another led to great clashes between the old and the new, which in turn further radicalised many of the participants.

It was during these revolutions that ideas about what could loosely be called women's freedom and equality came to the fore. During the English Revolution of the 1640s radical ideas about love, relationships and marriage were discussed and sometimes put into practice.[8] The French Revolution of 1789, with its slogan "Liberty, equality, fraternity", saw a radicalisation of many women, both as active participants in the revolution and as thinkers. Women such as Olympe de Gouges and Theroigne de Mericourt developed new ideas which challenged the old male/female relationships.[9] The actress Claire Lacombe and Pauline Leon, a worker in a chocolate factory, formed a women's organisation, the Société des Républicaines Révolutionnaires, in 1793. It was composed of poor women in Paris who organised for militant demands in defence of the revolution and for bread. The more moderate French revolutionaries were threatened both by the content of these demands and by who made them.[10] The historian Daniel Guerin described it thus: "The Revolutionary Women were eliminated because they wanted to sow too soon the seeds of a revolution that would liberate women".[11] In Britain perhaps the best known early feminist writer, Mary Wollstonecraft, was influenced by the French Revolution, and her statement on women's liberation, *A Vindication of the Rights of Woman*, was first published in 1792.[12]

While those ideals were marginalised by the defeat of the French Revolution and the reaction in Europe after 1815, a new radicalism, much of it in opposition to the brutal effects of industrialisation and the new factory system in Britain, grew again in the 1830s and 40s. Women played a prominent part in protests in these years. The working class Chartist women in the north of England were known for their strong views and political involvement:

> During the riots, disturbances and demonstrations of the 1830s the presence of women in the crowds was remarked by all observers. In the movement against the New Poor Law of 1834, for example, which swept through the manufacturing districts of the north in 1837, women and girls were to the fore, as they were in the public demonstrations of the short-time committees.[13]

Some of the first socialist ideas emerged at this time. In France the utopian socialist followers of Charles Fourier had an image of a new and better society, with free love and women's equality as an important component. In Britain the early socialist, and founder of the model factory settlement of New Lanark, Robert Owen also took up these ideas.[14] The utopian socialists in turn influenced the form of socialism adopted by Karl Marx, who developed what he called scientific socialism. So socialism was from the beginning identified with the idea of new and changed human relationships between men and women freed from the tyranny of capital.

In 1848 revolution swept Europe from one end to the other as the emerging working classes and the liberal middle classes jointly attempted to drive feudalism and its representatives from the political stage. Many socialists were actively involved in the revolutions, including Marx and Engels in their native Germany. The revolutionary movement fragmented on class lines, and the old order was able to hang on in many places. The defeat of the revolutions of 1848 left the new ideas of socialism and liberation pushed once again to the margins, subscribed to by a relatively small number of people who often could not agree among themselves. At the same time the expansion of capitalism which marked the second half of the 19th century allowed much more conservative ideas to take hold. From the 1850s onwards in Britain there was, as we have seen, the strengthening of the family as an institution of capitalist society and the triumph of an ideology of femininity which stressed woman's place was the home.

This only began to be challenged in the 1880s with the revival of socialism in Britain and internationally. One result was the emergence of a new type of woman, free and independent, and epitomised in the pages of radical literature such as the plays and novels of George Bernard Shaw, the work of the Norwegian playwright Henrik Ibsen, the novels of George Gissing or the writings of Olive Schreiner. These literary subjects were expressions of a narrow layer of middle class women who began to experience education and sometimes paid work. They expressed extreme frustration at the conventional lot of 19th century women, especially the idle decorativeness of wealthier women, and developed ideas of female emancipation.[15] Many of these "new women" were socialists. Eleanor Marx, for example, mixed with Shaw, translated Ibsen and wrote a pamphlet about women and socialism with her partner, Edward Aveling.[16]

Marx, Engels and women

Karl Marx and Frederick Engels began their lifelong collaboration in the 1840s and wrote about women from the very beginning. In one of Marx's earliest works, *The Holy Family*, he paraphrases from Charles Fourier this statement about women:

The change in a historical epoch can always be determined by women's progress towards freedom, because here, in the relation of woman to man, of the weak to the strong, the victory of human nature over brutality is most evident. The degree of emancipation of woman is the natural measure of general emancipation.[17]

Engels came to the subject from a different angle. He had travelled to Manchester in 1842 to work at the family firm of Ermen and Engels, where he had caught the end of the 1842 general strike which swept the north of England, and was impressed with the English working class, about whom he wrote a valuable book.[18] It helped him (and Marx) understand the importance of the working class as an agent of revolutionary change. It also helped give him an insight into the lives of working class women and of the working class family.

Marx and Engels believed that the basis for the working class family would eventually cease to exist. All previous families had been based on property and on the woman's subordination to the man within the family. Marx and Engels made a class distinction here:

On what foundation is the present family, the bourgeois family, based? On capital, on private gain. In its completely developed form this family exists only among the bourgeoisie. But this state of things finds its complement in the practical absence of the family among the proletarians.[19]

The family of the bourgeoisie and their associates was still based on property, and the subordination of family members to its head continued. The working class, on the other hand, had no property and every member of the working class family – men, women and children – had to sell themselves on the labour market in order to live. They no longer needed to depend on a husband or father for support. As Engels wrote, "The employment of the wife dissolves the family utterly and of necessity".[20]

Their analysis was based on the rapid industrialisation of England in the early decades of the 19th century, and the creation of a working class where women and children were often employed at the expense of men. This, they argued, would lead to the family's disappearance or at least its severe weakening as an institution. However, as we have seen above, that dissolution did not take place.

Instead the ravages of the factory system and the workhouse led to a strengthening of the working class family in the second half of the 19th century.

Engels returned to the question much later in life, when he published his *Origin of the Family, Private Property and the State* in 1884. Here Engels linked the division of society into classes with the development of the family and the rise of women's oppression. He describes this oppression as "the world historic defeat of the female sex" and argues that the overthrow of class society will also entail the ending of women's oppression. While there has been much criticism of Engels' work, and especially his reliance on the work of the anthropologist Lewis Henry Morgan, the book is a remarkable attempt to understand women's oppression and its roots, and to make the case that the way in which women lived and were treated in late Victorian society was in no way typical of how women have lived in most of human history. That alone makes it a valuable and extremely advanced contribution.[21]

The care with which both Marx and Engels indicated the condition of women in capitalist society, their scathing attacks on the hypocrisy of bourgeois society in its double standards towards women, and their egalitarian views are largely ignored or dismissed today. Yet they were genuinely radical, and in the case of Engels pathbreaking, in their understanding of women.

Their attitude to personal relations was also unconventional. Engels had two long unmarried relationships, first with the Irish woman Mary Burns, then after her death with her sister Lizzie. He and they saw no need to marry, with Engels marrying Lizzie Burns only on her deathbed. It is assumed that Mary Burns was illiterate and sometimes it is implied that the relationship was unequal, so Terrell Carver remarks that "in love Engels does not seem to have gone searching for his intellectual equal".[22] It is impossible to tell whether Mary or Lizzie were Engels' intellectual equals, but we do know that they were highly political Irish nationalists and socialists. Mary Burns was almost certainly involved in Chartist politics when Engels met her in the early 1840s.

Marx was more conventionally married to Jenny von Westphalen. They lived in great poverty for many years as he struggled with earning a living in exile, the whole family in two rooms over what is now an expensive Italian restaurant in Soho. Several of their children died in childbirth or at a young age, the surviving three all being girls: Jenny, Laura and Eleanor. All were highly educated, independent young women and all were political, identifying as teenagers with the Irish nationalist Fenian struggle and the first workers' government of the Paris Commune in 1871. Marx's wife Jenny was also political, if ground down by a life of at best genteel poverty from which she was only in part rescued by Engels' great generosity towards the family. Jenny and Laura both married French socialists, exiled following the defeat of the Commune, while Eleanor became a major figure in British socialist and trade union politics.

There was one episode that was no doubt unhappy and troubling for the parties concerned, although it hardly represents the dastardly Victorian behaviour that it is sometimes portrayed as. Marx had an affair with the family servant, Helene Demuth, which resulted in the birth of a son, Freddie. Helene was also a friend of the family and their circle, and a committed socialist. It is clear that the affair caused great distress to the parties concerned.[23] As was the convention of the time, the affair and parentage were not admitted to and only became clear at the death of Engels. The Marx daughters had assumed that Engels was the father. Helene continued to live with the Marx family and then at Engels' house in Regents Park Road until her death, and Eleanor became close friends with Freddie.

The legacy of Marx and Engels

The history of socialism from below and the attempts at human liberation have been as hidden from history as the struggles of working women. Yet this history is a remarkable one as far as women are concerned.[24] Indeed, in the home of the biggest socialist movement in the years between Marx's death and the First World War, Germany, "feminism was as much a men's as it was a women's movement" and "in general, socialist men proved to be more consistent feminists than bourgeois women".[25] As Anne Lopes and Gary Roth, two historians of this period, observe:

> That gender equality was at first a working class phenomenon [in Germany] raises many questions about the often-assumed modernising influence of the middle classes...bourgeois thinking in part represented a reaction against ideas of gender equality as then understood within the lower orders of society.[26]

The success of August Bebel's life's work, *Women and Socialism*, was astonishing. Bebel was one of the leaders of the German SPD (Social Democratic Party) and his book was the most sought after of any socialist book in the German movement. Once it became easily available after the repeal of the Anti-Socialist Laws in 1890 it was reprinted 22 times over the next decade.[27] The leader of the German socialist women's movement, Clara Zetkin, "began her career as an orator in the late 1880s by speaking about Bebel's book to illegal gatherings of socialist men".[28] All this demonstrates how seriously the German male socialists took the question of women's equality.

In the period before the First World War both German and Russian socialists brought women's issues onto the political agenda internationally, as we have seen with the establishment of International Women's Day. The strike that inspired it the year before in New York was one of the most remarkable ever seen. Known as "The Uprising of the 30,000" it involved many young women workers, the large majority of them Russian Jewish teenagers, often only speaking Yiddish. It was led by the young Jewish socialist Clara Lemlich, and the strikers faced beatings by gangsters and by prostitutes, arrest, sexual abuse, hardship and freezing cold conditions, all with a courage which still inspires today.[29]

The fight for women's suffrage developed into an international movement, and International Women's Day was part of the agitation over this question. In every country, however, there were divisions as to how to approach the "woman question." Should it be on the basis of demanding equality with men along existing lines, or should the fight for the vote, for women's full education and other issues of legal equality, be combined with a fight against the whole class divided society – where the fruits of its immense wealth were denied to most of its citizens, whether men or women? This was a period of growing radicalisation of both middle class and working class women.

There was at least some identification between the women of different classes, as middle class women also wanted to alleviate some of the misery of working class life. However, their sympathy didn't usually extend to anything which might threaten property. So extremely rich women such as Alva Belmont (married first to a member of the Vanderbilt family and then to the heir of the New York subway system) and Anne Morgan, daughter of one of the most predatory capitalists, J P Morgan, were ardent suffragists. Belmont believed that the suffrage was the answer to all the problems facing women. They initially supported the women garment workers in their strike, driving them in a cavalcade round the narrow streets of the Lower East Side in their expensive cars, but urged compromise on them when it came to talk of a settlement. After the strikers rejected this, Anne Morgan attacked the conduct of a public meeting held to protest at police brutality, saying, "It is very reprehensible for Socialists to take advantage of these poor girls in these times, and when the working people are in such dire straits, to teach their fanatical doctrines".[30] No wonder one socialist activist had already drawn the conclusion that it was not worth trusting these women:

> the girls would probably be better off in the long run if they did not take their money. They would the sooner realise the great contrast and division of classes. The women gave us a thousand dollars, but what does this amount to? Not even a quarter apiece for each striker.[31]

Marxist women rejected a narrow approach to suffrage and stressed the importance of organising working women, and this led to sharp divisions. Some of the sharpest were in Russia, where Tsarist repression meant that political involvement often resulted in imprisonment or exile. Alexandra Kollontai was a Russian socialist who came from a middle class background but whose left wing politics led her to first leave her husband and eventually to become a full time revolutionary during the Russian Revolution of 1905. She took up the cause of working women, who she wanted to organise for the socialist cause rather than for a feminism embracing all classes. She operated in the largely female Union of Textile Workers. Faced with political repression following the defeat of the 1905 Revolution, she organised a legal club for women workers and went into battle with bourgeois feminists in Russia.[32] At the first All Russia Women's Congress, a feminist conference that took place in December 1908, only a tiny number of working women were represented (only 45 out of over 1,000) but arguments about class continually erupted.[33] One working woman argued, "What do you know of our lives, bowling along in carriages while we get splashed by the mud?" When a feminist replied that this was why bourgeois women were better qualified to fight for women's rights, Kollontai got to her feet to argue. She risked arrest by doing so and it was her last highly controversial appearance before she was forced into exile.[34] Repeatedly the forceful demand for suffrage seemed to create unity across the different classes, but in every case the unity was broken as class divisions and economic issues came to the fore.

This was true of the Women's Social and Political Union in Britain, known ever after by its popular name of Suffragettes. Formed in Manchester in 1903 by Mrs Emmeline Pankhurst and her daughter Christabel, the suffragettes rapidly gained prominence for their mass organisation and determination to hound government ministers and other politicians who adamantly refused the demand for women's suffrage. Again issues of class came to the fore. One question was whether the vote should be granted to women on the same basis as then existed for men, or whether there should be universal suffrage. This was not an academic question when the majority of male unskilled workers were still denied the vote, just as were all women. Emmeline and Christabel were concerned only that they gained women's suffrage on the existing property qualifications, and this led to conflicts with much of the left, who generally favoured universal suffrage. The Pankhursts became increasingly anti working class and more hostile to the emerging Labour Party, even though their political roots had been in the Independent Labour Party, one of Labour's forerunners.[35] In one notorious example, when the Labour MP George Lansbury resigned his seat in the East End of London in 1912 to stand in a by-election on an Independent Labour ticket supporting votes for women, wealthy women suffragettes refused to lend their cars on election day and he lost his election.[36]

Britain entered a major social and economic crisis in the years before the First World War, facing suffrage agitation, a mass strike wave and calls for Irish Home Rule. The younger Pankhurst daughter, Sylvia, identified with these other issues and based herself in the East End of London, organising working class women over issues such as childcare. This brought her into conflict with her mother and sister, especially when she spoke at a meeting in London's Albert Hall in support of workers in Dublin who were locked out by a vicious employer. Christabel made her choose between the working class and socialist organisations and the suffragettes. She chose her East London Federation and continued to campaign, welcoming the Russian Revolution of 1917 and for a short while after the First

World War joining the new Communist Party. Mrs Pankhurst and Christabel now opposed universal suffrage and become keen supporters of the First World War.

Revolution and women's liberation

The revolutionary wave which swept Europe after the First World War led to the establishment of Communist Parties in most countries. These incorporated ideas of women's equality and contained within their ranks some of the best militant women of their generation.

Russia's Revolution in February 1917 was led by women agitating over bread shortages around International Women's Day.[37] The Soviet government set up after the October Revolution led to changes for women which were more advanced and radical than anywhere in the world. The Russian government recognised that women's equality had to be fought for if socialism was ever to be possible. It set up a women's department headed first by Inessa Armand, who died suddenly, and then by Alexandra Kollontai.[38] The Russian Revolution led to real gains for women: civil marriage, divorce, abortion and contraception, legal equality, free childcare and the socialisation of many aspects of housework, with communal restaurants and laundries. Open relationships and free love flourished especially among young people. It is hard to imagine now, nearly 100 years later, the impact of such changes. Many of these reforms were only established elsewhere in the 1960s and 1970s, and some of them are still denied to millions of women around the world even now. The achievements were awe inspiring in an economically backward, largely peasant country.[39] However, their fate was tied to that of the revolution itself. Even in its early years the country was too poor and backward to be able to achieve the implementation of all these reforms. Washing sent to the laundry was stolen, many orphan children had no family and lived in destitution, prostitution re-emerged and by 1921 there were an estimated 17,000 prostitutes in Petrograd and 10,000 in Moscow.[40] So the changes were a brave but short-lived experiment in a country racked by poverty, famine and civil war and where the revolution itself had been destroyed by the late 1920s. Under Stalin the gains for women went into reverse, with attacks on abortion rights, the ending of many socialised functions of the family, and the practice of awarding medals to mothers of large families. All this went alongside economic, political and social retreat throughout Russia:[41]

The triumphal rehabilitation of the family, taking place simultaneously – what a providential coincidence – with the rehabilitation of the rouble, is caused by the material and cultural bankruptcy of the state. Instead of openly saying, "We have proven still too poor and too ignorant for the creation of socialist relations among men, our children and grandchildren will realise this aim", the leaders are forcing people to glue together again the shell of the broken family, and not only that, but to consider it, under threat of extreme penalties, the sacred nucleus of triumphant socialism. It is hard to measure with the eye the scope of this retreat.[42]

One measure of this change was that between 1917 and 1930 there were 301 party resolutions or party decrees on the subject of women – during the next 30 years there were only three.[43]

Yet the Russian Revolution had a profound effect on those organising for women's liberation. So in the 1920s and 30s the Communist tradition led to a significant level of commitment and organisation over questions facing women in various countries around the world, and especially in Germany before the Hitler came to power in 1933. The Communist Party was the only party in Germany to defend married women's right to work, in opposition to the leaders of both the trade unions and the Social Democratic Party.[44] Often this commitment to women's rights, as with the German socialists of Bebel's time, was stronger than that of certain feminists, who saw women's rights simply as an extension of legal rights within bourgeois society, rather than a challenge to the whole oppressive and exploitative system. The mainstream left parties, and many feminists and liberals in Spain, Italy, France and Belgium were all reluctant to support the extension of the franchise to women on the grounds that the mass of Catholic peasant women would vote as the priests directed them and therefore could not be trusted.[45] Equal relationships, sexual experimentation and unconventional attitudes to morality were of great interest to Communist and left socialist women and men, and there is some evidence that they tried to put such ideas into practice.[46]

This tradition was largely submerged following the Second World War, until the explosion of radicalism in the 1960s. When the children of the post-war generation rejected the dominant social values which still tolerated gender and racial oppression and war they also began to search for a tradition to help explain how and why people had struggled over such issues before. They discovered the forgotten names of Alexandra Kollontai, Clara Zetkin, Sylvia Pankhurst and dozens of other strikers, campaigners and writers. Those individuals and the causes they organised round inspired a new generation, and International Women's Day was revived.

The defeats of the late 1970s marginalised many of these ideas once again, but the renewed interest in radical ideas in recent years has seen a greater consciousness of the need not just to fight for women's rights but to go beyond that and create a society based on economic and social equality. The socialist tradition of women's liberation should be an integral part of that consciousness.

Conclusion: how do we get there?

K ARL Marx writing in the 1860s in his great study *Capital* pointed to "the enormous mortality, during the first few years of their life, of the children of the [factory] operatives". He showed that, while in areas of the lowest infant mortality less than one in ten children under the age of one died, in the factory areas that rose to around one in four:

> The high death rates are...principally due to the employment of mothers away from their homes, and to the neglect and maltreatment, consequent on her absence, such as... insufficient nourishment, unsuitable food, and dosing with opiates.[1]

Nearly a century and a half later these same issues confront women around the world. Take Lorna, a garment worker and mother who works in one of the Export Processing Zones in the Philippines:

> Her workday begins well before dawn when she rises to cook her children rice and leftover vegetables for their lunch. After she leaves for work, the eight year old tries to look after his younger siblings. She knows the children often stray into the streets to play

with their friends... Her eldest son cannot attend school since she lacks money to buy supplies and books... Tragically, Lorna's attempt to walk the tightrope between the conflicting demands of economic survival and motherhood failed when she returned to work after the birth of her youngest child. The seven month old was left at home with her older siblings who tried to bottle feed her. The baby died from complications of diarrhoea.[2]

Or look at the case of another factory worker in the Philippines, Malou:

Desperate to earn a paltry 22 pesos (83 US cents) per hour in overtime, she was forced to remove her child from the factory nursery...and arrange a rota of well meaning but inadequate childminders to look after him at home during her long working day. Taking Ogie out of the nursery – where she could breastfeed him during nursing breaks from the shopfloor meant she also had to abandon breastfeeding. Although neighbours and older children of relatives tried to take care of him, they did not sterilise water for his infant formula. Ogie – often left propped up in his cot with a bottle – developed a life-threatening bout of diarrhoea.

Malou lost the income from her factory job while looking after him and spent more than a week's earnings on medicines alone. Her monthly salary is only 4,200 pesos (US$140), which she earns sewing fashionable Nike and Reebok jackets for Western consumers.[3]

Women and families around the world are being forced into circumstances which the Victorian reformers in Britain would have found all too familiar. But today governments pay lip service to reform but support a system where company profits are based on such exploitation and oppression. For most of the time the labour that goes into producing the commodities consumed in the richest countries is invisible; hence, despite some very valuable research and reporting on such questions, the lives of the women behind the mass production of these goods remain pretty invisible too.

However, any account of women's liberation in the West has to make these issues visible. What does liberation mean today for women factory workers such as the ones described above, the new working class in countries such as China or the Philippines, many living in dormitories next to their place of work, and living in order to work? What does liberation mean for a young woman in Thailand, forced to choose between a factory job and a life of prostitution? In Thailand, a country the size of Britain, there are, according to different estimates, between half a million and two million prostitutes, some of them bought from their families in effective slavery.[4] What does liberation mean to an East European prostitute trafficked to Western Europe and with no prospect of a job back home?

What does liberation mean for the call centre workers, supermarket cashiers, cleaners and cooks? What does it mean for migrant women, sucked into booming economies in countries such as Britain and Ireland? These women are forced to put up with poor wages and conditions in some of the least valued jobs such as cleaning and caring. They are often in a precarious state, lacking job or housing security and subject to racial and sexual harassment as well. Their status as immigrants increases the pressures on them and, of course, they face separation from their families, including their children. None of these women can talk about liberation in isolation from the economic and social conditions which dominate their lives.

Neoliberalism has changed their lives – destroying old industries and creating new ones, opening up markets where once they did not exist, creating a huge new commercialisation of sexual exploitation in which they can work. The options on offer to these women simply do not begin to deal with their problems. For women in the global south, highly exploited work is the only alternative to emigration or prostitution. Rebellion or revolt is met by repression. The market can easily coexist with forms of dictatorship or at best the democracy neoliberal style which allows freedom and choice as long as you accept the right freedom and the right choice.

This form of democracy is encroaching on the traditional Western democracies as well. A narrow form of political equality only means much to a small number of already privileged women, and who now find themselves accepted into the men's club, if not on equal terms, then near enough. But their privilege depends on the exploitation of men and women who produce the wealth and service the wealthy. The path of individual advance has only admitted a select few.

The creation of welfare states in many parts of the West in the course of the 20th century marked a real advance for working people, as well as enabling capital to increase productivity through developing an educated and healthy workforce. While it was never a reality for many parts of the world, it did form the basis on which many of those feminists from the 1960s and 70s were able to advance themselves. But it is now on the retreat as the neoliberal agenda attacks health, pensions and education provision. In Britain nearly 30 years of Thatcherism and Blairism have taken their toll. UNICEF in a 2007 report put the wellbeing of Britain's children at the bottom of 21 rich countries.[5] The poor suffer more than the rich: a survey of 30,000 parents of 19,000 children born in 2000/01 found that mothers and fathers in poorer families were less likely to spend paid time off around the birth of their children, and very few used formal childcare. Fathers in low income families are less likely to take two weeks paternity leave than the better off; 63 percent of working fathers felt they did not spend enough time with their nine to ten month old baby.[6]

The ideological response to the retreat from the welfare state is as grim as the response to sweatshop labour in the global south. Around 100 years ago the Fabians, the Cooperative Women's Guild and other pro-Labour reformers wrote important studies that argued for state intervention to help alleviate the position of working class families, and against the idea of blaming mothers for social ills.[7] Today New Labour and its neoliberal co-thinkers on an international scale blame the poor for poverty and, like those who thought up the Poor Law and the workhouse, believe that work is the solution to poverty. In 2007 the Labour government's welfare reform minister, Jim Murphy, greeted the shocking increase in the most recent child poverty figures in Britain with the statement that work was the only route out of poverty. Despite the protestations of child poverty experts, faced with 2.8 million children living in poverty, Murphy's approach met with no opposition from his colleagues.[8]

So women are expected to work longer hours, juggle with childcare, and carry the can if anything goes wrong in their lives. The pressure does not, of course, stop at work.

Major corporations operating in the age of mass information technology help to ensure anxiety among women on a mass scale. The opening up of work to women and the greater openness about sexuality have created or brought to light new and very harsh pressures, especially on young women. They see the gap between the idealised image depicted in the women's fashion magazines and reality as too great to bridge but too painful to put up with. The diet industry with its multi-million pound turnover is a reflection of the constant battle between women's actual looks and size and their desire to look very different. In a rich society obsession with food creates some strange manifestations, including bingeing and then starving oneself, constantly finding new ways of dieting or looking thinner, and relentlessly comparing oneself with images of women who look totally different from any woman one actually knows.

Unhappiness and dissatisfaction with actual looks are endemic. So rising numbers of women undergo the extremely costly job of "making over" those parts which need it – usually nearly all of them. This is highly profitable for the corporations involved, with the global cosmetic industry worth $20 billion, with the US sector alone constituting $13 billion to $15 billion a year. In 2004, 478,251 Americans had liposuction, 334,052 had breast augmentation and 166,187 had nose jobs. Depressingly, the author of a study on cosmetic surgery concludes that, "vulgar and shallow as it sounds, looks matter more than they ever have – especially for women".[9]

It isn't too hard to see that something big has to happen to change all this. There is so much wrong in women's lives, and by implication in the lives of men and children as well, that only some fundamental changes can begin to put things right.

How do we achieve those changes? It is not sufficient simply to repeat old slogans. We live in different times from the 1960s and 70s. This whole book has been an attempt to explain the different ways in which people live, think and act today, and any plan for the future has to take into account of those changes. But there are also certain reference points that remain constant.

We have a long tradition of women organising to fight back against their oppression. Indeed, women's movements and struggles have always arisen when social change is on the agenda, and have developed as part of a more general questioning of society. For hundreds of years women have defied the feminine image of their role and have campaigned at various times for bread, the staple food to feed their families, for the right to work, and for political rights. The revolutionary movements and political campaigns of the 19th century – Chartism, the revolutions of 1848, the Paris Commune – all saw women take their place alongside men in the fight for a better world and raise demands to improve their position.

Women have always taken inspiration from other campaigns. The term "women's emancipation" takes as its reference point the movement for emancipation from slavery:

> The movement for the emancipation of slaves thus not only inspired the American women's movement [of the 19th century], it also provided a concept that could express an aspiration for individual self-determination, along with social, economic and political change.[10]

The "first wave" of feminism – the international movement for women's suffrage and legal rights – coincided in countries such as Britain and the US with a growing political awareness and militancy within the working class. The "second wave", which began in the late 1960s, was very directly the product of the student, black and anti-war movements. The present growing interest in issues surrounding women and campaigns involving women also has its roots in the radicalisation caused by neoliberalism and war.

Below I put forward ten demands which should be eminently achievable but which we still have not won, and in many cases are still a long way from doing so. A charter for working women, it would begin to redress the balance of women's lives, but also would mean a redistribution of wealth and power away from those who hold them at present, and an opening up of possibilities of women's liberation.

★ The right to equal work and pay
★ The right to control our own bodies
★ The right to sexual self-determination
★ An end to discrimination against single mothers
★ For a 35-hour week and national childcare service
★ The right to marriage and divorce freely entered into by the agreement of both parties without coercion
★ The right for women to dress as they want
★ Against all violence against women, including domestic violence and rape
★ Against all racism and discrimination against migrant women
★ No to sexual harassment at work

Such demands could form the basis of new campaigns and movements.

However, there is no automatic progress towards equality. Again a theme of this book has been how victories have to be guarded and extended and how, if they are not, they can be put into reverse. Women and men cannot assume that what their parents fought for has been won forever. In a time when many of the gains of the 1960s and 70s are under attack, we need to understand why. The fight for women's liberation cannot be divorced from the question of class. The present form of class society, capitalism, has recreated women's oppression. It daily reinforces that oppression through the family and the system of exploitation which ensures that the needs of women are subjugated to the needs of capital.

These needs – for immigrant labour, low paid flexible labour and childcare on the cheap – and capital's ability to turn even the most personal emotions into goods which can be bought and sold, guarantee the continuing exploitation and oppression of working people. The only means of ending this exploitation and oppression is to end the exploitative system itself with its replacement by one based on producing goods that the people of the world really need, rather than on what makes profits for a tiny minority. This is the connection between women's liberation and socialism: the end of class society would create the preconditions for women's liberation. Not all women have an interest in this change coming about. Class society divides women as well as men between the tiny minority who live by the exploitation of others, and the vast majority who produce the wealth but have it taken from them.

Many women reject the equation of women's liberation and socialism, believing that this relegates women's demands to lower down the political agenda, or to waiting "till after the revolution". However, it is precisely in the course of these struggles and protests that women's demands are brought to the fore and that real change can be achieved. Some of the most obvious changes that would result would lay the basis for real liberation. Equal pay, full and free childcare, social provision for feeding people, cleaning clothes and houses, and caring for all members of the family who need it would make a start in paving the way for liberation. There would be a presumption against sexism in the media, in the legal system, in education and in other areas of life which would begin to alter attitudes towards women and relations between the sexes.

This isn't just about economics, of course. It's about changing ideas so that women and men look at themselves and the world in a new way. One of the fallacies of feminism is that Marxist ideas only explain the economy but cannot help us to understand how society works or ideas develop. On the contrary, for Marx, revolution was essential not simply to take economic control into the hands of those who produced the wealth; it was also because only in the process of making a revolution could working people change themselves: "The class overthrowing [capitalism] can only in a revolution succeed in ridding itself of all the muck of ages and become fitted to found society anew".[11]

We have seen how women do change in the process of battling to change the world. All the gains made in the past century have come about because people campaigned, organised and sometimes made great sacrifices in order to achieve them. This is true of access to education, women entering "male" jobs, the fight for abortion and contraception, improved rights at work and, of course, the vote for women. The key to achieving the long term goal of transforming women's lives does not lie in just dreaming about it, but in what we do now to achieve change, and in how that can be turned into a wider challenge to the existing order. As we have seen in previous chapters, many of the most consistent and far ranging fighters for women's rights were those who had an alternative vision of a socialist society, based on production for need and not profit. The key to change is connecting the many campaigns in which women and men are engaged to that alternative vision. If we can do that, it will bring women closer to their liberation. It will also mean that women can become not spectators on history, but its subjects, part of the struggle to change the world for the better.

Notes

1 Introduction: a revolution stalled

1 Betty Friedan, *The Feminine Mystique* (New York, 1963). "The Problem That Has No Name" is the title of chapter 1.

2 "Size of Gender Gap in Top Jobs 'Woeful'", *Financial Times*, 5 January 2007.

3 "Labour Force Survey", see www.statistics.gov.uk/STATBASE/Source.asp?vlnk=358

4 "Women with Children 'Working Longer Hours Than Ever'", *Financial Times*, 8/9 September 2001.

5 Rosie Cox, *The Servant Problem* (London, 2006) ch2 pp13-34.

6 "Mothers Bear Brunt of Discrimination at Work", *Guardian*, 1 March 2007.

7 Sue Sharpe, *Just Like a Girl* (London, 1987).

8 Frederick Engels, *Origin of the Family, Private Property and the State* (New York, 1975). While much of Engels' writing is dated today, this was a pathbreaking book for its time. I return to this point in the chapter on socialism below.

9 Unicef, "Report Card 7, Child Poverty in Perspective: an Overview of Child Wellbeing in Rich Countries", 14 February 2007. See www.unicef.org.uk

2 Sex: the peculiarities of the English

1 Abigail Self and Linda Zealey (eds), *Social Trends*, 37 (London, 2007), p16.

2 Jil Matheson and Carol Summerfield (eds), *Social Trends* 30 (London, 2000), p37.

3 Abigail Self and Linda Zealey (eds), *Social Trends* 37, p19.

4 As above, p22. Out of 645,835 births in 2005, 276,505 were outside marriage.

5 *Guardian Education*, 16 January 2001.

6 *Guardian*, 22 February 2001. The rate of teenage pregnancies in Britain differs greatly from area to area, and the highest rates have a direct correlation with areas of poverty, unemployment and social deprivation. Those areas with the greatest number of conceptions per 1000 girls aged 15 to 17 include working class London boroughs such as Lambeth, Lewisham and Barking and Dagenham, as well as the declining industrial areas of Doncaster, Newcastle and Salford. Areas with the least teenage pregnancies were Surrey, the London

borough of Kingston, Richmond, and Oxfordshire. Rates here were around a third of rates in poor areas such as Southwark or Lambeth. Britain's relatively high level of such pregnancies compared with much of Europe appears to be at least in part connected with Britain's standard of living and welfare. Rates tend to be highest among some of the most vulnerable in society – those in care or in the poorest areas, while poverty and lack of work or educational opportunities seem to be connected to high rates.

7   Quoted in Angela Holdsworth, *Out of the Doll's House* (London, 1988), p158.

8   Geoffrey Gorer quoted in Ross McKibbin, *Classes and Cultures England 1918-1951* (Oxford, 1998), p296.

9   Steve Humphries, *A Secret World of Sex* (London, 1991), pp17-18.

10   As above, pp95-96.

11   John R Gillis, *For Better, For Worse* (Oxford and New York, 1985), pp286, 294.

12   See Eric Josef Carlson, *Marriage and the English Reformation* (Cambridge Mass, 1994), p126.

13   John Gillis, *For Better*, p198.

14   As above, p141. See also Eric Josef Carlson, *Marriage*, and Christopher Hill, *Society and Puritanism* (Harmondsworth, 1986).

15   John R Gillis, *For Better*, p231.

16   As above, p232.

17   Antonio Gramsci, *Selections from Prison Notebooks* (London, 1986), p297.

18   For a full study of this question see Ronald Pearsall, *The Worm in the Bud* (Middlesex, 1972).

19   Eustace Chesser, quoted in Jeffrey Weeks, *Sex, Politics and Society* (London, 1981), p209.

20   Study quoted in Kevin White, *Sexual Liberation or Sexual License* (Chicago, 2000), p41.

21   Quoted in Steve Humphries, *Secret World*, p130.

22   Diana Gittins, *Fair Sex* (London, 1982), p45.

23   Kevin White, *Sexual Liberation*, p68.

24   Jeffrey Weeks, *Sex, Politics and Society*, p200.

25   For much of the 19th century the poor had had to rely on their own resources in the care of their young and sick, with a whole network of women who gave advice, helped with lying in and performed medical and nursing tasks. By the 20th century this had begun to change with the state playing a much bigger part in health and welfare provision. The introduction of school inspections, which checked on the health of children, improved levels of hygiene and general health. Childbirth was much more under the control of the medical profession, with the number of maternity hospital beds rising from 210 in 1891 to 10,029 in 1938. Midwives had to be professionally qualified by 1910 and a maternity grant was provided under the legislation of 1911. All of this created a much safer environment for mothers and children. See Diana Gittins, *Fair Sex*, pp49-51.

26   As above, pp51-52.

27   See, for example, Michael Young and Peter Wilmott, *Family and Kinship in East London* (London, 1962), p20. My mother and other women who grew up in the 1920s and 1930s also used it, as in "I fell for a baby before I was married".

28   Angela Holdsworth, *Out of the Doll's House*, p133.

29   Steve Humphries, *Secret World*, p29.

30   Mass Observation Survey 1945 quoted in Liz Stanley, *Sex Surveyed* (London, 1995), p186.

31   Steve Humphries, *Secret World*, p188.

32   Liz Stanley, *Sex Surveyed*, p188.

33   Steve Humphries, *Secret World* pp181-182.

34   Liz Stanley, *Sex Surveyed*, p187.

35   Diana Gittins, *Fair Sex*, p114.

36   As above, p81.

37   Elizabeth Roberts, *Women and Families: An Oral History, 1940-1970* (Oxford, 1995), p70.

38   Elizabeth Roberts, *A Woman's Place: An Oral History of Working Class Women 1890-1940* (Oxford, 1985), p75.

39 Elizabeth Roberts, *A Woman's Place*, pp75, 77.
40 Diana Gittins, *Fair Sex*, p169.
41 Elizabeth Roberts, *Women and Families*, p79.
42 Steve Humphries, *Secret World*, p76.
43 See Ross McKibbin, *Classes and Cultures: England 1918-51*, p307.
44 Diana Gittins, *Fair Sex*, p173.
45 As above, p164.
46 Ross McKibbin, *Classes and Cultures*, pp305-306.
47 As above, p297.
48 Royal Commission on Equal Pay 1944-46.Cmnd 6564 Memo from AEU, Appendix 8 (London, 1946).
49 Steve Humphries, *A Secret World*, p65.
50 Angela Holdsworth, *Out of the Doll's House*, p145.
51 Sheila Rowbotham, *A Century of Women* (London, 1997), p240.
52 Quoted in Elizabeth Wilson, *Only Halfway to Paradise* (London, 1980), p89.
53 Ross McKibbin, *Classes and Cultures*, p303.
54 John Gillis, *For Better*, pp280-281. Less than a third of couples married within a year of first meeting in the 1950s; long engagements were connected to the need to save enough to furnish a home, and the groom was expected to earn a "man's wage".
55 As above, p304.
56 Jeffrey Weeks, *Sex, Politics and Society*, p252.
57 Kaye Wellings, Julia Field, Anne M Johnson and Jane Wadsworth, *Sexual Behaviour in Britain* (London, 1994) p37.
58 Liz Stanley, *Sex Surveyed*, p45, quoting a survey by Michael Schofield.
59 Jane Lewis, *Women in Britain since 1945* (Oxford, 1992), p44.
60 Abigail Self and Linda Zealey (eds), *Social Trends*, 37, p30. The figures for male undergraduates in the same year are 241,000.
61 Chris Harman, *The Fire Last Time* (London, 1988), p86.
62 For example, the 1967 Abortion Act, which made abortion legal under certain circumstances, could be liberally interpreted to allow abortion for social as well as physical reasons. Although this reform was very far from the free abortion on demand which became a key plank of women's campaigning in the 1970s, it did allow many women the choice to end unwanted pregnancy quickly and safely. Again many began to see that their sexuality and sexual activity did not have to be linked to marriage, motherhood or indeed monogamy.
63 Jeffrey Weeks, *Sex, Politics and Society*, p252.
64 As above, chs 12, 13 and 14, and Nicola Field, *Over the Rainbow* (London, 1995), for background.
65 See Anne Koedt, *The Myth of the Vaginal Orgasm* (originally published 1970 and reprinted in Rosalyn Baxandall and Linda Gordon, *Dear Sisters: Dispatches from the Women's Liberation Movement*, (New York, 2001); Germaine Greer, *The Female Eunuch* (London, 1970); Shere Hite, *The Hite Report* (New York, 1976); Susan Brownmiller, *Against Our Will* (London, 1976).
66 Kaye Wellings and others, *Sexual Behaviour*, pp71-72, shows that of those surveyed only 6.1 percent of men and 15.9 percent of women had their first intercourse in marriage, compared with 42.9 percent of men and 51.4 percent of women who had it first in a steady relationship.
67 John R Gillis, *For Better*, p307.
68 Kevin White, *Sexual Liberation*, p197.
69 John R Gillis, *For Better*, pp307-308.
70 Kaye Wellings and others, *Sexual Behaviour*, pp98-100.
71 As above, p77.
72 As above, pp156-157.
73 Figures in Wellings, of those asked about oral-genital sexual contact in the past year, were as follows: cunnilingus only: men 6.4 percent, women 5.5 percent; fellatio only: men 2.7 percent, women 3.3 percent; both: men 46.5 percent, women 40.7 percent. As above, pp149-151.

74 Decca Aitkenhead "Prudes rock", *Guardian*, 5 March 2002.
75 Ariel Levy, *Female Chauvinist Pigs* (New York and London, 2005), p34.
76 Shere Hite, *Oedipus Revisited* (London, 2005), p56.
77 Ariel Levy, *Female Chauvinist Pigs*, p198.
78 See Sheila Rowbotham, *A Century of Women*, p431.
79 Susan Brownmiller, *Against Our Will* (London, 1976).
80 Katie Roiphe, *The Morning After* (London, 1994), p52.
81 As above, p54.
82 "Rape Victims 'Failed by Police and Courts'", *Independent*, 31 January 2007, taken from joint report from HMI of Constabulary and Her Majesty's Crown Prosecution Service Inspectorate.
83 Ariel Levy, *Female Chauvinist Pigs*, p29.
84 Karl Marx, *Economic and Philosophic Manuscripts 1844*, quoted in *Writings of the Young Marx* (New York, 1967), p292.
85 As above, p292.

3   The family: the best of worlds, the worst of worlds

1   Leo Tolstoy, *Anna Karenina* (Harmondsworth, 1986), p13.
2   According to an NSPCC survey in 2002, nearly 80 percent of child murders were carried out by parents. See "Child murder rate 'a national disgrace'", BBC News website, 13 October 2002.
3   Home Office statistics available at http://www.homeoffice.gov.uk/crime-victims/reducing-crime/domestic-violence/?view=Standard
4   This is the essence of Frederick Engels' arguments in *Origin of the Family, The State and Private Property*.
5   See Ivy Pinchbeck, *Women Workers and the Industrial Revolution* (London, 1981).
6   This is what Karl Marx and Frederick Engels believed at the time. For more on this see the section "Marx, Engels and Women" in chapter 8.
7   See chapter 7 on the women's movement for a full discussion on this question.
8   Lindsey German, *Sex, Class and Socialism*, (London 1989), ch1; Jane Humphries, "Class Struggle and the Persistence of the Working Class Family", in *Cambridge Journal of Economics*, vol 1 (1977); Dorothy Thompson, "Women and 19th Century Radical Politics", in Juliet Mitchell and Ann Oakley (eds), *The Rights and Wrongs of Women* (Harmondsworth, 1976).
9   This is based on women listed as "unoccupied" in the census figures, which will almost certainly underestimate the number of women working for some sort of financial reward (and which of course assumes that the unpaid work carried out in the home is not an "occupation" because it does not command a wage). John Gillis, *For Better*, p245.
10 Bridget Hill, *Eighteenth Century Women: An Anthology* (London, 1987), p10.
11 John R Gillis, *For Better*, p246.
12 For details of this see for example Michael Anderson, *Family Structure in 19th Century Lancashire* (Cambridge, 1971), and Jill Liddington, *The Life and Times of a Respectable Rebel* (London, 1984).
13 See chapter 4 on work for a fuller explanation of this process.
14 Liz Steel and Warren Kidd, *The Family* (London, 2001), p63.
15 On this see John Gillis, *For Better*, p277.
16 www.statistics.gov.uk/pdfdir/marr0205.pdf
17 *Population Trends*, Office of National Statistics (Winter 2006). Available at www.statistics.gov.uk/downloads/theme_population/PopTrends126.pdf
18 Abigail Self and Linda Zealey (eds), *Social Trends 37*, p18.
19 See http://www.statistics.gov.uk/cci/nugget_print.asp?ID=170. See also Abigail Self and Linda Zealey (eds), as above, p18 (figure 2.9).
20 See http://www.statistics.gov.uk/cci/nugget_print.asp?ID=170.
21 Len Cook and Jean Martin (eds), *Social Trends 35*, pp23-24.

22 As above, pp23-24.
23 *British Social Attitudes* 17, 2000-2001 (London, 2001), p3.
24 As above, p112.
25 As above, p111.
26 www.ipsos-mori.com/polls/1997/m_971027.shtml
27 www.oneplusone.org.uk/marriedor not/Factsheet2.htm. This is referenced from *British Social Attitudes* 18 (London, 2002).
28 Elizabeth Roberts, *Women and Families*, pp72-74; John Gillis, *For Better*, pp187, 294.
29 John Gillis, as above, p187.
30 Elizabeth Roberts, *Women and Families*, p72.
31 Diana Leonard Barker, "A Proper Wedding", in Marie Corbin (ed), *The Couple* (Harmondsworth, 1978), pp56-77.
32 As above, p57.
33 As above, p58.
34 www.daycaretrust.org.uk/mod.php? mod=userpage&menu=1
35 "£164,000 cost of bringing up children", *Guardian*, 4 May 2004.
36 "£43,056 – the cost of bringing up a child", *Guardian*, 16 February 2006.
37 "High cost of bringing up baby", BBC news http://news.bbc.co.uk/1/hi/business/3223896.stm
38 Lindsey German, *Sex, Class and Socialism*, ch4, "The Sexual Division of Labour". Also see Sheila Lewenhak, *Women and Work* (London, 1980), p229.
39 Maud Pember Reeves, *Round About a Pound a Week* (London, 1994), pp104-112.
40 Ben Fine and Ellen Leopold, *The World of Consumption* (London, 1993), p302.
41 As above, p302.
42 See Rosie Cox, *The Servant Problem*. She estimates that there are perhaps 2 million domestic workers in Britain today, and quotes a source for 2.7 million British households who employ some sort of domestic help (see p3).
43 As above, ch2.
44 *Independent*, 12 December 2006.

45 Michael Mitterauer and Reinhard Sieder, *The European Family* (Oxford, 1982), p35.
46 Margaret Thatcher, interviewed in *Women's Own*, 31 October 1987.
47 BBC News website on 07 December 2006, available at http://news.bbc.co.uk/1/hi/england/6215566.stm
48 Len Cook and Jean Martin (eds), *Social Trends 35*, p23.
49 Figures are from the Joseph Rowntree Foundation. See http://www.jrf.org.uk/knowledge/findings/socialpolicy/0366.asp
50 http://www.daycaretrust.org.uk/mod.php?mod=userpage&menu=2601&page_id=8
51 Joseph Rowntree Foundation, see http://www.jrf.org.uk/child-poverty/
52 As above.
53 National Children's Home press release 4.12.2006, available at http://www.nch.org.uk/information/index.php?i=77&r=524
54 Joseph Rowntree Foundation, see http://www.jrf.org.uk/knowledge/findings/socialpolicy/0366.asp
55 As above.

4 **Work: all day, every day**
1 "The Importance of Sex", *Economist* 15 April 2006.
2 See, for example, Madeleine Bunting, *Willing Slaves* (London, 2004), and the description of flexitime and super-exploitation in retailing and other industries in Jane Hardy, "The Changing Structure of the British Economy", *International Socialism*, 106 (Spring 2005).
3 See, for example, the TUC Equality Audit 2005, which draws on the government's Labour Force Survey. Available at www.lrd.org.uk/services/tuceq/womenstats.html. In 2003 women made up 44 percent of the UK workforce with female employment standing at 12.36 million compared to 15.58 million for men.
4 "The Thing-ummy-bob (That's Gonna Win The War)", Thompson/Heneker, 1942:

I'm the girl that makes the thing that
*   drills the hole*
that holds the ring that drives the rod that
*   turns the knob*
that works the thing-ummy-bob
I'm the girl that makes the thing that
*   holds the oil*
that oils the ring that takes the shank that
*   moves the crank*
that works the thing-ummy-bob.

http://www.lyricsplayground.com/al
pha/songs/t/thethingummybob.shtml

5   Rochelle Gatlin, *American Women Since 1945* (London, 1987), p1.

6   Leila J Rupp, *Mobilizing Women for War* (New Jersey, 1978), pp76-78.

7   As above, p75.

8   For the story of such women in Italy, see Jane Slaughter, *Women and the Italian Resistance* (Denver, Colorado, 1997).

9   Alan S Milward, *War, Economy and Society* (Harmondsworth, 1977), p219.

10 Penny Summerfield, *Women Workers in the Second World War* (Beckenham, 1984), p10.

11 Lindsey German, *Sex, Class and Socialism*, pp102-105.

12 Penny Summerfield, *Women Workers*, p31.

13 Penny Summerfield, "Women and War in the Twentieth Century", in June Purves (ed), *Women's History Britain: 1850-1945* (London, 1995), p321.

14 Sue Bruley, *Women in Britain Since 1900* (London, 1999), p96.

15 Penny Summerfield, *Women Workers*, p29.

16 As above, p34; Lindsey German, *Sex, Class and Socialism*, pp102-103.

17 Sue Bruley, *Women in Britain*, p94.

18 Richard Croucher, *Engineers at War* (London, 1982), p253.

19 Penny Summerfield, *Women Workers*, p36.

20 Alan S Milward, *War*, p219.

21 Penny Summerfield, *Women Workers*, p47, and Richard Croucher, *Engineers*, p268.

22 Sue Bruley, *Women in Britain*, pp101-102.

23 Penny Summerfield, *Women Workers*, p38.

24 As above, pp18-19.

25 As above, p84.

26 As above, p94.

27 As above, p82.

28 As above, p114.

29 Pat Kirkham, "Beauty and Duty: Keeping up the (Home) Front", in Pat Kirkham and David Thoms (eds), *War Culture* (London, 1995), pp15-17.

30 Penny Summerfield, *Women Workers*, pp126, 135.

31 As above, p140.

32 Richard Croucher, *Engineers*, p255.

33 As above, p255.

34 As above, p277.

35 As above, p279.

36 Lindsey German, *Sex, Class and Socialism*, p103.

37 AEU Memo to Royal Commission on Equal Pay 1944-46, appendix 8, from *Statistics Relating to the War Effort* Cmnd 6564 (London, 1946).

38 Norbert Soldon, *Women in British Trade Unions 1874-1976* (London, 1978), p156.

39 AEU memo to Royal Commission on Equal Pay 1944-46.

40 Richard Croucher, *Engineers*, p264.

41 Lindsey German, *Sex, Class and Socialism*, p134.

42 As above, pp105-106; Jill Walker, "Women, State and Family", in Jill Rubery (ed), *Women and Recession* (London, 1988), p220.

43 Pearl Jephcott with Nancy Seear and John H Smith, *Married Women Working* (London, 1962), p20.

44 As above, pp66-67.

45 As above, p21, quoting a survey by Richard Titmuss.

46 Chris Harman, *Explaining the Crisis* (London, 1984), p104.

47 Sarah Boston, *Women Workers and the Trade Unions* (London, 1980), p242.

48 Plans for nurseries and nursery schools on the new post-war housing estates simply did not materialise. See Steven Fielding, Peter Thompson and Nick Tiratsoo, *England Arise* (Manchester, 1995), p106.

49 Sarah Boston, *Women Workers*, p221.
50 Lesley Rimmer and Jenny Popay, "The Family at Work", in *Employment Gazette* (June 1982).
51 General Household Survey 1983 (London, 1985), published by HMSO.
52 Jean Martin and Ceridwen Roberts, *Women and Employment: a Lifetime Perspective* (London, 1984), table 2.3.
53 Tanvi Desai, Paul Gregg, Julian Steer and Jonathan Wadsworth, "Gender and the Labour Market", in Paul Gregg and Jonathan Wadsworth (eds), *The State of Working Britain* (Manchester, 1999), pp170-171.
54 Jill Rubery and Roger Tarling, "Women's Employment in Declining Britain", in Jill Rubery (ed), *Women and Recession*, p125.
55 Patricia Hewitt, *About Time* (London, 1993), p15.
56 *Financial Times*, 8 February 2001.
57 Patricia Hewitt, *About Time*, p14.
58 Penny Babb, Hayley Butcher, Jenny Church and Linda Zealey, *Social Trends* 36 (London, 2005), p52.
59 Shirley Dex (ed), *Families and the Labour Market* (London, 1999), p33.
60 As above, p35.
61 Jill Walker, "Women, the State and Family in Britain: Thatcher's Economics and the Experience of Women", in Jill Rubery (ed), *Women and Recession*, p221.
62 Doria Pilling, "Engels and the Condition of the Working Class Today", in John Lea and Geoff Pilling (eds), *The Condition of Britain* (London, 1996), p23.
63 Shirley Dex (ed), *Families*, p42.
64 As above, p42.
65 *Guardian*, "The Mother Load", 26 March 2002.
66 Shirley Dex (ed), *Families*, p43.
67 See Daycare Trust childcare costs survey 2006, available at www.daycaretrust.org.uk
68 "Multiplicity of Childcare Options", *Financial Times*, 20 March 2002.
69 *Financial Times*, 19 April 2002.
70 "Multiplicity of Childcare Options", *Financial Times*, 20 March 2002.

71 "The Mother Load", *Guardian*, 26 March 2002.
72 "More Women in Paid Employment", *Financial Times*, 8 February 2001.
73 "Childcare Gap Stops Mothers Working", *Guardian*, 26 March 2002.
74 Howard Meltzer, *Day Care*, pp56-57.
75 As above, p18.
76 Sarah Boston, *Women Workers and the Trade Unions*, p279.
77 Tanvi Desai and others, "Gender", p179.
78 http://www.womenandequalityunit. gov.uk/pay/payfacts.htm,2006. Also see *Just Pay* (London, 2001), p1. This report is from the Equal Opportunities Commission's equal pay task force.
79 *Just Pay*, p1.
80 http://www.womenandequalityunit. gov.uk/pay/payfacts.htm,2006
81 *Just Pay*, p7.
82 Jil Matheson and Penny Babb, *Social Trends* 32 (London, 2002) p76; table 4.14.
83 As above, p93.
84 Tanvi Desai and others, "Gender", p168.
85 As above, p178
86 Jill Rubery and Roger Tarling "Women's Employment", pp126-127.
87 Rosalind Coward, *Sacred Cows* (London, 1999), p49.
88 See: http://timesonline.co.uk/tol/ news/uk/article1496865.ece
89 Tanvi Desai and others, "Gender", p176.
90 "Childcare Benefits Count for Nothing", *Guardian*, 1 March 2001.
91 See the survey of contact centres from 2003 available at http://www.e-skills. com/cgi-bin/go.pl/research/public ations_library/article.html?uid=606
92 Hakim's controversial views on this question have been rebutted by various feminist academics. See Catherine Hakim, "The Myth of Rising Female Employment", in *Work, Employment and Society*, 7:1 (March 1993), pp97-120; Catherine Hakim "Five Feminist Myths About Women's Employment", *British Journal of Sociology* 46:3 (1995), pp429-455; Jay Ginn and others, "Feminist

Fallacies: A Reply To Hakim On Women's Employment", *British Journal of Sociology* 47:1 (1996), pp167-173; Irene Bruegel, "Whose Myths Are They Anyway?", *British Journal of Sociology* 47:1 (1996), pp175-177; Catherine Hakim, "The Sexual Division of Labour and Women's Heterogeneity", *British Journal of Sociology* 47:1 (1996), pp178-188.

93 Jean Martin and Ceridwen Roberts, *Women and Employment*, chs 3 and 4.

94 Susan Harkness, "Working 9 to 5?", in *The State of Working Britain*, p106.

95 Jay Ginn and others, "Feminist Fallacies: a Reply to Hakim on Women's Employment", *British Journal of Sociology*, vol 47:1 (March 1996), p170.

96 See Irene Bruegel, "Whose Myths Are They Anyway?", p176; "How Safe Is Your Job?", *Independent*, 16 May 1996, reported that since 1992 175,000 more part time workers had said they would rather work full time.

97 Jean Martin and Ceridwen Roberts, *Women and Employment*, p41.

98 "UK's work burden grows fastest in Europe", *Guardian*, 21 June 2000.

99 Jil Matheson and Penny Babb, *Social Trends 32*, (London, 2002), pp78-79 (chart 4.18).

100 Susan Harkness, "Working 9 to 5?" in *The State of Working Britain*, pp104-107.

101 As above, p107.

102 Clare Ruhemann, "Women in Unions Face Glass Ceiling", *Labour Research* (March 2002), pp10-12.

103 Abigail Self and Linda Zealey (eds), *Social Trends*, 37, p54. In 2005, 30 percent of female employees were trade union members, while 28 percent of male employees were.

104 www.tuc.org.uk. Also see *Labour Research*, as above.

5   Men: how Mr Right became Mr Wrong

1   Quoted in *Metro*, 5 July 2000.

2   "Beating Eating Disorders", available at http://www.beat.co.uk/NewsEvents PressMedia/PressMediaInformation/ Somestatistics

3   Melanie Phillips, *The Sex Change State* (London, 1997), p15.

4   Quoted in Geoff Dench, *The Place of Men in Changing Family Cultures* (London, nd), p62.

5   Steve Humphries and Pamela Gordon, *A Man's World* (London, 1996), p7.

6   As above, p171.

7   As above, p173.

8   As above, p177.

9   As above, p39.

10 Susan Faludi, *Stiffed* (London, 1999), pp19-20.

11 Betty Friedan, *The Feminine Mystique* (1963); Simone de Beauvoir, *The Second Sex* (first published in French in 1949 and in English in 1953); Doris Lessing, *The Golden Notebook* (1962) and the Martha Quest novels (1952-1969).

12 Perhaps the best known of this genre is John Osborne's *Look Back in Anger* (first performed in 1956), but it occurred in a range of 1950s literature from Kingsley Amis's *Lucky Jim* (1954) to Alan Sillitoe's *Saturday Night and Sunday Morning* (1958).

13 Susan Faludi, *Stiffed*, p29.

14 Kathleen Gerson, *No Man's Land* (New York, 1993), p5.

15 Barbara Ehrenreich, *The Hearts of Men* (New York and London, 1983), p120.

16 W D Rubinstein, *Capitalism, Culture and Decline in Britain* (London, 1993), p15.

17 Eithne McLaughlin (ed), *Understanding Unemployment* (London, 1992), p3.

18 W D Rubinstein, *Capitalism*, pp33-34.

19 See Jill Rubery and Roger Tarling, "Women's Employment in Declining Britain", in Jill Rubery (ed), *Women and Recession*, on women's job losses.

20 For the unemployment rates in 2005 see Abigail Self and Linda Zealey (eds), *Social Trends 37*, p51 (figure 4.15). The TUC Equality Audit, as above, gives the percentages of female and male workers working part time in 2003 as 43 percent and 9 percent respectively (p2).

21   See footnote 3 in "Work".

22   *Social Trends* 30 (London, 2000), p71.

23   "In Search of New Dad", Guardian, 14 June 2000.

24   Patricia Hewitt, *About Time*, p58.

25   As above, p57.

26   As above, pp57-58.

27   As above, p61.

28   "In Search of New Dad", *Guardian*, 14 June 2000.

29   Shirley Dex (ed), *Families*, p37.

30   As above, pp38-39 from unpublished tables by Elsa Ferri and Kate Smith, *Parenting in the 1990s* (London, 1996), from the Family Policy Studies Centre.

31   Study by Helene Couprie of the University of Toulouse February 2007. The study was of British data. Available at http://news.independent.co.uk/business/comment/article2302933.ece

32   Shirley Dex (ed), *Families*, pp38-39.

33   Geoff Dench, *The Place of Men*, p63.

34   "In Search of New Dad", *Guardian*, 14 June 2000.

35   Susan Faludi, *Stiffed*, p154.

36   Trevor Blackwell and Jeremy Seabrook, *Talking Work: An Oral History* (London, 1996), p141.

37   As above, p161.

38   "When Boys Can't Be Boys", *Independent on Sunday*, 23 July 2000 (from a transcript of "Men in Crisis" due for broadcast on Radio 4 on 25 July 2000).

39   Rosalind Coward, *Sacred Cows* (London, 1999), p59.

40   *Crime in England and Wales* 2005-6, p8. This is a report produced by the Home Office and is available from http://www.homeoffice.gov.uk/rds/pdfs06/crime0506summ.pdf

41   Simon Nye, *"Act Your Age!" The Observer Encyclopaedia of Our Times*, vol 1 (London, nd), p3.

42   "Staying Active on a Diet of Sex and Sport", *Financial Times*, 14 April 1997.

43   As above.

44   Letter in *Socialist Review*, January 1997.

45   *Loaded*, May 2007.

46   *FHM*, May 2007.

47   "We Are the World", *FHM*, June 1997.

48   *Nuts*, May 2007.

49   Imelda Whelehan, *Overloaded* (London, 2000), p65.

50   Barbara Ehrenreich, *The Hearts of Men* (New York and London, 1983), ch4.

51   Susan Faludi, *Stiffed*, pp144-145.

52   As above, pp145-146.

53   A study of male autoworkers in 1960s and 1970s Michigan shows how one particular male pursuit took on a heightened value as social uncertainty grew. Lisa Fine discovered that deer hunting was a major ritual for (mostly white) men working in the car plant she was studying. The proportion of the population in Michigan in 1968 who hunted deer was seven times the proportion in 1920, partly as a result of greater mobility. A fifth of all Michigan males went deer hunting in 1968 and all but 6 percent of the hunters were male. They were mainly manual working class, with a 1966 survey showing that almost half of deer hunters with firearms were craftsmen, foremen, operatives or kindred workers. The number of workers engaged in this pursuit increased in the late 1960s, suggesting a greater defensiveness about the right to bear arms and to hunt, but also perhaps an assertion of traditional and masculine values at a time of great change, uncertainty and challenge to those values. These were the young men who didn't protest at the Vietnam War; indeed many of them would be drafted to fight. Their factory closed in 1975 – Lisa Fine, "Rights of Men, Rites of Passage", in Roger Horowittz (ed) *Boys and their Toys* (New York and London, 2001), pp256, 259.

54   Melanie Phillips, *Sex Change State*, p7.

55   Beatrix Campbell, "Missing the Target", *Guardian*, 3 July 2000.

56   As above.

57   Angela Phillips quoted in Rosalind Coward, *Sacred Cows*, p180.

58   Sandy Ruxton, "Boys Won't Be Boys", in Trefor Lloyd and Tristan Wood (eds), *What Next For Men* (London, 1996), pp77-78.

59 As above, p78.
60 As above, p86.
61 As above, pp84-85.
62 See the crime information website:
    http://www.crimeinfo.org.uk/topic
    ofthemonth/index.jsp
63 Sandy Ruxton, "Boys Won't Be Boys",
    p82.
64 "Ladies who Lift", *Guardian*, 5 March
    2002.
65 http://www.retailresearch.org/
    crime-and-fraud/shoplifting-for-
    xmas.php
66 Quoted in Lynne Segal, *Slow Motion*
    (London, 1997), p263.
67 *Social Trends* 30 (London, 2000), p58.
68 Abigail Self and Linda Zealey (eds),
    Social Trends 37, p30.
69 Barry Hugill, "Britain's Exclusion
    Zone", *Observer*, 13 April 1997.
70 *Social Trends* 30, p56.
71 As above, p59.
72 Lilian Rubin, *Families on the Faultline*
    (New York, 1994), p112-113.
73 Engels described the plight of a male
    worker in St Helens, Lancashire, who
    was interrupted darning his wife's
    stockings. The worker, Jack, describes
    how he has had no work for three
    years, while his wife works from dawn
    till night in the factory and so is too
    tired to do anything at home. He says
    to his friend, "Thou knowest when I
    got married I had work plenty, and
    thou knows I was not lazy... And we
    had a good furnished house, and
    Mary need not go to work. I could
    work for the two of us; but now the
    world is upside down. Mary has to
    work and I have to stop at home,
    mind the childer, sweep and wash,
    bake and mend; and when the poor
    woman comes home at night, she is
    knocked up" – Frederick Engels, *The
    Condition of the Working Class in
    England* (Moscow, 1973), p183.
74 As above, p184.
75 As above, p184.
76 Shere Hite, *Oedipus Revisited* (London,
    2005), p101.
77 Frederick Engels, *Origin of the Family,
    Private Property and the State*.

6   **War: liberation, like it or not**
1   Radio Address by Mrs Bush,
    Crawford, Texas. Available from
    http://www.whitehouse.gov/news/
    releases/2001/11/20011117.html
2   "Cherie Blair attacks Taleban 'cruelty'",
    BBC News, 19 November 2001,
    available at http://news.bbc.co.uk/2/
    hi/uk_news/politics/1663300.stm
3   Laura Flanders, *Bushwomen* (London,
    2004), p267.
4   Iris Marion Young, "The Logic of
    Masculinist Protection: Reflections on
    the Current Security State", in *Signs:
    Journal of Women in Culture and Society*
    29:1 (2003), p18.
5   Laura Flanders, *Bushwomen*, p267.
6   Eleanor Smeal quoted in Iris Marion
    Young, "Logic", p18.
7   Laura Flanders, *Bushwomen*, p268.
8   As above, pp268-269.
9   As above, p269.
10 Zillah Eisenstein, *Against Empire*
    (London, 2004), p155 (footnote).
11 As above, p154.
12 George Bush, State of the Union
    speech 29 January 2002, quoted in
    New York Times, 30 January 2002.
13 Natasha Walter, "We Are Just
    Watching Things Get Worse",
    Guardian, 28 November 2006.
14 "Taking Stock: Afghan women and
    girls five years on", Womankind
    Worldwide, October 2006, p7.
    Available at
    http://www.womankind.org.uk
15 As above, p29.
16 Sheldon Rampton and John Stauber,
    Weapons of Mass Deception (London,
    2003), pp69-75.
17 As above, pp76-77.
18 Anne Alexander and Simon Assaf,
    "Iraq: the Rise of the Resistance",
    International Socialism 105 (2005).
19 UNIFEM Gender Profile – Iraq –
    Women, War and Peace http://www.
    womenwarpeace.org/iraq/iraq.htm
20 UNIFEM, as above.
21 All examples from "Iraq: Decades of
    Suffering, Now Women Deserve
    Better", Amnesty International, 22
    February 2005. Available at

http://www.amnesty.org/library/ind ex/ENGMDE140012005?open.

22 Amnesty International, as above.

23 James Denver, "Horror of US Depleted Uranium in Iraq Threatens World", 29 April 2005. Available at http://www.resne.com/general64/du.htm

24 BBC poll at http://news.bbc.co.uk/2hi/middle_east/6464277.stm

25 Haifa Zangana, "We have not been liberated", March 6 2007. Available at http://commentisfree.guardian.co.uk/haifa_angana/2007/03

26 Farida, quoted in Elaheh Rostami Povey, "Gender, Agency and Identity: the case of Afghan Women in Afghanistan, Iran and Pakistan", *Journal of Development Studies* (2004).

27 Elaheh Rostami Povey, *Afghan Women, Invasion and Identity* (London, 2007), ch5 [forthcoming].

28 Quoted in "Feminism as Imperialism", *Guardian*, 21 September 2002.

29 As above.

30 Iris Marion Young, "Logic", p20.

31 Elaheh Rostami-Povey, *Afghan Women*, ch5.

32 Elaheh Rostami Povey, "Workers, Women and the Islamic Republic", *International Socialism* 105 (2005), pp43-62.

33 See Shirin Ebadi, *Iran Awakening* (London, 2006). For debates on feminism in Iran see Elaheh Rostami-Povey, "Feminist Contestations of Institutional Domains in Iran", *Feminist Review* 69 (2001).

34 "United in support of Iranian Women", *Financial Times*, 28 March 2007.

35 Roksana Bahramitash, "The War on Terror, Feminist Orientalism and Orientalist Feminism: Case Studies of Two North American Bestsellers", *Critique: Critical Middle Eastern Studies* 14:2 (2005), pp223-237.

36 See, for example, Humayan Ansari, "Muslims in Britain", in *Minority Rights Group International Report* (London, 2002); for Europe, see the report of the European Monitoring Centre on Racism and Xenophobia, European Union, 18 December 2006.

37 Final report of the Equalities Review, EOC London, 28 February 2007.

38 "Minister's Call to Choose Outrages British Muslims", *Guardian*, 22 November 2003.

39 Jack Straw quoted in the *Lancashire Evening Telegraph*, BBC News, 6 October 2006. Available at http://www.bbc.news.co.uk/1/hi/uk_politics/5413470.stm

40 In the general election of 2005 Labour lost a million votes compared with the previous election, the anti-war party Respect won a seat and achieved four of the top ten swings from Labour in the whole of Britain. Straw was humiliated when he brought Condoleezza Rice to his home town in 2006 and was met by large demonstrations.

41 See Antoine Boulange, "The Hijab, Racism and the State", *International Socialism* 102 (2004).

42 "Opposition Condemns Dutch Governments 'stunt' in election dominated by race and religion", *Observer*, 19 November 2006.

43 Saied R Ameli, Manzur Elahi and Arzu Merali, *British Muslims' Expectations of the Government* (London, 2004) p42.

44 As above, pp49-51.

45 As above, p52.

46 Deborah Orr, "Why This Picture Offends Me", *Independent*, 8 July 2006.

47 Sarah Hussein, "I Shouldn't be Dictated to", *The Independent on Sunday*, 8 October 2006.

48 Haleh Afshar, Rob Aitken and Myanwy Franks, "Feminism, Islamophobia and Identities", *Political Studies*, vol 53 (2005), pp262-283.

49 As above.

50 Joan Smith, "The Veil is a Feminist Issue" *Independent on Sunday*, 8 October 2006.

51 Shahed Saleem, "A New Era", in Lindsey German and Andrew Murray, *Stop the War: the Story of Britain's Biggest Mass Movement* (London, 2005), p59.

52 As above.

53 Lindsey German and Andrew Murray, *Stop the War*, pp57-63.

54 See Philip S Foner (ed), *Clara Zetkin: Selected Writings* (New York, 1984), pp158-165; Dave Crouch, "The Bolsheviks and Islam", *International Socialism* 110 (2006); John Riddell (ed), *To See the Dawn: Baku, 1920, First Congress of the Peoples of the East* (New York, 1993).

7   Feminism: the limits of liberation

1   Rebecca West, 1913, http://www.quotationspage.com
2   Quoted in "Got it, bought the T shirt", *Guardian*, 9 March 2007.
3   Survey, Girls Shout Out! 26 February 2007, http://www.girlguiding.org.uk
4   As above.
5   As above.
6   Dianne Feinstein, quoted in "Maternity leave law found illegal by judge", *New York Times*, 22 March 1984.
7   Sara Evans, *Personal Politics* (New York, 1979), p190.
8   Lise Vogel, *Woman Questions* (London, 1995), p6.
9   As above, p14.
10 Sara Evans, *Personal Politics*, pp198-199.
11 As above, p179.
12 As above, p87.
13 As above, p192.
14 As above, pp60-66; Lise Vogel, *Woman Questions*, pp6-11.
15 For a useful overview see Michelle Barrett, *Women's Oppression Today* (London, 1980), especially chapter 1.
16 The best book, in my opinion, is Sara Evans, *Personal Politics*, but Jo Freeman, *The Politics of Women's Liberation* (New York, 1976), is also a very useful account.
17 The socialist historian Sheila Rowbotham wrote three important and accessible books in the early 1970s which influenced socialist feminists in Britain: *Hidden from History* (London, 1974), *Woman's Consciousness, Man's World* (London, 1973) and *Women, Resistance and Revolution* (London, 1972).
18 The first conclusion tended to be held by theorists who argued that domestic labour contributed to the profits of the capitalists because it produced surplus value, through the production of labour power, which could be sold on the labour market; while the argument that domestic labour only produced use values often underpinned the second position. For this very extensive debate see Jean Gardiner and others, "Women's Domestic Labour", in *On the Political Economy of Women* (London, 1976); Mariarosa dalla Costa and Selma James, *The Power of Women and the Subversion of the Community* (Bristol, 1976); John Harrison, "The Political Economy of Housework", Bulletin of the Conference of Socialist Economists 4, (1974); Wally Seccombe, "The Housewife and her Labour under Capitalism", *New Left Review* 83 (1974).
19 See Lindsey German, *Sex, Class and Socialism*, pp70-73, for my fuller view.
20 See Lindsey German, "Theories of Patriarchy", in *International Socialism* 12 (1981).
21 Heidi Hartmann, "The Unhappy Marriage of Marxism and Feminism: Towards a More Progressive Union", *Capital and Class* 8 (1979).
22 Reprinted in Johanna Brenner, *Women and the Politics of Class* (New York, 2000), pp11-58.
23 As above, p20.
24 As above, p24.
25 Anna Clark, *The Struggle for the Breeches* (Berkeley, 1997), p129.
26 As above, pp205-206.
27 Johanna Brenner, *Women and the Politics of Class*, p23.
28 Margaret Hewitt, *Wives and Mothers in Victorian Industry* (London, 1958), p25.
29 Ivy Pinchbeck, *Women Workers and the Industrial Revolution 1750-1850* (London, 1981), p244.
30 Jane Humphries, "Class Struggle and the Persistence of the Working Class Family", in Alice H Amsden (ed), *The Economics of Women and Work* (London, 1980), p154.
31 Johanna Brenner, *Women and the Politics of Class*, p29.
32 As above, p30.

33 Barbara Sinclair Deckard, *The Women's Movement* (New York, 1979), p385.

34 Celestine Ware, *Women Power* (New York, 1970), p50.

35 See Jo Freeman, *Politics of Women's Liberation*, p143.

36 As above, p143.

37 See Lindsey German, *Sex, Class and Socialism*, p200.

38 See "Women's liberation 1977", *Spare Rib* 58, May 1977.

39 See *Spare Rib* 70-73, May, June, July and August 1978.

40 Marnie Holborow, "Women in Italy", *Socialist Review* 13, (July/August 1979); Paul Ginsborg, *A History of Contemporary Italy: Society and Politics 1943-1988* (London, 1990), pp366-370. See also Chris Harman, *The Fire Last Time*, pp345-355.

41 Elizabeth Wilson, *Hidden Agendas* (London, 1986), p17.

42 Rosalind Coward, *Sacred Cows* (London, 1999), p42.

43 Sheila Rowbotham, Lynne Segal and Hilary Wainwright, *Beyond the Fragments* (London, 1979).

44 See, for example, the writings from the early women's movement in *Liberation Now!* (New York, 1971), especially the final section on "Sisters in Revolution".

45 Johanna Brenner, "The Best of Times, the Worst of Times", in *Women and the Politics of Class*, p233. Brenner's essay is an overview of what has happened to feminism which locates its fortunes in the ups and downs of the class struggle. It paints two pictures of women's lives by the early 1990s: one is of women breaking into new fields, gaining education, forming organisations to defend women; the other is of worsening conditions at work, the trials of the double burden, continued male domination in the home and violent images of women seeming all pervasive. She comments, "Both pictures are true" (p220).

46 As above, p228.

47 Martin Smith, "The Shape of the Working Class", in *International Socialism* 113 (2007).

48 See chapter 4.

49 Rosalind Delmar, "What is Feminism?", in Juliet Mitchell and Ann Oakley (eds), *What is Feminism?* (Oxford, 1986), p9.

50 Naomi Klein, *No Logo* (London, 2001), pp121-122.

51 Juliet Mitchell, "Reflections on Twenty Years of Feminism", in Juliet Mitchell and Ann Oakley (eds), *What is Feminism?*, p48.

52 Naomi Wolf, *Fire with Fire* (London, 1993), p108.

53 William Morris, *A Dream of John Ball* (1886), available at http://www.marxists.org/archive/morris/works/1886/johnball/johnball.htm

8   Socialism: the rising of the women

1   The phrase, "the rising of the women", comes from the song "Bread and Roses" written by James Oppenheim for women textile strikers in Lawrence, Massachusetts, in 1912.

*As we come marching, marching in the
    beauty of the day,*
*A million darkened kitchens, a thousand
    mill lofts gray,*
*Are touched with all the radiance that a
    sudden sun discloses,*
*For the people hear us singing: "Bread
    and roses! Bread and roses!"*

*As we come marching, marching, we
    battle too for men,*
*For they are women's children, and we
    mother them again.*
*Our lives shall not be sweated from birth
    until life closes;*
*Hearts starve as well as bodies; give us
    bread, but give us roses!*

*As we come marching, marching,
    unnumbered women dead*
*Go crying through our singing their
    ancient cry for bread.*
*Small art and love and beauty their
    drudging spirits knew.*
*Yes, it is bread we fight for – but we fight
    for roses, too!*

As we come marching, marching, we bring
the greater days.
The rising of the women means the rising
of the race.
No more the drudge and idler – ten that
toil where one reposes,
But a sharing of life's glories: Bread and
roses! Bread and roses!

Meredith Tax, *The Rising of the Women* (Illinois, 2001), p241, quoting Joyce Kornbluh (ed), *Rebel Voices: An IWW Anthology* (Michigan, 1964), p196

2   See Philip S Foner (ed), Clara Zetkin *Selected Writings*, pp31-32. On the garment workers' strike, see Sheila Rowbotham, *A Century of Women*, pp45-53.

3   For details of Eleanor Marx's remarkable life see Yvonne Kapp, *Eleanor Marx, vol 2: The Crowded Years, 1884-1898* (London, 1976).

4   August Bebel, *Women and Socialism* (New York, 1910). Bebel's book was originally published in German in 1879.

5   For details of the strike and campaign see Sheila Rowbotham, *Century*, pp348-352.

6   See "The Night Cleaners' Campaign", in *Shrew*, December 1971, reprinted in Michelene Wandor (ed), *The Body Politic: Women's Liberation in Britain* (London, 1972).

7   Frederick Engels, "The Book of Revelation", in *Progress*, vol 11 (1883), quoted in Christopher Hill, *The World Turned Upside Down* (London, 1984), p306.

8   Tony Cliff, *Class Struggle and Women's Liberation* (London, 1984), ch1; Christopher Hill, *The World Turned Upside Down*, ch15, p306 onwards.

9   Tony Cliff, *Class Struggle*, pp20-22.

10 As above, pp27-33.

11 Quoted in Tony Cliff, as above, p30.

12 Mary Wollstonecraft, *A Vindication of the Rights of Woman* (London, 1992).

13 Dorothy Thompson, "Women and Nineteenth Century Radical Politics", in Juliet Mitchell and Ann Oakley (eds), *The Rights and Wrongs of Women* (London, 1976), pp118-119.

14 See Barbara Taylor, *Eve and the New Jerusalem* (London, 1983).

15 There are many books on this subject, but for the political and social background see Yvonne Kapp, *Eleanor Marx*, vol 2.

16 As above.

17 Karl Marx and Frederick Engels, *Collected Works*, vol 4 (London, 1975), p196.

18 Frederick Engels, *The Condition of the Working Class in England* (London, 1987).

19 Karl Marx and Frederick Engels, *The Communist Manifesto*, in *Selected Works* (Moscow, 1968), pp49-50.

20 Frederick Engels, *Condition of the Working Class*, p182.

21 Frederick Engels, *Origin of the Family, Private Property and the State*. For debate on this see, for example, Lise Vogel, *Marxism and the Oppression of Women* (London, 1983), pp74-92; Chris Harman, "Engels and the Origin of Human Society", *International Socialism* 65 (1994).

22 Terrell Carver, *Frederick Engels: His Life and Thought* (Basingstoke, 1989), p159.

23 For some detective work on this see Francis Wheen, *Karl Marx* (London, 1999), pp170-176.

24 Anne Lopes and Gary Roth tell the story of one part of it in *Men's Feminism: August Bebel and the German Socialist Movement* (New York, 2000). They point out that many of the socialists in the German Social Democratic Party were deeply committed to the theory and practice of women's rights.

25 As above, p31.

26 As above, p31.

27 As above, p37.

28 As above, p70.

29 See Meredith Tax, *The Rising of the Women*, pp205-240.

30 As above, pp229-231.

31 Quoted in Meredith Tax, as above, pp230-231.

32 See Richard Stites, *The Women's Liberation Movement in Russia* (Princeton, 1991), chs 7 and 8 (pp191-227); Cathy Porter, *Alexandra Kollontai: A Biography* (London, 1980), ch6 (pp125-147).

33 Tony Cliff, *Class Struggle*, p96.

34 Cathy Porter, *Alexandra Kollontai*, p146.

35 See Paul Foot, *The Vote* (London, 2005), pp171-237; Sheila Rowbotham, *Century of Women*, pp13-14.

36 For more on this see Lindsey German, *Sex, Class and Socialism*, ch7.

37 The Russian calendar was 13 days behind that used in Western Europe at the time, so International Women's day in 1917 in Russia was celebrated on February 23rd.

38 See Cathy Porter, *Alexandra Kollontai*, pp190-191.

39 For a full analysis of this period see Richard Stites, *The Women's Liberation*, pp317-422.

40 As above, p372.

41 As above; see the section on "The Sexual Thermidor" pp376-391.

42 Leon Trotsky, *The Revolution Betrayed* (New York, 1972), pp151-152.

43 Helmut Gruber and Pamela Graves (eds), *Women and Socialism / Socialism and Women* (Oxford, 1998), p521.

44 As above, p155.

45 As above, p513.

46 Sara Evans, *Personal Politics*, pp116-119.

9 Conclusion

1 Karl Marx, *Capital* vol 1 (London, 1974), p375.

2 Roselle Leah K Rivera, "Business Orphans", in Judith Mirsky and Marty Radlett (eds), *No Paradise Yet* (London, 2000), p194.

3 As above, p193.

4 Kevin Bales, "Because She Looks Like a Child", in Barbara Ehrenreich and Arlie Russell Hochschild (eds), *Global Woman* (London, 2003), p214.

5 See chapter on family, p71.

6 Equal Opportunities Commission, "EOC calls for more support for the modern family", 6 March 2007, and available at http://www.eoc.org.uk/default.aspx? page+20038

7 See, for example, Maud Pember Reeves, *Round About A Pound A Week*; Margaret Llewellyn Davies (ed), *Life As We Have Known It* (London, 1977).

8 "Work is the Route Claimants Must Take, says Murphy", and "Child Poverty Sees Shock Increase", *Financial Times*, 28 March 2007.

9 Alex Kuczynski, *Beauty Junkies* (London, 2007), quoted in Edwina Ings-Chambers, "Unreal Beauty", *FT Magazine*, 31 March/1 April 2007.

10 Sheila Rowbotham, "Facets of Emancipation", in Sheila Rowbotham and Stephanie Linkogle (eds), *Women Resist Globalization* (London 2001), p16.

11 Karl Marx, *The German Ideology* (London, 1965), p86.

Further reading

Below are 50 books which have helped me to write this book and which give different insights into women's lives:

25 non-fiction books

Lillian Rubin, *Worlds of Pain: Life in the Working-Class Family* (New York, 1977)

Sara Evans, *Personal Politics* (New York, 1979)

Ivy Pinchbeck, *Women Workers and the Industrial Revolution 1750-1850* (London 1981)

Pearl Jephcott with Nancy Seear and John H Smith, *Married Women Working* (London, 1962)

Alice Clark, *Working Life of Women in the 17th Century* (New York, 1983)

Barbara Taylor, *Eve and the New Jerusalem* (London, 1983)

Meredith Tax, *The Rising of the Women* (Illinois, 2001)

Frederick Engels, *Origin of the Family, Private Property and the State* (New York, 1975)

Sheila Rowbotham, *Women, Resistance and Revolution* (London, 1982)

John R Gillis, *For Better, For Worse* (Oxford and New York, 1985)

Diana Gittins, *Fair Sex* (London, 1982)

Helmut Gruber and Pamela Graves (eds), *Women and Socialism / Socialism and Women* (Oxford, 1998)

Jo Freeman, *The Politics of Women's Liberation* (New York, 1976)

Anonymous, *A Woman in Berlin* (London, 2005)

Richard Stites, *The Women's Liberation Movement in Russia* (Princeton, 1991)

Maud Pember Reeves, *Round About a Pound a Week* (London, 1994)

Barbara Ehrenreich and Deirdre English, *For Her Own Good* (New York, 1989)

Alice H Amsden (ed), *The Economics of Women and Work* (London, 1980)

Alice Kessler Harris, *Out to Work* (Oxford, 1982)

Eleanor Leacock and Helen I Safa, *Women's Work* (New York, 1986)

Lise Vogel, *Marxism and the Oppression of Women* (London, 1983)

Elizabeth Roberts, *A Woman's Place: An Oral History of Working Class Women 1890-1940* (Oxford, 1985)

Bridget Hill, *Eighteenth Century Women: An Anthology* (London, 1987)

Eleanor Burke Leacock, *Myths of Male Dominance* (New York, 1981)

Philip S Foner, *Clara Zetkin: Selected Writings* (New York, 1984)

Joyce Marlow, *Votes for Women* (London, 2001)

25 novels

Doris Lessing, *The Golden Notebook* (London, 1962)

— *The Four Gated City* (London, 1969)

— *Martha Quest* (London, 1952)

Fay Weldon, *Down Among the Women* (London, 1973)

Edna O'Brien, *The Girl with Green Eyes* (London, 1981)

Simone de Beauvoir, *She Came to Stay* (Glasgow, 1975)

George Bernard Shaw, *The Unsocial Socialist* (London, 1988)

Marge Piercy, *Woman on the Edge of Time* (New York, 1981)

Leo Tolstoy, *Anna Karenina* (Harmondsworth, 1986)

Zadie Smith, *White Teeth* (London, 2001)

Edith Wharton, *The Age of Innocence* (London, 1990)

Gustave Flaubert, *Madame Bovary* (London, 1992)

Nell Dunn, *Poor Cow* (London, 1968)

Lewis Grassic Gibbon, *The Scots Quair* (Edinburgh, 1995)

Alexandra Kollontai, *Love of Worker Bees* (London, 1991)

Andrea Levy, *Small Island* (London, 2004)

Honore de Balzac, *A Harlot High and Low* (London, 1975)

Hilary Mantel, *A Place of Greater Safety* (London, 1993)

Patrick Hamilton, *Twenty Thousand Streets Under the Sky* (London, 1987)

Randa Abdel-Fattah, *Does My Head Look Big In This?* (London, 2006)

Rohinton Mistry, *A Fine Balance* (London, 1997)

Gabriel Garcia Marquez, *Love in the Time of Cholera* (London, 1989)

Monica Ali, *Brick Lane* (London, 2004)

Alice Walker, *The Colour Purple* (London, 1986)

Vassily Grossman, *Life and Fate* (London, 2006)

Index

bookmarks

Bookmarks is Britain's leading socialist bookshop –
just around the corner from the TUC and the British Museum

We stock a huge range of books
- anti-racism and Black struggle
- education and trade union resources
- anti-war and anti-imperialism
- classic and contemporary Marxism
- excellent children's section plus radical fiction, art and culture
- DVDs, audio CDs and political journals together with a well stocked secondhand section
- and much more

Our trade union book service provides comprehensive bookstalls for conferences. We are official booksellers to the TUC.

Any book in print can be ordered through us and we have a full mail order service.

- Bookmarks,
  1 Bloomsbury Street,
  London WC1B 3QE
- 020 7637 1848
- www.bookmarks.uk.com